WOMEN
An
Anthropological
View

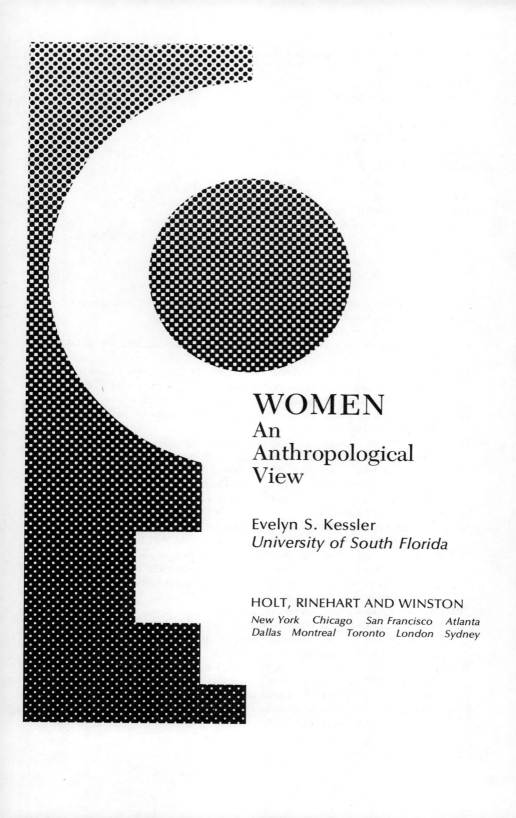

WOMEN
An
Anthropological
View

Evelyn S. Kessler
University of South Florida

HOLT, RINEHART AND WINSTON
New York   Chicago   San Francisco   Atlanta
Dallas   Montreal   Toronto   London   Sydney

Library of Congress Cataloging in Publication Data

Kessler, Evelyn S.
  Women: an anthropological view

  Includes index
  1. Women. I. Title
  GN479.7.K47   301.41'2   75–41355
  ISBN 0–03–014876–6

COPYRIGHT ACKNOWLEDGMENTS

The author wishes to thank the following copyright holders for permission to reprint extracts from their listed works:

Columbia University Press for *Women of the Forest* by Yolanda Murphy and Robert F. Murphy.

E. P. Dutton & Co., Inc. and Souvenir Press, Ltd., for *Child of the Dark: The Diary of Carolina Maria de Jesus*. Translated by David St. Clair. Copyright © 1962 by E. P. Dutton & Co., Inc., and Souvenir Press, Ltd.

Dorothy Eber for *Pitseolak: Pictures Out of My Life*, from recorded interviews by Dorothy Eber (Washington).

Holt, Rinehart and Winston for *The Isthmus Zapotecs: Women's Roles in Cultural Context* by Beverly L. Chiñas. Copyright © 1973 by Holt, Rinehart and Winston, Inc. For *Women and Men: An Anthropologist's View* by Ernestine Friedl. Copyright © 1975 by Holt, Rinehart and Winston. For *Fun City: An Ethnographic Study of a Retirement Community* by Jerry Jacobs. Copyright © 1974 by Holt, Rinehart and Winston, Inc.

M. J. Meggit for "*Male-Female Relationships in the Highlands of Australian New Guinea*" by M. J. Meggitt, *American Anthropologist*, 66 (4).

William Morrow and Company, Inc., for *Sex and Temperament in Three Primitive Societies* by Margaret Mead. Copyright 1935, 1950, 1963, by Margaret Mead.

Oxford University Press, Oxford, for *Honour, Family and Patronage* by J. K. Campbell, © Oxford University Press 1964.

Random House and William Heinemann Ltd., for *Report from a Chinese Village* by Jan Myrdal, translated by Maurice Michael. Copyright © 1965 by William Heinemann Ltd. Reprinted by permission of William Heinemann, Ltd., and of Pantheon Books, a Division of Random House, Inc.

Random House and Martin Secker & Warburg Limited For *La Vida* by Oscar Lewis. Copyright © 1965, 1966 by Oscar Lewis. For *The Children of Sanchez*, by Oscar Lewis. Copyright © 1961 by Oscar Lewis.

Simon & Schuster, Inc., for *The Mountain People* by Colin M. Turnbull. Copyright © 1973 by Colin M. Turnbull.

To the women who have shaped my life:
my grandmother, my mother, my daughter, and Margaret Mead.

Preface

No one can write an anthropological study of women without recognizing the enormous debt to the pioneers in anthropology who studied women and their condition long before women's studies became known as such. In their pioneering studies, anthropologists like Margaret Mead showed that the temperament of women is more closely constrained by factors of culture than those of biology. Audrey Richards proved that women in non-Western society could, through ritual, be molded into people who met their societies' criteria of what women should be like. Certainly one of the most important pioneers in this area was Oscar Lewis, who, by using tape recorders, permitted women in a subculture of modern society to tell their own stories.

Today, the pioneers are being followed by a generation of young women who are doing penetrating studies, and deriving new theoretical approaches to many of the problems in the area of women's studies. Carol Stack has provided us with a new model of the matrifocal family as adaptive strategy. Beverly Chiñas, Louise Spindler, Sherry Ortner, and Ernestine Friedl have all made significant contributions in this area. The future waits in the wings.

I should like to thank my students, both men and women, for their unflagging interest in the anthropology of women, and the insight they offered into their lives and attitudes. I hope that from among them more anthropologists will be enlisted to study the status of women cross-culturally.

My personal gratitude is extended to Louise Spindler and George Spindler, who have encouraged me in writing this book. I would also like to thank David Boynton for his patience and encouragement. Special thanks are due Beverly Chiñas for master editing, and I owe an enormous debt of gratitude to Margaret Mead for her unfailing help and understanding, as well as her existence as a model of the professional woman.

On a more personal level, I am indebted to my grandmother and my mother, who taught me that I was not "merely" a woman. Most of all, I am grateful for the friendship of my daughter, through whom I have been able to empathize with the young women facing adulthood in a world of changing goals and standards.

E. S. K.

Tampa, Florida
January 1976

Contents

WOMEN
An
Anthropological
View

Introduction

Times of fundamental change bring about the reexamination of values, roles, and behavior. By breaking down cottage industries and the peasantry which preceded, the industrial revolution produced alternative modes of subsistence as well as basic changes in the structure of the family and personal values. Similarly, the fall of the great ancient empires and the rise of feudalism changed not only the character of the larger society, but also the roles and structure within the family.

We live in times that can in many ways be compared to those mentioned above. Fundamental changes are apparent both within nations and in our international relationships as well. Those powerful industrial nations which had previously existed as opposing blocks are now drawn into accord because of their common reliance upon basic raw materials, which can be obtained only from so-called "underdeveloped" nations. These underdeveloped nations are no longer remaining isolates, but are becoming part of economic blocks as a strategy for dealing with the great powers.

In addition, problems such as overpopulation and air and water pollution cannot be solved by individual nation-states alone, and must be dealt with in the context of worldwide solutions. Industrial corporations have already recognized the necessity for international contacts and have developed the multinational corporation as a response for the need to control all aspects of production, from the acquisition of raw materials to the marketing of the finished product.

Basic to these changes is the intensification and proliferation of industrial technology. Changes in technology include such factors as the ability of machinery to do the bulk of heavy manual labor and the development of computer technology. Such changes have produced the need for different types of skills and different types of workers.

Even more drastic changes have been worked through the changes in medical techniques. People can now live and be productive longer than at any earlier time. Moreover, people are now able to control fertility and childbearing by methods which are safe, effective, and convenient.

In response to such dramatic changes, it should be expected that people of all kinds must seriously reexamine their roles, their status, and their relationships to society and to each other. Minority groups of all kinds have been actively involved in this reexamination and the painful struggle toward a more equitable position in society.

Although women do not constitute a numerical minority, their status in modern Western society has largely been a subordinate one. They have been encultured to avoid competition with men and to take satisfaction in their roles as wives and mothers. With equality of educational opportunities and a labor market that requires mental rather than sheer physical abilities, more women have been reexamining their positions, and have found that mothering uses only a portion of their lives, and that many years can be devoted to other things. A change in sexual attitudes has made it more acceptable for the single woman to live alone, or at least independent of the larger family unit. Other changes resulting from role reexamination include such phenomena as the young married woman who does not want to have children and the young single woman who does, and can support them without a husband.

The institution of marriage has been questioned in terms of economic and emotional advantages measured against loss of freedom and assumption of obligations. In its present form, many women have found marriage wanting.

For those women who seek alternative or supplementary careers, there have been other frustrations. Many have found unfair practices in employment and have been subject to overt and subtle discriminations; some men have felt threatened by equal opportunity employment practices. Even in universities, some professors doubt a woman's ability to pursue a career as aggressively as a man. In some professions, women must achieve far higher standards than men in order to be admitted to professional schools or to earn respect as colleagues. Women who have attempted to combine careers and marriage are often confronted with an unfair distribution of chores, in that the full-time working wife must also be the full-time housekeeper, while her husband uses his free time for relaxation or the further pursuit of his professional goals.

In their struggle to free themselves of these archaic encumbrances and to find new and satisfying roles, women have at times adopted a rhetoric, or style, which some men find threatening. However, the rhetoric of any activist or power group, no matter what color, at first seems frightening. Also, certain elements within the women's movement have used their platform to espouse what can only be called "female chauvinism." This, along with the lesbian influences, has caused many thoughtful women as well as men to turn away from the movement itself. This is a tragic loss, because in turning away from strident rhetoric, people are also turning away from the very real needs that women are especially equipped to meet.

The aggressive male attitudes which have so long characterized national and international relationships seem singularly inappropriate at present. Whether it is a missile confrontation or a "war on poverty," the mood of society is not in tune with the aggressor; the need now is for the conciliator. The survival of our culture depends upon our ability to reach agreement with other nations, to compromise rather than threaten. We must be able to reach out to the "underdeveloped" nations upon whom we depend for vital resources, and evolve ties that are meaningful to them as well as to us. Warfare is not the solution, although it is the traditional way in which men have met any impediment to their purpose.

Women have long been encultured, perhaps even culturally selected, for their skills as healers of wounds. They have had to learn the diplomatic skills of tact and compromise in order to survive. The world needs these skills, even at the expense of the family, and women must find new ways to make them available to the larger community and to structure their lives and new relationships both within and outside the traditional family.

Men will have to accept women in their new roles. Both women and·men of good will have to reach deeper understandings of themselves and each other. We can no longer exist as the exploiter and the exploited.

The anthropological view presented in this book is an attempt to explore the origins of present role-determination, and to offer a view of alternative relationships as they are structured in various societies both past and present. Only when the full panoply of relationships is displayed can one make a valid choice as to either a model or model segments from other societies as patterns with which we can work toward a newer, more fulfilling relationship, on both an interpersonal and intersocietal level.

The fight for women's rights must be stated in positive rather than negative terms. It is a fight *for* equality of opportunity, *for* better distribution of obligations, *for* the right to contribute sorely needed skills to society. This need not degenerate into a fight *against* men, *against* marriage, or *against* male prerogatives. And finally, it is a fight that must enlist both men and women, because the survival of society is equally important to both.

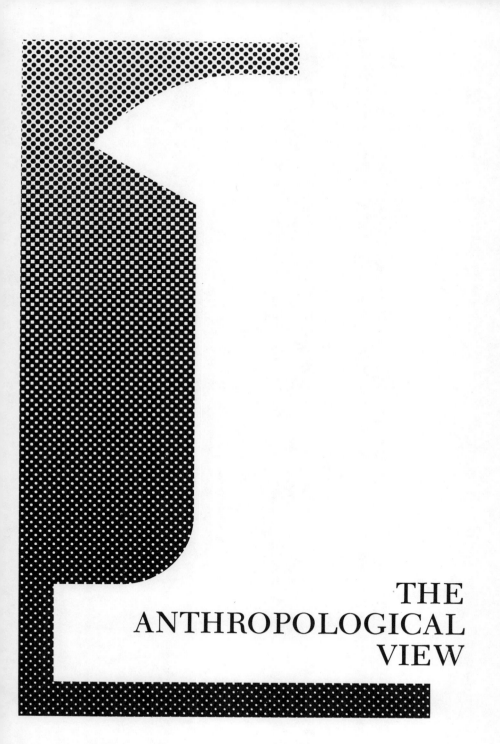

THE
ANTHROPOLOGICAL
VIEW

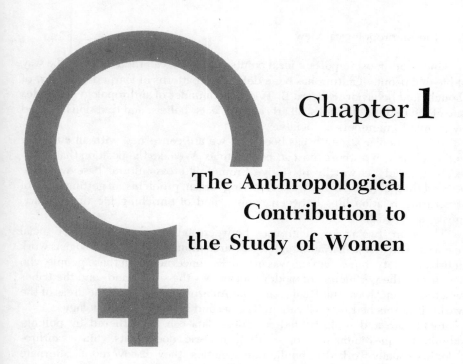

Chapter 1

The Anthropological Contribution to the Study of Women

With the growth of interest in women and their roles and statuses, there has been a concomitant proliferation of studies related to aspects of women's lives. Literature by women about women, the psychology of women, and the history of the feminist movement, are all worthy subjects for study, but they necessarily lack a dimension which only anthropology can supply.

What Anthropology Is

For most people, the term anthropology connotes such exotic subjects as the study of fertility rites, the exploration of mysterious temples covered by jungle vegetation, or expeditions to far away places. It is true that anthropology does contemplate these and other topics for serious scientific purposes. Anthropology is the study of humanity; it is concerned with the origin of human beings, their evolution from earlier forms, and the present biological makeup of human populations. As anthropologists we are interested in how people structured their communities, how they lived, what foods they ate, and what cities they built in the dim past; we are interested in peoples who left no written records and whose lives must be reconstructed from stone and bone implements and long silent buildings; in the language people speak, its origins, and its meanings; and with the way people structure their relationships to each other.

One of our most important focal points is what we call their culture, the way of life of a people. Culture has been defined as patterns of learned behavior, of thought and behavior. Edward B. Tylor, the founder of anthropology, provides one of the better definitions: all arts and artifacts, beliefs, and traditions learned by people as members of society.

Our particular strength has been that we are concerned with all cultures, not only our own or those most accessible to us. We take the position that every existing society is worthy of study. From this cross-cultural base we have learned that there are many ways of solving human problems, of getting food, of structuring relationships between people, and of enriching life through art, music, and ritual.

There are two major differences between anthropology and other social sciences. The first is that, although today large numbers of anthropologists work in urban society, our discipline was originally concerned with those people who lay outside the perimeters of modern society — the small bands and the tribes which lived in Africa, the Pacific, and the Amazon jungle — all the areas of the world little touched by civilization. The second is one of methodology.

In literate and sophisticated societies, data can be gathered by polling, submitting questionnaires, or reading historic documents. Since anthropologists usually worked in nonliterate societies, they discovered an alternate method of gathering information, called "field work."

Anthropological Method

Each anthropologist, as part of his or her required training, goes to live with a group of people whose culture is different from our own, or who belong to a subculture; that is, a culture that exists as part of a larger society. In this new environment, the anthropologist acts as both participant and observer. Thus the anthropologist is exposed to daily events, sees and hears the reactions of people to each other, and comes to know intimately matters which for other scientists remain mathematical statistics. A good anthropologist quickly learns to separate what people really do from what they say they do, and observes the way a society actually works, which is often quite different from the way it appears on paper.

The data thus accumulated is then compared with other data compiled either by anthropologists working on the same problem in different areas, or by anthropologists who have worked in the same area at a different time. Out of such comparisons, the anthropologist hopes to derive an idea of the regularities that exist in the human condition, as well as reasons for the differences between cultures. Anthropologists are not mere collectors of antiques or exotica; they are social scientists who firmly believe that knowledge gained solely from the study of modern industrial society is only partial knowledge. The entirety of human experience must be explored. For example, an exhaustive study of the role of women in the United States is not adequate to present the various forms which male-female interaction can take. The relationships between the sexes in such far-off places as New Guinea, Australia, and Africa must also be studied in order to depict the full range of human variability.

Since we are primarily concerned with the study of women, we should realize that the data for such a cross-cultural study varies in quality. In many societies other than our own, men and women live side-by-side, yet separately, and therefore male anthropologists have little access to the world of women and would be most unwelcome there. Fortunately, anthropology has had such great women as Margaret Mead, Audrey Richards, Ruth Benedict, Carol Stack, Beverly Chiñas, and countless others who have been able to function both as women and as anthropologists in the field, and have brought out of their research much of the woman's view of the society studied. It should also be stated that many male anthropologists, like Oscar Lewis, have been sensitive to the condition of women in the societies they studied, and have recognized the gap in their own work because they were unable to penetrate the world of women and include that dimension. Responsible anthropologists attempt to present a full and complete study of their society. Due to the fact that there have been more male anthropologists than female ones, enthnographies and descriptions of cultures often seem to be weighted to the study of the male functions and status. For example, in hunting and gathering societies, the male role of hunter in supplying subsistence for band societies has been stressed. The newer studies are beginning to show that women, in their gathering activities, actually supply the major portion of the subsistence in these societies.

It is also true that male activities, which constitute the public life of the culture, are more visible to the anthropologist, and are thus more likely to be documented than the private domain in which women carry on their activities.

Characteristics of Culture

There are two major characteristics of culture which are crucial to the understanding of any aspect of it. First, culture is cumulative; and second, culture is a system composed of subsystems.

The fact that culture is cumulative is obvious when we examine the technology of a society. Uses of the wheel and of fire were discovered early in human history, and today are basic to the production of most modern machinery. We could not have modern devices without this prior knowledge. Similarly, but somewhat less obvious, is the fact that attitudes and beliefs are cumulative. Many attitudes that men and women bear toward each other are the result of the cumulative nature of culture. The stereotype of the woman driver, for example, persists contrary to the evidence of insurance statistics, unbiased observers, and reality. This is probably the result of earlier experience at a time when women, confined to their homes, did not drive the family car.

Another more serious survival is the male concept that intercourse is dangerously weakening to men, and that menstrual blood is defiling. Both Mexican-Indian men and the Mae Enga men exhibit such fear, as do many others. As we shall see, this belief is widespread among traditional societies and, in some cultures, is perpetuated simply because it is part of the cultural baggage we have carried from early times.

Perhaps most serious are the ideas that women cannot do men's work competently or make decisions, or that they are inclined to emotionalism. These views are not simply a result of the cumulative nature of culture. More likely, they are a rationalization based upon attitudes developed in earlier times when the division of labor between men and women was more rigid than it is now.

The fact that culture is a system has been amply demonstrated by studies of culture change, in which it can be seen that variations in any one subsystem reverberate throughout. Although this idea of culture being a system composed of subsystems is an abstract one, it is necessary to the study of culture. For example, in such a concept as the divine right of kings, it may be very difficult to distinguish between the sociopolitical subsystem and the ideological subsystem. However, in order to study any culture, the anthropologist finds it necessary to make the abstraction of seeing culture as a system of subcultures so that one may better study the impact of one subsystem upon the other.

Subsystems of Culture

Anthropologists describe culture in terms of three subsystems or "universals," to use Marvin Harris's (1975) term. We shall study women cross-culturally in terms of each of the three subsystems and their relation to the role and status of women. The first is the technoenvironmental subsystem, which describes culture in terms of its adaptation to the environment. It explains how people get their food, what resources they have, and what tools they use, as well as how food and other goods are distributed through the culture.

The second or sociopolitical subsystem describes the essence of relationships between people of one culture and those of another culture, and also the relationships among people within a given culture. The nature of families, the political organization, and associations are all dealt with.

Finally, in the ideological subsystem, anthropologists study religious beliefs, values, myths, legends, art, music, dance — all the aesthetic components of culture.

Although the basic needs of all human societies are the same — to feed itself, reproduce itself, and have affective relationships — the ways in which individual societies express each of the three sybsystems varies enormously with the environment, the technology, and the historical experience of each culture.

All three subsystems of a culture interact with each other so that, as stated earlier, a change in one usually causes changes in both the other subsystems. In studying the status of women in individual cultures, we would expect changes in social organization and in values and beliefs as women's roles in subsistence change. Similarly, conversion to a new religion may affect the economic role of the women. In the Islamic religion, where women are veiled and secluded, it is highly unlikely to find them taking an active part in agriculture or commerce.

As we proceed to look at women cross-culturally, we shall observe examples within each of the subsystems, attempting to view the diversity of adaptations to environment and history within each subsystem. We can expect to find great variety in women's status as well. By looking at the many facets of women's lives in cultures other than our own, we can hope to understand our own culture better. When we recognize that other cultures have alternative modes of structuring the family or the division of labor, we can begin to seek imaginative solutions to the problems of our own culture.

But, before, we adventure into individual cultures, there are certain generalities about women which pertain to all cultures. The next chapter will discuss some of these and suggest theoretical explanations.

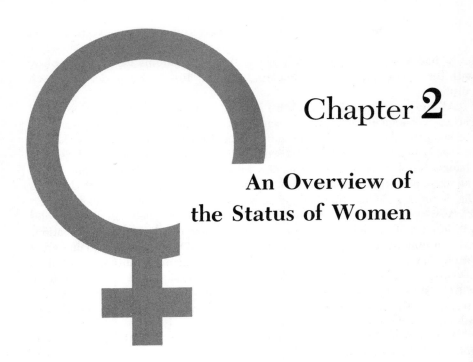

Chapter 2

An Overview of the Status of Women

At this point it is essential to distinguish between individual cultures and culture generically, that is, culture as a whole. Each society possesses and uses an individual culture, adaptive to its own environment and its own history. Culture as a whole refers to the sum of all present cultures and cultures of the past, as far back as we can go. More than the sum of these cultures, culture as a whole presents trends that can be analyzed, universals that are found in each of the individual cultures. Culture as a whole is the unique tool of humanity.

Women's Status in Culture

There is, unquestionably, a great deal of variety in the status and role of women in various cultures. However, in considering culture as a whole, it is universally true that women occupy a secondary status. Despite myths pertaining to Amazons, matriarchies, and the like, no anthropologist to date has ever found a culture in which women rule.

This is quite different from individual women rulers who often were called to power in the absence of an adult male heir. In such cases, it was recognized that the aberrant female was playing a male role. This is eloquently portrayed by the statuary of Queen Hatshepsut of Egypt, who is shown wearing a beard, in order to be recognized as holding a position of authority normally held by a male.

In a brilliant article, Sherry Ortner (1974) speaks of the factors by which the position of women in society can be measured. These three factors are:

1. Statements of cultural ideology which explicitly devalue women, their products, and their roles.
2. Symbolic devices, such as the concept of defilement, associated with women.
3. The exclusion of women from participation in the area believed to be most powerful in the particular society, whether religious or secular.

Although some societies practice all three, others may practice only one or two. Ortner states (1974:69) that "everywhere, in every known culture, women are considered, in some degree, inferior to men." There is no question but that women differ from men, physically, functionally, and perhaps psychologically. However, it is strange that everywhere such differences should be marked as a badge of inferiority.

Nature versus Culture

In his seminal "The Raw and the Cooked," Lévi-Strauss has proposed the dichotomy between men and women as one between nature and culture, where men interact with nature to provide the raw food, and women act as culture-bearers by using fire to cook the raw food. In some way this is implicitly recognized by members of both sexes. Men fear the loss of their manhood, their naturalness, and their raw strength and virility through contact with women; women constantly strive to enculture their men, by taming the rawness of their natures. Ingham (1971), elaborating on this theme, writes of the Siriono of Bolivia. He demonstrates through custom and myth how the Siriono integrate their society around the fact that male hunters provide raw meat to the matrilineages into which they marry. Ingham states (1971:1098):

> Marriage between the Siriono might be understood as a unilateral exchange of game for sexual favor and cooked food, an exchange so practical and self-sufficient that it engendered little additional transaction between social groups. Women simply acquired hunters, who were symbolically cooked (dyed red, smoked, etc.) because they were considered raw and natural. A nature/culture dialectic in primitive myths may mirror an uncertain effort to win culture from nature.

Ortner disagrees with this analysis. She points out that physically women are more closely tied to nature than men. Their bodies are so constructed that many organs and internal secretions exist, not for the benefit of the individual, but rather for the breeding of young. Women are tied to a menstrual cycle for much of their lives; this cycle is regulated by natural rather than cultural time. Men, on the other hand, have bodies that are relatively free from natural time cycles. Most importantly, men have survived by their ability to control and manipulate nature, whether by technology or ritual. Men recognize, consciously and unconsciously, that maleness is tied up with control of both their own bodies and their environment. Man is measured by his ability to control nature. The world presents a challenge to man which he meets by bending nature, even his own, to his will. Woman, according to Ortner, is seen by the community as deriving her womanliness by bending to the forces of nature and to man. They, like children, have been viewed as closer to nature, in that they have not learned the conditioned male responses to stress, have not learned to inhibit natural responses for cultural ends, and do not have the ability to respond to nature aggressively, as men do, because they are smaller and less muscular. In other words, Lévi-Strauss sees men as representative of nature as opposed to women who are representative of culture, while Ortner sees women as representative of nature and men as the products of, as well as the contributors to, culture.

Ortner is careful to point out that women are not regarded as "nature," but rather as being more closely *controlled* by nature and on more intimate terms with it. Thus they fall into an ambiguous category which makes them appear unequal to men, and perhaps even a bit dangerous.

Ortner's idea of how men see themselves in relationship to women would more validly explain the existence of male puberty rituals in which boys must be "made" into men. Girls grow naturally into women, which fact is sometimes recognized in a puberty ceremonial. Women must constantly work to achieve a balance between nature and culture. This is evident today where young women who wish to participate fully in a career are often forced to make choices and decisions regarding the rearing of a family, a problem that does not usually concern men.

Women Bound by Biology

Human biology cannot be completely restrained by culture. Even today, when we have perhaps come closer to this type of control than ever before, we are still conscious of biological necessities, particularly as these apply to reproduction of the species. In every human society women bear and raise children, at least for a short time. This places certain limitations upon the activities of women. The erect posture of the human species has created a narrower birth canal than in other species, and the large brain of the infant also makes birth difficult.

The human infant, therefore, is smaller and far more immature than infants of other species. The birth process itself is more painful and more dangerous, a fact of which man has been manifestly aware for at least 40,000 years. Pregnancy, birth, and infant care, have all operated to bind women more closely to a home place. In fact, the creation of a home place had great survival value for the human species because it was a place to which food and water could be brought, and in which the ill, the very young, or the very old could rest and be cared for. The only way such a home could exist was if there were a division of labor where certain individuals felt obligated to bring food and water to those who remained. The division of labor in simple societies was based upon need and biological factors. Need dictated that labor be divided between the young and the old, the male and the female. Freed from biological imperatives, the young males could roam from the home place to hunt, to find better caves and campsites, and to meet other groups of young males. Women foraged too, but they were constrained by the necessities of carrying and nursing babies and of traveling at the pace of toddlers and small children. They therefore stayed closer to home. At this very early stage, then, the division of labor into a public and a private domain became a human universal. The males, particularly those who were young and active, made contact with other bands and became knowledgeable about a larger geographic area; the females, especially those of child-bearing age, stayed closer to home and had less contact with the outside world. The horizons of the woman thus became more limited and seem to have cast the role of the female as a member of a private sphere, a domestic world, whereas that of the male was a public one, open to greater contact with the outside world and its inhabitants. This still does not explain why the private sphere of women should carry with it the stigma of second-class citizenship. An analysis of the functions of marriage may clarify this.

Marriage

What is this institution? Is it analogous to the pair-bonding of other species? Indeed, it is not. Marriage is a cultural invention, conceived by the human species as an adaptation to its own particular needs. One need only look at marriage as it occurs in many societies to recognize it is not the fulfillment of a romantic dream as it is so often portrayed in our society, but as a powerful, cultural invention created for very specific purposes. The institution of marriage is a public one. Among many people in our time, marriages are arranged by relatives of the bride and groom for purposes which have little to do with mutual affection or romance, although these are often taken into consideration. The function of marriage may be seen in terms of three categories: (1) the division of labor; (2) reproduction; and (3) the formation of alliances. We shall discuss the division of labor and the formation of alliances.

As the division of labor developed, elaborations, the hallmark of culture, developed as well. Among band societies today, one finds that women gather most of the vegetable food used by the group, whereas men provide the meat. This is in keeping with the fact that gathering can be done slowly and relatively close to home, while the hunting pace and hunting range are set by the animal hunted. Although in many societies women kill lizards and small game close to home, the elaboration of this initial division of labor is to be found as a human universal. In fishing societies, women often gather shellfish or fish the waters close to shore while men venture out in boats to fish. Further elaborations of the division of labor are based on traditions. In some societies, women, and women alone, carry water. In most societies, men make tools, even the digging implements used by women, although women may make baskets and nets for their own use; thus the interdependency of the sexes is reinforced. One society follows a tradition where men make pottery and women weave; a neighboring society may observe the opposite tradition. Why this arbitrary division between what is man's work and what is woman's?

As mentioned earlier, the establishment of a home place was of great adaptive advantage to the human species, in that it forced the individuals involved to feel under obligation to share their productivity through the institutionalization of the division of labor along sexual lines. But such an exchange of products can still take place within the nuclear family or as a result of group activity, without the necessity of marriage. Why then marriage?

Most definitions of the term include such concepts as the legitimization of children, the regularization of property ownership, and inheritance. A proper definition should also include the idea of a mutuality of obligations. Again the question arises as to why all these properties cannot exist within a limited group; in other words, why do incest laws force individuals to seek such legitimization and regularization outside the home group? The answer to this is best expressed by Lévi-Strauss (1969a), who thinks of women as gifts to create alliances.

Marriage, in its function of legitimizing offspring, serves to create lasting bonds among separate groups. Certainly, in nonliterate societies, treaties between neighboring groups are limited in value; however, recognition of mutual kinship is a binding force. It is for this reason that until very recently marriages among European royalty were arranged in order to create alliances between particular nations. Mutual descendents, it was hoped, would make the alliance binding beyond the lifetime of the present allies. Thus marriage was — and sometimes still is — an institution created to forge bonds of mutual obligation between disparate groups. By reserving one's women for trading purposes, one enlarges the network of potential allies one can call upon in need. Hart and Pilling (1960) report that the Tiwi of north Australia still create alliances among men by the promise of wives. The older men in this society, having lived long enough to redeem the promises, are powerful because they command the labor of many wives as well as the loyalties of many younger men — sons-in-law — to whom they have promised the daughters of these wives. Women are the ones who must be promised and exchanged because they bear the next generation. As childbearers, women can serve not only to perpetuate the species, but also to create networks of alliances among potentially hostile groups. The function of marriage as an alliance is so important that it is conceivable that the elaborations of the natural divisions of labor were cultural inventions devised to enforce the necessity to marry. As such, marriage can only work in the presence of incest laws, which are nearly universal in human societies. They are variously defined in terms of the degree of relationship regarded as incestuous, but with few exceptions most societies prohibit marriage within the nuclear family: father-daughter, mother-son, or sister-brother. Such laws are neither biologically nor psychologically derived, but firmly rooted in cultural needs. This can be illustrated by the fact that some societies encourage marriage between a man and his mother's brother's daughter, while they regard marriage between a man and his mother's sister's daughter as incestuous.

In patrilocal societies, a "hostage" is given in order for marriage to function as an alliance between two potentially hostile groups. That hostage is a woman, who forever remains an alien in her husband's group. Among traditional Indian families, little girls are treated with great affection because it is recognized that very early in their lives they will pass to the control of a potentially hostile household. Moreover, once in that household, the only way in which a woman can justify her existence is to produce male heirs. Many societies will grant divorce to a man whose wife fails to produce children. In some societies, divorce will be granted if a woman fails to produce male children, no matter how many girls she bears. Even in societies where people live separately, as we do, or with the woman's family, husband and wife are products of different families of orientation, with the differences of enculturation this implies.

Such an analysis of marriage indicates the extent to which women became instruments to be manipulated in the activities of the public sphere. In fairness, it should be stated that once the rules of the game became clear, women, in many societies, became adept at manipulating the marital institution to' their own best interests. However, such manipulations usually were carried out unofficially, within the private sphere which remained the woman's domain.

Authority

We come finally to the question of authority in the public sense, and we see how rarely women wield such authority. In our own time, when women are beginning to assert their right to authority and to challenge the structures which deny them such authority, some men are asserting that women are generally unable to function in such capacities due to hormonal or psychological deficiencies. Anthropologists, however, propose quite another reason for the general powerlessness of women. By definition, incest laws cause marriage to be contracted between men and women of different, though not necessarily hostile, groups. Each, however, has individul obligations and loyalties. In some societies, each retains a good deal of independence, while in others, particularly in patrilocal and neolocal societies where women are isolated from th kin, women are forced to achieve their goals indirectly. Because t' excluded from channels of authority, women have often had to means to safeguard their own interests and those of their ch'

Women thus were stigmatized as enigmatic and potentially dangerous, both magically and practically. Each man found himself in a double bind. He needed women to perpetuate his group, but the women society made available to him were aliens, and often viewed ambivalently and perhaps as magically endowed with "power." The Mae Enga of New Guinea and the Sarakatsani of Greece recognize and verbalize this attitude. Mead reports that among the Arapesh, where infant girls are adopted and reared within the family of the potential husband, witchcraft is thought to be practiced by the mountain people, since no one in the immediate group could be guilty of ill-will toward his own people. Women, then, cannot wield authority because of a heritage of exclusion from legitimately conceived power. Although modern marriages among most people no longer serve the original purposes, and although individual women may feel very much at home among their affines (families by marriage), the folk-ethic of man's ambivalence toward women in general, and his conception of their ways as inscrutable, remains.

Women's Status in the Modern World

It would be a gross over-simplification to suggest that the dilemma of modern women in Western society is due entirely to the adaptation of the formation of alliances and the division of labor as it was constituted in earlier times. Nonetheless, as Rosaldo (1974:36) points out:

> Women's status will be lower in those societies where there is a firm differentiation between domestic and public spheres of activity and where women are isolated from one another and placed under a single man's authority, in the home.

Through time, the anomalous and powerless position of the domestic woman became translated into whatever idiom was current. It is not very long ago in our own society that a woman's body, her sex, was regarded as the work of the devil, to be hidden beneath layers of cumbersome clothing. In some societies this is still the case today. One has but to think of the veiled Moslem women or the peasant women of Europe.

Rosaldo also points out (1974:42) that today, although in our own society we give lip service to the idea of equality of the sexes and woman's body has been largely freed from its encumbrances, we tend to place priority and greater value upon the work of men than the work of women. It is considered normal procedure for a woman to cease work to care for small children or to give up her career to facilitate her husband's. In this way, we continue to relegate women to the domestic, private domain, while men remain in the public sphere.

The universal classification of women to secondary status can thus be seen as the result of cultural adaptations made possible by the nature of women and their biological heritage. Let us now examine this biological base in an effort to determine not only the nature of the obvious differences between males and females, but also the significance placed by culture upon those differences.

Chapter 3

The Biology of Womanhood

It was mentioned earlier that in many societies men can and do divorce wives who do not produce sons for them. The cruelty of this act sharply points out two things: the secondary position of women, in that the wife is always assumed to be willfully withholding the desired heir, and also the ignorance of the biological fact that maleness can only be passed on by men.

X and Y Chromosomes

Every human being possesses twenty-three chromosomes in one's sex cells. Only one is a sex chromosome, which determines the sex of the child to be born. Females produce eggs containing sex chromosomes of only one kind — the X chromosome. Males produce sperm of two kinds, some containing the X chromosome, others containing the Y chromosome. Thus, in the act of reproduction, the embryo necessarily receives an X chromosome from the ovum of the mother, but may receive either an X or a Y chromosome from the sperm of the father. A female is determined by the combination XX; a male by the combination XY.

The X chromosome is a relatively large one and bears genes that influe the development of many traits. The Y chromosome, on the other han small, and we do not know at this time precisely what genes it c know, however, that the Y chromosome does not carry the s chromosome, because certain diseases, such as hemophilia, appear only in the male, but are passed on by the female. Evidently the gene for hemophilia appears only on the X chromosome and is a recessive trait. This explains why a female who has a gene for hemophilia on one X chromosome and a gene for normal blood clotting on the other X chromosome does not develop the disease herself, but a son that she bears who receives the X chromosome carrying the defect will show the disease, since there is no alternative gene on the Y chromosome. Work is proceeding to determine which genes are carried on the Y chromosome. It has been suggested that males who, through defective cell division, carry several Y chromosomes tend to be more aggressive than other males; however, this theory needs much further testing.

Since the Y chromosome is very small and light as compared with the X chromosome, its light weight makes the sperm carrying it more mobile than the sperm carrying X chromosomes. As a result, the actual number of male fertilizations which occur is higher than female fertilizations.

Differential Viability of Males versus Females in the United States

Ashley Montagu (1974:84) estimates the number of male embryos as 120 to 150 compared to 100 female embryos at fertilization. However, during the embryological process, these embryos show less viability. During gestation, many die so that at birth the number of males born is 106 to 100 females. This suggests that there may be a disadvantage to the embryo possessing the Y chromosome. Such a disadvantage may be of the type known for hemophilia, an inability to counter recessive deleterious genes on the X chromosome. Or the disadvantage may lie in some as yet unknown quality. Whatever that disability is, it continues throughout the population curve, in that more males than females die in every age grouping, until, in old age, the predominant number of survivors are females. Montagu (1974:85) states that in the first year of life, three male infants die for every female; by the age of 21 the ratio is down to two to one. At 35, 1,400 males die for every 1,000 females; at 55 the ratio is up to 1,800 to 1,000. After that the ratio declines; however, the life expectancy of the female is always greater than that of the male.

For the Western world, Montagu (1974:87–88) lists 63 diseases which appear in males more frequently than in females, whereas there are only 31 diseases which afflict women more frequently than men. The diseases to which males are subject are diseases of stress.

Coronary insufficiency occurs 30 times more frequently in men than in women. Coronary sclerosis affects men 25 times as often as it does women. Ulcers are six times more prevalent among men than women. Angina pectoris affects men five times more frequently than women. Women appear to be slightly more subject to carcinomas of the gall bladder and genitalia.

Hormones

It has been shown that the possession of the Y chromosome alone is not sufficient to create maleness. The differentiation of the sexes is a process which occurs *in utero*, during fetal development. In the embryological process, various biological systems develop at various times. Apparently, early in pregnancy the reproductive tissue of the embryo is undifferentiated. During the course of development, anatomical sexual differentiation of the male occurs in response to androgens secreted by the fetal testis. Hamburg and Lunde (1972:19) state:

> The recent, but already classic experiments of Jost have shown that there is a critical period during which the development of internal reproductive structures takes place. The testis must secrete a masculinizing hormone (androgen) during this period if differentiation is to take a male course.

Both sexes are exposed to female hormones secreted *in utero* by the mother. It has been noted that in cases where pregnant women have been treated with a synthetic form of testosterone (the male hormone) in order to prevent miscarriage, there have been reports of masculinization of the fetus. This has been shown by Wilkins *et al.* (1958) in 18 out of 21 cases of female pseudohermaphrodism (the enlargement of the clitoris and partial fusion of the labial folds) which causes the female sexual organs to resemble male sexual organs. Wilkins (1965) has shown that in cases where the embryo starts out as a genetic male, and the masculinization continues so that the internal genitalia are differentiated, a failure of androgen secretion by the fetal testes causes the external genitalia to develop in feminine fashion.

It may be that the role played by androgens during pregnancy contributes to the discrepancy between the number of males conceived and those born. A male may fail to develop normally due to lack of androgens. With the exception of the artificial introduction of testosterone during the pregnancy, the course of sexual differentiation for the female is less hazardous than that for the male.

At birth there are notable differences between males and females. Male neonates raise their heads higher than females. Females are more sensitive to the removal of covering, showing a higher degree of skin sensitivity.

The role of sex hormones in patterning the behavior of males and females is less clearly understood. Since there is a feedback mechanism in operation between the glands which secrete hormones and the hypothalamus which is part of the brain, it is not clear what role in human behavior is played by hormones alone. Thus Money (1961) reports that sex hormones have little or no influence in patterning human behavior, but that such behavior is culturally defined and taught. Hamburg and Lunde (1966:21) are less certain of this *a*do seem to see some basic hormonal patterning, although they state *t*"complexity of the inter-reactions between genetic, endocrin*e'* environmental variables" needs further study.

Throughout childhood there is a minimal secretion of gonadotrophins, regulators of sex hormones. Research (Donovan 1963) tends to show that certain cells in the hypothalamus portion of the brain lose their sensitivity to gonadotrophins gradually throughout childhood, and eventually allow the presence of sufficient amounts of these regulators to stimulate puberty; environmental factors may be involved in the timing of this event. It has been noted that the onset of puberty has decreased from the ages of 16 to 17 one hundred years ago to 12 to 13 years at present. The reasons for this are unknown at present, although better nutrition has been suggested. In any event, the onset of puberty is marked in both sexes by the development of secondary sexual characteristics. These include the growth of body hair characteristic of each sex, lowered pitch of the voice in boys, and the development of the breasts in girls. This is also accompanied by a spurt in growth which usually occurs a year or two earlier in girls than in boys. According to chemical assays (Hamburg and Lunde 1972:6), both boys and girls secrete estrogens, the female hormone, and testosterone, the male hormone. The difference between the sexes is marked by the proportion of each. Moreover, estrogens become cyclic for the female, with the onset of the menstrual cycle, but not for the male.

The female menstrual cycle is marked by a buildup of the estrogen levels, followed by a cessation of estrogen production and the onset of progesterone secretion. During pregnancy, progesterone levels remain high. It is possible that the minor fluctuations in behavior, which mark both the menstrual cycle and the birth cycle for some women, might have their origin in the sudden cessation of progesterone production with the onset of the menses or immediately post-partum.

Experimentation on monkeys has shown that monkeys maintained on a high level of testosterone tend to be more aggressive than untreated monkeys. They have a higher level of threat behavior; they initiate more play, and their play tends to be rougher. Since human behavior is always mediated by culture, it cannot be stated that the presence of testosterone alone will suffice to make the human male more aggressive. As to the effects of estrogen-progesterone cycles on females, much less is known. Aside from the occasional swings in mood and minor discomforts which accompany the alternations of the cycle, little in female behavior can be directly attributed to hormonal activity. Progesterone has been found to raise the pain threshold in the brain, a most adaptive feature for childbirth. Sex motivation in the female seems to be influenced by androgens, a secretion of the adrenal glands, rather than either estrogen or progesterone. Maccoby (1972) and others have measured intellectual activity, intelligence, creativity, and areas of intellectual interest among males and females for evidence to support a claim that what differences exist are either consistent or biological in nature. The fact that some boys may excel in science while some girls excel in literature or art is a result of the cultural norms of male–female behavior established in our society rather than of hormonal influence.

Puberty

There are, however, certain differences which are intrinsically biological, and upon which culture has elaborated. Primary among these is the fact that the female reproductive period is marked by the visible symptoms of menarche and menopause. The male reproductive period is not. This has had an effect upon the means used by various cultures to establish adult status in its members. Many societies have found it necessary to create elaborate puberty rituals to mark the passage from boyhood to manhood. Since the time used is culturally rather than biologically determined, the age varies from culture to culture.

Puberty Rituals for Boys

Almost all such puberty rituals for boys are marked by several common phenomena.

First, the boys are removed from home and taken to stay for a variable period with boys of about the same age. This custom deserves considerable discussion. Until the age at which the society defines the onset of male puberty, boys identify with their mothers, as do girls; they remain at home and are treated as the small children they are. The abrupt rupture of these relationships is seen among many people as necessary to the creation of men.

Among the Mae Enga people of New Guinea, the men consciously express the fact that they "marry their enemies" (Meggit 1964). Thus, boys, who will become men of the patrilineage, must be removed from this potentially dangerous and alien environment of the mother-dominated home, and taught to fear and disdain females. Physical separation is seen as a necessary first step in this process. Initially this must be a frightening experience for young boys, but is probably somewhat mitigated by the potential achievement of adult male status. However, there are numerous field reports of the traumatic experience that this can be to many young boys.

Second, during this period of enforced separation, the boys are instructed by the men. In simple societies this is usually the only formal schooling period. All the lore and knowledge of the particular society is imparted to the youths. They are taught the origin of myths, as well as the precepts and the codes of their society. In addition, they are taught that such knowledge must never be imparted to women or uninitiated boys.

Third, after the learning period is over, the boys are usually subjected to some physical test of courage, and then, in some way (circumcision, tatooing, removal or filing of teeth), physically marked to show their initiation is complete. In many societies, boys are forbidden to cry out in order to show their bravery. Tests of courage range from silently sustaining a beating to killing one or several designated animals. Among some people, obedience to older men is also inculcated at this time: arbitrary rules are enforced by the older men with whom the boys are taught to comply automatically.

And finally, having successfully completed the tests, proven obedience, and been marked as men, a feast is held to celebrate the achievement of manhood. The young males now reenter the group as men, with all that this implies: separation from the world of women; alliance with other men of the society, beyond immediate kinship bonds; and, above all, the fact that men have been made. One does not grow to manhood; one must achieve it.

Puberty Rituals for Girls

Far fewer societies hold similar puberty rituals for girls. Attempts to correlate female puberty rituals with matrilineality have been largely unsuccessful. Puberty in women is marked by undeniable physical symptoms. At menarche, many societies segregate the young woman in a hut used especially for this purpose. She is instructed by older women in the particular patterns of behavior her society assigns to menstruating women. These usually take the form of prevention of defilement. The blood of menstruating women is often regarded as dangerous, particularly to men and to objects used by males. In some societies, a menstruating woman is forbidden to cook for her family. In others, she must not walk unrestricted through the forest, but must confine her steps to a particular path lest she spoil the hunting prospects.

Some societies, such as the Bemba of Rhodesia, hold elaborate ceremonials for girls at menarche, but this is the exception. Such a Chisungu ceremonial will be described in a later chapter. Usually, girls are closely confined, apprised of the taboos involved, and after bleeding has ceased, resume their ordinary duties. For some people, marriage is either contracted at this time or, if already contracted, it is consummated.

In most societies a woman is forbidden access to her husband or his possessions for fear that she will taint them. This is expanded in some societies to include the woman herself, so that she may not scratch herself, but must use a stick for this purpose.

Views of Menstruation

Hogbin (1970:88) reports that on the island of Wogeo in New Guinea men regard menstruation as purification. At regular intervals men initiate mock menstruation in themselves as follows:

First the man catches a crayfish or crab and removes one of its claws which he keeps wrapped up with ginger until it is required. He also collects various soothing leaves including some from a plant whose fruit has a smooth skin of deep purple color. From dawn onwards on the day he has fixed, he eats nothing. Then late in the afternoon he goes to a lonely beach, covers his head with a palm spathe, removes his clothing, and wades out until the water is up to his knees. He stands there with legs apart and induces an erection either by thinking about desirable women or by masturbation. When ready, he pushes back the foreskin and hacks at the glans, first on the left side, then on the right. Above all, he must not allow the blood to fall on his fingers or his legs. He waits until the cut has begun to dry and the sea is no longer pink and then walks ashore. After wrapping the penis in leaves, he dresses and goes back to the village where he enters the club. Here he remains for two or three days. Sexual intercourse is forbidden till the next new moon — the soreness, in any event, may take that long to wear off (Hogbin 1970:88)

Hogbin notes that it is believed that such "menstruation" must be done at regular intervals in order to maintain good health. Some societies regard menstrual blood as a physically dangerous fluid in itself. All contact with it must be avoided on pain of very severe illness or possible death. Menstrual blood is also believed to have properties which endanger the well-being of the entire group. The inadvertent passage of a menstruating woman through a pasture or a field can endanger growing animals and plants. It is interesting to note that menstrual prohibitions apply not only to women marrying into the society, but also to its daughters. Coult (1963:32–35) has attempted to explain menstrual taboos in terms of perceptual reality. He claims that menstrual discharges have "depressant effects on organic substances," a fact which man perceived early in history.

Few societies take any particular ritual note of menopause. In all probability, not many women in early societies lived long enough to achieve this stage. Today when women do live past menopause, they are also past the danger of defilement and can take positions of power. Particularly in modern peasant societies, some women even venture into the public sphere. For example, in Indian villages in Mexico, the curandera is often a woman past the menstrual cycle. The mother of grown sons in nearly every society wields a great deal of power, but in patrilocal societies particularly this power is confined to the private sphere.

Birth and Lactation

Birth lactation are also biological attributes of women, and here too, the ritual involved is manifold, and will be dealt with at a later time. Despite the fact that childbirth in itself is a natural process, most societies recognize that it is fraught with danger for both mother and child under primitive conditions. Pregnant women are often permitted special foods, and denied others in order to ease childbirth. There are few societies which do not have a ritual specialist, either a man or, more frequently, a woman, whose task it is to see a woman through a difficult childbirth. In some societies, men are strictly barred from the house in which a woman is giving birth. In others, as in Mexico, the husband is often asked to hold the wife, to support her through the final stage of parturition. There are various rituals connected with the disposal of the afterbirth, as well. In many societies, it is buried either in the floor of the house or close by.

Finally, there are often restrictions on intercourse between husband and wife during pregnancy and lactation. These range from the extreme of complete abstinence during the entire period, which may last as long as six years, to the milder injunctions against intercourse during the final months of pregnancy and almost always during lactation.

Biologically, then, the differences between males and females are real and of significant order. Cultural elaborations have served to widen the gap. In one instance, however, there is evidence of decreasing differentiation between men and women. This brings us to the question of sexual dimorphism.

Sexual Dimorphism

In most species, it is possible to distinguish the male from the female visually. Almost always, particularly in mammals, the male is significantly larger. He is often endowed with certain physical traits which differ from the female, such as the mane of the lion or the larger canine teeth of baboons. Most of these traits, including greater physical strength, are correlated with the function of the male as protector of the females and young. Although sexual dimorphism is less obvious among humans than among other species, men usually have heavier bones and muscles than women. They also have a higher rate of heart efficiency. Such differences are not highly significant in the light of modern complex technology. However, they must have been much more significant for early humans, and thus men were endowed with the responsibility of acting as protectors of women and children. Some anthropologists have argued that *Australopithecus robustus* may be the male of the same species of which the smaller, more gracile *Australopithecus africanus* is the female. This theory has not been generally accepted by anthropologists. Certainly, by the time we deal with *Homo erectus*, the differences between males and females are more difficult to discern, except, of course, in the pelvic structure. This implies that, for man, culture replaced physical weapons for defense. A woman armed with a heavy stick could do as much damage to an intruder as a man. With the development of cultural means of defense and offense, the differences in physical stature between men and women became relatively less important. In discussing athletic training programs for women, De Vries (1966) notes that those sports which depend upon power more than skill have fewer women as star performers. However, he also notes that women athletes respond to a conditioning program in much the same way as men. Barron, Heeschen and Widman (1968) state that men have heavier muscles and bones than women, that they tend to be five to six inches taller than women, and that they have less subcutaneous fat. Women have more rapid pulse rates. In a measure of heart efficiency, known as the oxygen pulse, men and women show the same efficiency until the age of about 15. At that time, the male efficiency triples, while that of the female remains the same; this factor may have been very significant to early man. De Vries (1966:405), however, points out that women have greater manual dexterity than men:

> A review of the literature in this area (physical training) seems to indicate that there are probably no real sex differences in regard either to motor learning rate or capacity, unless strength is a factor.

In contemporary life, strength plays a smaller role than it did in the past. Few modern industries depend upon brute strength, and dexterity is probably at least as important.

Today, there are women who are taller than men, and men who are lighter in weight than women. Some women show greater athletic ability than some men. Both men and women of one society may be taller than both men and women of other societies. The question of greater physical strength is also debatable. In many societies, the women do the heavy work, carry the heavy loads, and walk while men ride. Therefore, sexual dimorphism in humans is less significant now than in the earlier times. This can be regarded as the result of the development of cultural strategies for survival.

The Relation between Culture and Biology

Although this chapter has dealt primarily with the physical, biological differentiation between the two sexes, it should be noted how frequently cultural factors have been mentioned. The human species, although certainly a biological entity, has, through the use of culture, divorced itself from biological imperatives to a greater extent than any other species. Humans are preeminently creatures of learning and culture, which modifies even the most demanding needs of biology. We fulfill our need for nourishment according to the dictates of our society as to appropriate food and proper time to eat. Our sexual desire similarly follows culture's guidelines, which attempt to restrict it to a lasting emotional attachment that has adaptive value for the culture. Even the ultimate biological fact of death has for many people been culturally translated into a transferral to a new and better life. The important factor in this cultural involvement with biology is that the culture sets up a feedback system between the biological fact and the societal values.

If we use the simple factor of the biological attainment of puberty, we can readily see how culture constrains the biological effects. Weatherley (1964) reports that boys who show signs of an early puberty readily become leaders among their peers in middle-class Western society. Group acceptance is easily granted to the taller, stronger, more masculine boy. Late maturing boys are less dominant and more in need of reassurance. Precocious boys are sure of themselves; they are sure of society's approval, they become confident, secure men. Precocious girls, on the other hand, often feel the weight of their society's approbation. They are often frightened and embarrassed by the early onset of menstruation and tend to be timid and withdrawn; however, girls who matured late showed anxiety. This proves the point that a thoroughly encultured member of a society incorporates the values of that society. Women themselves have been taught by tradition that being a woman is not desirable, despite the biological facts which tend to disprove this.

Summary

There are very real biological differences between men and women. Although men are usually larger and stronger, evidence shows that in our society women tend to live longer and be less subject to diseases of stress. This condition may change as more women enter the stressful public sphere.

The factor of maleness is due not only to the presence of a Y chromosome, which must be inherited from the father, but also to the production of androgens by the fetal reproductive system.

Boys attain manhood through a culturally defined ritual or form of recognition; girls reach womanhood through menarche. Many societies regard menstrual blood as dangerous, and therefore women are considered potential defilers during menstruation.

Concern with childbirth and lactation is evident in most societies. Specialists exist to aid the mother, and most cultures observe specific customs during this period. Central to the differentiation of men and women is woman's function as a childbearer. Many of the attitudes and behavior patterns of the sexes are structured around this core.

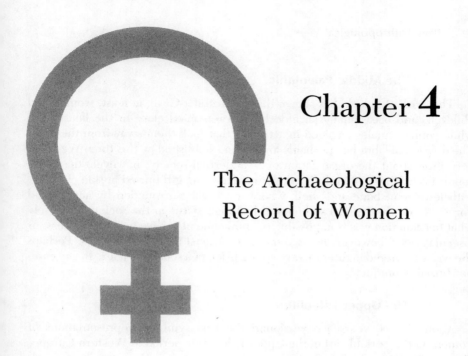

Chapter 4

The Archaeological
Record of Women

Some archaeological finds of whole populations have made the determination of sex of skeletons easier and more secure, although not absolute. It is difficult to determine the sex of a single, individual skeleton, since most measurements are comparative and therefore require more than one skeleton before the relative size of the skull, massiveness of the spinal column, length and narrowness of the pelvis can be evaluated. In the case of an individual skeleton, any assignment of sex must be tentative. Physical anthropologists, for example, changed their minds three times in the past generation with respect to the sex of the famous Tepexpan skeleton in Mexico.

In keeping with the distinction already made between the activities of males in the public sphere and females in the private sphere, the archaeological evidence points out that ceremonial burials, accompanied by grave goods, occur more often for males than for females, although there are notable exceptions.

The Lower Paleolithic

We know too little to make any kind of statement regarding the role of women in Australopithecine or *Homo erectus* populations. With the appearance of *Homo sapiens neanderthalensis*, however, we begin to find more cultural evidence.

The Middle Paleolithic

The work of Solecki has shown that in Shanidar Cave, at least, women and children, and occasionally an elderly man remained close to the hearth fire while younger males engaged in activities that took them away from the cave. The division of labor had probably long been established by this time. We know very little about the organization of Neanderthal society; however, there is a report from Siberia of finding a skeleton of a young girl buried in skin clothing, with jewelry of bone and shell, whose grave was surrounded by antlers and horns. No doubt this girl so honored had high status in the society. Precisely what her function was is impossible to know. She may have been a priestess, or a secular ruler; however, her age mitigates against these possibilities. Perhaps she was a favored daughter or very young bride of a societal leader. In any case, her burial is unique.

The Upper Paleolithic

About 25,000 years ago we found the first symbolic representations of women, in the portable art of the Upper Paleolithic period in Western Europe. These statuettes, which anthropologists humorously call "Venuses," are rough portrayals of females in which the sexual and secondary sexual characteristics are greatly exaggerated, while faces, arms, and legs are merely sketched in or are missing altogether. Until very recently, these "Venuses" were categorized as "fertility figurines" and dismissed. Alexander Marshack (1972) undertook the analysis of both cave and portable art from this period, using a process that may be called cognitive archaeology. By very fine microscopic examination of the artifacts concerned, he has derived some interesting insights into their uses and general meanings.

Venuses

Marshack divides the "Venuses" into three categories: (1) those which are carved on rock walls; (2) those which are finely made, but portable; and (3) those which seem to have been sketchily made, and portable.

Some of the female figures in the first category seem to indicate the use of the area as a shrine, perhaps a place where women went for magic help in conceiving or carrying through a successful pregnancy. However, the two figures carved on the rock surface at Laussel (Marshack 1972:334–335) indicate a much more complex interpretation. These female figures are heavy, but not pregnant and faceless; they seem to have been rubbed with red ochre. Both figures carry curved horns, one of which has thirteen lines on it. Marshack interprets these figures as goddesses, with the thirteen lines on the buffalo horn indicating the lunar months.

Females and Seasonal Fertility

Much of Marshack's interpretation of Upper Paleolithic art is concerned with showing that man was capable of what Marshack calls "time-factoring," an awareness of the passage of time either through counting phases of the moon or through some other astronomical observation. Marshack relates these female figures to a ceremonial or myth connected with seasons of rutting, migration, and calving of animals and believes the female figures to have been central to that ceremonial (Marshack 1972:335). In Marshack's view, man at this time had an accurate calendrical notion about the behavior and seasonal appearance of various animals and plants. It seems very likely that this periodicity should be related to the natural periodicity of the female cycle. Do we, at Laussel, have the prototype of all the later Mother-Earth goddesses?

Childbirth and Figurines

Marshack has made a fine analysis of the various types of portable art. He suggests that some of the more finely made figurines were the property of specialists who used them in magical rites to assist women in childbirth. Of the more crudely made figurines, he proposes that some may have been made for purposes of aiding in one specific case, and then discarded. However, his analysis is actually far more refined and gives us greater insight into the symbolic nature of femininity at this time. Marshack shows that there are many types of portable art, such as tiny female figurines, made of coal, from Petersfels, Germany, which have holes in them and were evidently worn and used as amulets or finely carved, small statuettes showing a female figure at an early age of development. The use of these figurines is speculative; Marshack guesses that they might have been used during a puberty ceremonial.

Abstract Female Figurines

There are, as well, symbolic presentations of parts of female anatomy which bear every resemblance to the most abstract of modern art. The buttocks and the vulva are stylized and abstracted to form symbols which appear, not only in sculpture, but also in cave paintings. The breasts are often presented alone, on a single stem, and often are marked with lines which suggest the counting or factoring of time. Marshack concludes that these breast pendants were worn by women, and the counting may have been either the menstrual cycle or the cycle of pregnancy.

The use of these stylized female representations was not, however, limited to women. In northern Italy, the grave of a young man of the Upper Paleolithic is relatively rich in grave goods; it contains a cap of seashell beads, pendants of deer tooth, a stone knife, and four batons of commandment, which are rods of antler with a hole at the top, often highly carved with animal, plant, and fish signs. The use of these batons is not known. There is speculation that they may have been arrow-straighteners. Marshack (1972:317) says:

> Near the upper part of the body there lay a decorated bone pendant in the shape of the buttock's image, with a hole at the top. The microscope showed it was highly polished and was worn inside the hole from long use. The female buttock's image had been used in life by the youth or someone else, and it was being used now in burial to extend its meaning into the afterlife.

Mother-Goddess

A great many of these images, particularly the stylized ones, have lines and arcs drawn on them. It is not possible to decipher what meaning such marks had; we do know that these were not merely created by the society as fertility or pornographic objects. As far as we can tell, they were distributed throughout the entire continent of Europe, from the U.S.S.R. to the borders of the Atlantic, from the northerly reaches of Siberia to Italy and the Iberian peninsula. Wherever they are found, they seem to indicate the existence of a belief system and a ritual which involved aspects of womanhood. Abramova (1962), a Soviet archaeologist, interprets these figurines and symbols in terms of a "Mother-Goddess" cult, which is perhaps linked with matrilineal clans and the concept of the woman as "mistress of the home and hearth, protectress of the domestic fire, responsible for the well-being of the household and the bearing of children."

Marshack's analysis (1972:339) leads him to the following summation:

> I point out that my study of the "female" images indicates a mythology and the use of the image more complex and diverse than that of goddess of the hearth and hunt and ancestress of the clan, although these are not excluded as aspects of the myth and ceremony. Analysis of the archaeological evidence and a beginning attempt to reconstruct certain basic cognitive and symbolic psychological processes have indicated that the images were extremely variable in meaning and use and that they played a number of specialized and generalized roles across the complex, integrated, time-factored culture.

It is important to note here that 25,000 to 30,000 years ago, all across Europe, evidence shows that culture recognized and incorporated the woman and her cyclic regularity in a complex belief system. Since such complex mythology does not spring from a vacuum, earlier finds may some day give a clue as to the development of such concepts. It is unlikely that we shall ever be able to know the precise meanings these objects had for the wearers or users, but there is every reason to see in them the beginnings of later cults.

Goddesses and Agriculture

In later times female deities are most conspicuously connected to the agricultural cycle. If we accept the notion that early division of labor was based on the needs of babies and young children it seems obvious that women would have to be more concerned with obtaining those food items which were found in permanent positions, not too far from home. Among societies of hunters and gatherers, women do the gathering of roots, nuts, and vegetable foods. Lee (1968:33) states that among the Bushmen, women provide two to three times as much food by weight as men. In this society, the vegetable foods provided by the women comprise 60 to 80 percent of the total diet. Under such circumstances, women will obviously become better acquainted with the nature and needs of plants, and it is not unlikely that initial efforts at plant domestication were made by women. It is also true that the rounds of agriculture are seasonal, cyclic in nature, like the female pattern. Women and earth are potentially fertile, have dormant seasons, and will, in due time, reproduce. In fact, the analogy is so obvious that in Peru, one of the major gods of the Mochica people is depicted as casting seed upon the ground from his penis. Thus, there is relatively easy transfer of images from woman to earth-mother. Virtually every agrarian society has such a figure — Isis, Demeter, and countless others. With each there is a legend to account for the barren season: Isis travels through Egypt seeking parts of the body of her destroyed husband; and Demeter goes to the underworld in hopes of finding her missing daughter.

An interesting paradox can be seen in the fact that those societies which worshiped female deities and had castes of priestesses and female oracles did not necessarily give higher status to the ordinary women. In Greece, women were housebound; they did not participate in public events of any kind except as onlookers. In Rome, the situation was similar. Although we have read about Caesar's wife and know from history about Cleopatra, we are also aware of the fact that the Roman paterfamilias had the right of life or death over his wife and children. Consistency has never been a human strong point; perhaps our heritage would be less rich if it were.

Summary

Archaeologically, then, early man seems to have recognized the particular ability of women to produce children. Lacking scientific skills, rituals which involved the use of female figurines were used to invoke the aid of the supernatural to help in the process. Early man extrapolated the potential fertility of women from human to animal populations, thus bridging the gap between the male and the female concerns, at least, ideologically. The potential fertility of women is a human universal and has been universally recognized and used. The particular ways in which this has been used will be explored from this point on.

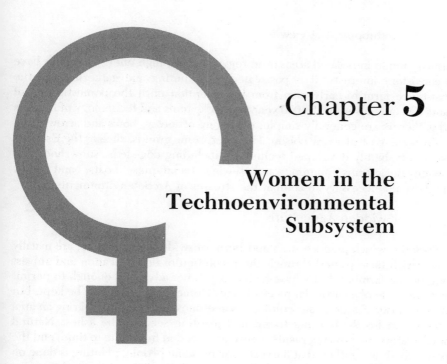

Chapter 5

Women in the Technoenvironmental Subsystem

One of the basic tasks confronting any society is that of subsistence. This requirement involves not only obtaining food, but also distributing it. As mentioned before, a division of labor between men and women seems to have existed in this activity.

Ranking of Societies

Societies may be ranked on a scale according to the efficiency with which they produce energy. Those which use very little manpower in proportion to their population for food production are called high-energy societies; those which depend primarily upon manpower and utilize much of their population for subsistence production are called low-energy societies. Depending on the environment and the efficiency of technology, anthropologists may classify societies on the basis of subsistence methods.

Hunters and Gatherers

Hunters and gatherers, or foragers, consist of those people who make no effort to change their environment, but simply make use of what is found. These people live in a variety of climatic zones and their activities vary in accordance with ecological demands. Although today such groups are small and normally found in isolated areas or in regions where high-energy societies have no consistent interests, it is postulated that hunting and gathering was the subsistence form of early man from his inception until the domestication of plants and animals some 10,000 years ago. The tools and technology of hunters and gatherers are generally simple, consisting of spears, bows and arrows, and usually some type of arrow poison. However, some groups, such as the Eskimo, have a very highly developed technology including dog-sleds, snowshoes and snow-goggles, traps, tanning and sewing techniques, boats, and other paraphernalia necessary to combat the stresses of Arctic environments.

Swidden Agriculture

Societies which practice slash-and-burn, or swidden agriculture, are usually those which have passed through the revolution of domestication and subsist primarily on farming, but whose technology is not advanced enough to permit permanent use of a particular piece of land. Domestic animals may be kept, but not in quantity. Swidden agriculture is sometimes practiced by clearing an area of trees and brush, burning them, and planting seed in the ashes. Natural rainfall waters the growing plants, which are weeded from time to time, and the ripened foods are gathered at harvest. Among some people, planting is done on the alluvial soil near a river, and the natural rising of the river in the spring waters the plants. In some areas fields must be allowed to lie fallow for quite a long time or else the soil becomes depleted, and consequently, new areas must be cleared every two or three years. Most of the food raised is used for subsistence, although some may be set apart for trade or ceremonial use. Technology is still relatively simple — the digging stick serves as the most common agricultural implement. Today these societies are found in parts of the Pacific, Africa, and the New World, and are in fact quite widespread. Until high-energy societies encroach upon them, they seem to be stable and well adapted.

Developed Agriculture

Developed agricultural societies have devised the means of intensifying agriculture, either through the use of the plow and fertilizers or through irrigation works. Domestic animals are kept on land that cannot be cultivated, while the rest of the land is permanently cultivated. This is the most widespread form of subsistence now known and is used throughout the continents of the world. The special kind of herding society found in desert and steppe environments, in which the herding of animals is the major subsistence form, although some agriculture also takes place, is considered a subcategory of this type of society.

Industrialization

Although we tend to think of industrialization as the most prevalent form of subsistence, it is not. Industrialization is found primarily in Western civilization, which includes such modern nation-states as Japan and the Soviet Union. Here agriculture and animal raising tend to take place on a large scale. The technology is very elaborate, and includes the use of complicated machinery. Chemicals are used both as fertilizers and as pest eradicators, in what Galbraith has called the "agrochemical" industry. Work is done by fewer people, and these are employees rather than individual landholders. The basic products of the society are not considered agricultural, but industrial.

A subtype of this industrialized society are the "developing nations," which pass from colonialism (where a cash crop is raised for export and the majority of the people also practiced subsistence agriculture) to independence (where political stress is on industrialization and market-cropping as opposed to subsistence farming).

We shall discuss the role and status of women as they appear in each of these societies. The technoenvironmental subsystem must be adapted to the environment in order for the society to function. One of the basic adaptations, the division of labor, becomes more complex as the technoenvironmental subsystems become more complex. In such cases, the role of women varies with the differences in their responsibilities, and with differences in the nature of the group in which they find themselves.

Women in Hunting and Gathering Societies

The nature of the hunting and gathering band is such that it is very closely controlled by the environment. There are, of course, major differences among societies, depending upon their particular ecological niche. We shall summarize, as far as possible, the role of women in two different types of hunting and gathering societies: the Hadza and the Tiwi of Australia.

Hadza

The Hadza of Africa inhabit a rift valley not far from Lake Eyasi in Tanzania. They are important to us because, contrary to many hunters and gatherers, they do not live in an area of sparse food resources, but seem to enjoy plenty of food with relatively little effort. This probably simulates the conditions under which human society evolved more closely than does the band living under conditions of extreme scarcity. It seems logical that before the development of high-energy societies, the low-energy societies had their choice of suitable environments. Woodburn (1968:49) states that the Hadza utilize many species of plants and animals in their environment. Vegetables consist primarily of the roots of four particular plants and the berries of six others. However, this food is not greatly valued, partially because the roots are fibrous and the berries are bitter. Hunting is done exclusively by men and boys. The game usually hunted is small, although large game is taken when possible. Honey is used both as food and in trade. Although the Hadza know the technique of drying their meat in the sun to preserve it, they do not, in fact, do so, but consume the meat as it is brought into camp. Similarly, no attempt is made to store vegetable food.

Nevertheless, little time is spent either by men or women in subsistence-related activities. Woodburn (1968:54) remarks that these hunter-gatherers seem to have an easier time of it than neighboring agriculturalists, since the wild food upon which they depend is more resistant to drought and other harsh conditions than the cultigens which have been introduced to the agricultural societies.

Division of Labor

Woodburn states that women go out to gather alone, with their children, or in small groups. The women and children usually go to an area within an hour's walk of the camp, where they not only gather, but also eat berries, and lightly roast and eat roots. They bring back to camp only that which remains above their subsistence needs. In hunting, men also bring back only that portion of the food which remains after they have eaten. They seldom capture large game, but when they do, they bring it back to the camp. Women seem to live and work with little or no interference by the men. In light of the degree of independence in terms of food-getting, what are relationships between men and women?

Camp Life and Marriage

No territorial rights are proclaimed by the Hadza (Woodburn 1968:50). Since people have few possessions, moving is not a difficult task and is done with great frequency, limited only by the desire to remain close to potable water. Woodburn (1968:105) states that the average camp contains 18 adults who live together for a few weeks and then either move on as a group, or break up, with various families going in different directions. The only rule that seems to be followed is that the camps are small in the wet season and larger in the dry season.

Marriage is relatively unstable. Woodburn gives figures of 49 divorces per 1000 years of marriage, as compared to 10.4 for the United States in 1949–1951. However, marriage is the rule; few men or women prefer to remain single. One of the obligations of marriage is that a couple must reside for at least a good part of the time with the wife's mother. Although the residential unit is focused on the wife's mother, these units are so flexible that the composition of the group changes often. A camp will normally contain one or several older women and their daughters, their daughters' husbands and children. Given the frequency of movement, such camps break up from time to time, and couples go to live with the husband's mother for a while.

Another binding obligation of marriage is that the husband must keep his wife and mother-in-law supplied with meat, beads, tobacco, and cloth. The last three are, of course, obtained through trade. Obligations between the sexes exist in that women need men to provide them with meat and trade goods and men need women to produce offspring and to provide the vegetable food which makes up the bulk of their diet.

Relations between the Sexes

In such a society we would expect the status of women to be relatively high. Woodburn remarks that in the small, wet season camps there is little sex discrimination. However, in the larger, dry season camps, which are concentrated near available water supplies. men tend to spend their time in gambling games with other men, while women spend their time gathering and exchanging information with other women. From viewing Woodburn's film, which was made in the field, one gets the impression that we are dealing with two entirely separate worlds — that of the men and that of the women — which do not impinge upon each other very much. One is not aware of a power struggle, or indeed, any other struggle between the sexes. It seems that the lack of stress involved in subsistence is extended to other subsystems of the culture, and therefore a generally relaxed and tolerant relationship between the sexes prevails.

Tiwi

The Tiwi of Australia, as described by Hart and Pilling (1960), live on Melville and Bathhurst Islands, in northern Australia. Their society is as different from the Hadza as could be imagined. Nine bands live on approximately 3,000 square miles of land, much of which is not rich for hunting or gathering. Each band consists of a group of 100 to 300 people who hunt, gather, and live in a distinct territory. Prior to the impact of modern civilization, these bands conducted harmless, sporadic raids upon each other.

Food Supply

The basic foodstuffs are *kwoka*, a porridge made of nuts, and *kolema*, a type of yam. Wallaby, lizards and fish are all used for food. Women hunt, as do boys and young men. Occasionally there is a communal wallaby hunt, but most of the time hunting is done individually or in small groups. The Tiwi acknowledge the fact that their basic food supply is gathered by the women. Hart and Pilling (1960:34) report a conversation between a Tiwi who had many wives and a missionary who tried to disparage polygyny: "If I only had one or two wives, I would starve, but with my present ten or twelve wives, I can send them out in all directions in the morning and at least two or three of them are likely to bring something back with them at the end of the day, and then we can all eat."

Exchange of Women

Perhaps because of her economic contribution, the Tiwi woman has become the object of a patronage system among the men. In order to attain wealth, in terms of surplus food and leisure time, a man must have many wives. Consequently, if a man wishes to place another man under obligation to him, or wishes to benefit from a younger man's efforts, he promises that man a wife. Men seldom acquire wives until they are 30 or 40 years old.

The first wife is seldom bestowed upon a man; she is usually acquired in a trade between two men who exchange their widowed mothers. This older woman, who is usually well past child-bearing age, manages the household and trains young wives when they come into the home. As the young man rises in power in the band, wives will be promised to him for the future. No woman is allowed to remain single, because it is feared that the spirit ghost will impregnate her and the child thus conceived will have no living father. Therefore, girl children are bestowed in marriage even before birth.

Since girls do not leave their families to go into their husband's household until they are about 14 years old, men must wait until they are quite elderly before their young wives come to live with them. Hart and Pilling report that formerly men were known to have 20 or more wives, although not all of them resided in the household at the same time. Moreover, the longer a man lived, the more wives he was likely to acquire. Obviously, since women were so much younger than their husbands they were widowed quite early and quite often. If the widowed girl was young, her mother's current husband retained the right to bestow her on another man; if she was older, her brother or son had this privilege. It was very good politics for a man to marry a woman who had several daughters, for in case they were widowed, he could then bestow them on a man or men of his choice.

Status of Tiwi Women

Hart and Pilling state (1960:52): "Women were the main currency of the influence struggle, the main trumps in the endless bridge game." Females had their fates decided for them before they were born. At marriage they entered new households, which were not of their choice. They were subject to the constant supervision and chaperonage of the older women who were first or second wives. Trysts with younger men occurred during the day when they were gathering and away from the scrutiny of the older women. Only when women reached old age could they have some say about their future, since they could usually persuade their brothers or sons to make an exchange which would be satisfactory from their point of view.

Whereas Hart and Pilling regard these women as objects of trade, Goodale (1971:9;335) takes a different view of the status of women. She states:

> Both male and female Tiwi view their culture's rules governing choice of mates as providing them with considerable freedom and variety throughout their life. Men achieve variety through acquisition of multiple wives, while females can anticipate a succession of husbands; and both sexes manage a limited amount of sexual variety outside of marriage.

Goodale goes on to say that normally a girl's first husband is considerably older than she is, and she often describes her relationship with this husband with phrases like: "He took me like a daughter"; or "He grew me up" (Goodale 1971:44).

With the advent of puberty, a woman's husband can bestow her as yet unconceived daughter upon a young man of his choice, who is then obliged to help bring food to the camp. Of puberty, Goodale says:

> This week is perhaps the most important period in a woman's life. She has become a woman, and she has become a mother-in-law.

Goodale (1971:160, 169) also points out that Tiwi women do small game hunting, sometimes assisted by young men. They hunt opossums and bandicoot and on at least one occasion a woman was credited with killing a wallaby.

Although Goodale (1971:338) claims that Tiwi women accept their successive marriages positively, she also notes:

> Beyond the fact that all females are considered as unique individuals during their life, opportunities for self-expression are less variable and less obvious.

She continues:

> Older women can gain a certain amount of prestige politically by expressing a dominating and forceful personality. Within a domestic group such women can control the lives of their sons-in-law, and to some extent those of their husbands through extra-marital affairs.

Summary

From what we have learned about Hadza and Tiwi society, we can conclude that woman's productivity as a gatherer in a hunting and gathering society does not necessarily confer egalitarian status upon her. We should also realize that no specific pattern of behavior toward women is embraced by all foraging societies. Among the Hadza, a woman can live with her mother for a good part of her married life. Her obligations to her husband are binding, but not oner- ous. She is quite free and independent in her life, which is spent primarily among other women who are related to her. Among the Tiwi, we get two points of view on women's status. According to Hart and Pilling, a woman is an object in a game played by men. Goodale, on the other hand, regards her as much more independent. She feels that woman's function as gatherer and hunter, as well as the bearer of daughters, makes her valued in Tiwi society. Neither Goodale nor Hart and Pilling reports instances of maltreatment of wives, al- though they do acknowledge that women's lives may be more circumscribed than men's.

Female Agriculture

With the development of swidden agriculture, changes occurred both in the division of labor and in the status of women. One wonders why people would give up the idyllic life described among the Hadza for the somewhat more difficult life of the swidden agriculturalist. Ester Boserup (1970) theorizes that increases in population on more favorable lands caused excess population to migrate into less favored areas, which had to be cultivated for the people to survive. There is no way to prove or disprove this suggestion, but certainly the shift from gathering to domestication did occur. Boserup (1970:16) refers to swidden or shifting cultivation as female agriculture. Using African tribes as her examples, she explains that today men grow cash crops, sometimes with the aid of hired help, rather than devoting their time to hunting and warfare, as they did prior to European contact. Men and primarily young boys help to fell trees, but all the other work is done by women, including sowing, weeding, and harvesting (Boserup 1970:17). Under this type of system a high incidence of polygyny exists. In the usual polygynous marriage, a man will take two or three wives. Each wife has her own hut in the compound, which she shares with her children. She is expected not only to feed herself and her children by her own efforts, but to share the task of feeding her husband with the other wives as well. However, the crops she raises are hers to do with as she pleases, and most women, particularly among the Yoruba, produce sufficient surplus to sell products in the market. Boserup (1970:43) states:

> In a family system where wives are supposed to provide food for the family, or a large part of it, and to perform the usual domestic duties for her husband, a wife will naturally welcome one or more co-wives to share with them the burden of daily work.

Where land is tribally owned and distributed, a man with several wives can put more acreage under cultivation than a man with one wife. This adds to his wealth and prestige.

Marketing and Women's Roles

According to Boserup (1970:93), marketing is done by two-thirds of the adult women of the Yoruba and 70 percent of the women of Ghana. Since women are allowed to keep the money they earn from selling their surplus crops, they can acquire a good deal of wealth. In addition, the marketing activities, which may occur on a daily or weekly basis, bring women into contact with other women outside their households. Each woman becomes part of a group which can, by concerted action, wield considerable power. This association of women can potentially become a quasi-political body. Women often derived sufficient income to wrest considerable power from this male-oriented society. For example, a woman could raise the bride-wealth necessary to acquire the bride of her or her son's choice rather than one her husband might choose for his own political purposes. Or, if she were judicious, she could influence her husband's choice of his future wives by agreeing to contribute to their bride-wealth. In this way she was able to surround herself with compatible co-wives, and could also direct the future of her children. Female power in Nupe society was so great that the woman's marketing association was perceived as a band of witches, with the head of the market as the chief witch. Beverly Chiñas (1973) found that the Zapotec women of the Isthmus of Tehuantepec also had considerable power and were quite respected as a result of their marketing activities. Nadel (1952), in his studies among the Nupe, noted that through their marketing activities women enjoyed remarkable access to the public sphere. They were long-distance traders and traveled far from home. They learned about such things as contraceptives and had the opportunity for illicit sex. During their child-bearing years, however, women sometimes confined their marketing activities to the local market. If a woman had competent co-wives, she could rely on one of them for child care and spend more time in the market. As her household burdens decrease, she could expand her marketing activities to include nonagricultural products such as cloth and household utensils. She thus could become a business woman who buys and sells goods, is concerned with profit margins, and comes in contact with strangers of both sexes in her buying and selling activities.

The role of the woman, then, is one of considerable status and freedom. She is a desired child because her marriage brings bride-wealth to her family; her husband will proclaim her value to him by making an investment in her which may represent a significant amount of goods or money.

Matrilocality

In areas where female agriculture is the major subsistence form, but where markets do not exist, the society may be organized around a residential unit which consists of a woman, her daughters, and their husbands. This arrangement is called matrilocality and is found in many areas of the Pacific and in the American Southwest, as well as in other parts of the world. The society may also determine group affiliation by tracing descent through the mother, rather than through the father. This practice is called matrilineality. Even in societies that are both matrilocal and matrilineal, women as individuals do not necessarily play a role in decision-making. This prerogative is usually held by the mother's brother. He makes all major decisions affecting the residential unit, in terms of land usage, crop distribution, and marriages. In such situations, the women form a cohesive work unit bound by kinship ties. A woman, her sisters, and their daughters live and work together. Marriages tend to be quite brittle and husbands come and go in the household. Although women do not have direct public power, they do have power as a group and thereby can influence many decisions. In the American Southwest, for example, women are necessary in ritual and curing ceremonials and consequently have a collective right to appear in public ritual.

Male Agriculture

The transition from female to male agriculture is marked by changes in technology — the introduction of the plow, the use of draught animals, fertilizers, and irrigation techniques. Boserup (1970:24) points out that as the woman's role in agriculture decreased, so her status changed dramatically. Although some women have been known to use the plow, most of the techniques associated with the intensification of agriculture are used by men. Women become confined to small kitchen gardens and to the care of some of the domestic animals. A shift from the man paying bride-wealth to the woman's family providing a dowry at marriage also occurs. Boserup points out that in societies where women are excluded from any productive work, as in the Moslem world, they are also veiled and removed from any contact with the world at large.

Variation in Status of Women in Developed Agriculture

The status and role of women in societies in which men do the agricultural work varies. Where farming is difficult and largely unproductive, men and women may work together to eke out a living from the soil. In this case women have greater access to the public sphere and are less formally constrained. In India, the Untouchable women work alongside the men and as a result, are allowed to be seen in public and have contact with other members of their own caste, as well as outsiders. Women of the upper castes, however, are more closely confined to the home and traditionally have little contact with the world outside their immediate families. The traditional European small farm is another example of the diminution of the status of women. In most peasant societies, although the woman has stipulated tasks to perform and works as long and as hard as her husband, her status is clearly inferior to his. Her concerns are restricted to "woman's sphere," which includes matters that concern the children, illnesses, church and religious ritual. She has little or no say in how the harvest is distributed, she has no voice in public affairs, and, on the rare occasions that she must appear in public, she is required to behave in an unobtrusive manner so as not to attract any attention.

Status of Women in Successful Male Agriculture

In societies where men can successfully produce consistent surpluses in agriculture with the aid of other men, the woman is simply the producer of sons. Few families welcome the birth of a daughter, because expensive dowries must be provided. In ancient Greece, prerevolutionary China, and India, female infanticide was practiced, as it still is in many foraging societies. When she married, a woman went from her natal home to her husband's home. She was seldom valued as a coproducer, although her capacity for hard work was important. Her value lay primarily in her ability to produce sons. In India, for example, a woman is not called by her proper name after marriage until she has borne a son, and then she is called "mother of John," or whatever the son's name is. Hence it is her sexuality which is considered valuable, and this must be guarded. Consequently, her appearance and behavior in public become extremely important, and any dress or action which might attract the attention of other people and thus threaten her husband's sexual exclusivity is severely punished. Women must wrap themselves in cumbersome shawls, ill-fitting outer garments, and, in extreme cases, appear completely veiled in public.

Since the woman in these societies is rigidly excluded from the public sphere, her ability to form cohesive groupings with other women is limited. Even in harems, where women are secluded together and cooperate with each other to some extent, competition still exists because there are no natural links among them. Each is concerned with bettering her own and particuarly her son's welfare, at the expense of co-wives and their sons. Such an improvement in status can come about only by winning the favor of the husband.

Obviously, there is a loss of status for women associated with the shift from female to male agriculture. When women become valued for their reproductive capacities rather than for their economic production the society tends to become more stringently divided along sexually defined lines, and women are more closely confined to the private sphere.

Nomadic Women

Robert Ekvall (1968) describes a seeming exception to this among the nomadic pastoralists of Tibet. Although subsistence is based upon yak and sheep herding, and dowries are provided for women at marriage, there are other factors which make the status of women somewhat different from what would be expected of a male-oriented society. For one thing, both men and women inherit equal amounts from their parents.

Most important, after marriage the woman becomes "tent mistress" (Ekvall 1968:60) in her husband's group. Although polygyny is permitted, it is confined to the wealthy, since a man must set up a separate tent for each wife. Once in her husband's household, a woman has certain defined tasks, including caring for the stock at birth, looking after the young stock, milking, and perhaps most important, churning butter.

Only the tent mistress can make butter, which is one of the most important commodities in this Tibetan society. Ekvall (1968:60) states:

> Butter is an important part of diet, and in economics it is the pastoralist's measure, in weight units, of price in the same way that the agriculturalist's measure is weight units of barley. Even when payment is not made in butter, the value of commodities and even currency are quoted in weight units of butter. It is, indeed, a currency based on its own utilitarian value in the economy. In technology, at its oldest, oiliest stage when no longer acceptable as food, it is the universally used tanning agent for softening all the hides used in making many artifacts of a pack-and-saddle existence, and for all the sheepskins used for clothing. In social relationships it is the preferred gift in the reciprocal attitudes and responsibilities created by the gift exchange system; in religious observances it is the universally preferred offering because it fuels the millions of butter-lamps in Tibetan shrines and temples.

Thus, women are the only members of Tibetan society who create a necessary commodity, one which is indeed the backbone of the subsistence, trade, and religious systems. A Tibetan woman, then, is in a position of power. Her ability to gain wealth balances her husband's productivity in tending herds. As a result, Tibetan women are quite independent and outspoken. They spend much of their life on horseback, as do men. They display equal or greater bravery in coping with the severe climate and the constant movement. They ride horses until the day they give birth, and shortly thereafter they travel again, carrying the baby inside their fur shirts. Ekvall notes that often women must be consulted before herd animals are sold and they play a lively part in business transactions. They are neither secluded nor compelled to observe particular behavioral patterns in the presence of outsiders.

Industrialization

With the development of industry, still greater changes in woman's status evolved. In the early days of the industrial revolution, families involved in the so-called cottage industries produced many of the commodities at home. In Java, the Batik industry is still run in this fashion (Boserup 1970:107). This type of set-up tends to erode the division of labor, since all adults, and even some children, participate. The work pace is governed by the needs of garden and stock as well as necessary household chores.

Particularly in England, when cottage labor was replaced by the factory, women and children worked in them under abominable conditions. During this time there were actually two distinct statuses for English women. The poor, who worked in factories or did other work in the large cities, had no status to speak of. They were powerless, driven only by their need to earn money. There were few social agencies, public or private, to look after women and children who were exploited.

At the very same time, women who were born or married into wealth led extremely sheltered lives and were treated with great courtesy. They occupied their time with frivolities, although some became aroused by the conditions under which other women lived. A number of changes took place. As the efficiency of machinery increased, fewer workers were needed. Social legislation aimed at relieving the conditions of women and children in factory work came into being, which in effect made it more troublesome for an employer to hire a woman, who had to receive benefits such as lighter work, shorter working hours, and maternity leaves, than a man. As a result, fewer women were employed, competition among men for available jobs increased, and women were virtually eliminated from the job market. Prosperity grew, and more men were able to support a nuclear family; they began to feel stigmatized if their wives worked. Moreover, factory conditions were still such that most married women preferred to stay home and raise their children. Today, the balance is changing in that current figures show 35,000,000 women have regular places in the work force. Women have used World War II manpower shortages as a lever to enter and stay in the world of working men *and* women.

Developed Industrialization

By the nineteenth century, industry had created a full-fledged class system which operated parallel to, and sometimes in accordance with, the preexisting class system based on land ownership. Wives of wealthy industrialists were expected to act as displays of their husband's success, consumers par excellence. This was considered the model of desirable behavior for women of both the middle and lower classes.

Middle-class women whose husbands' jobs were sufficiently lucrative to support the family, stayed at home and reared children. There were few "proper" jobs available for women who wanted to work. Marriage was the ideal, and if some hideous misfortune prevented this, these women continued to be dependents of their father, or later, their brothers. Women could not live alone, and the only jobs they could take were as librarians or elementary school teachers.

Poor women had to work, but even for them jobs were categorized as "proper" or "improper." It was proper to take in sewing or do domestic service in the homes of the rich, less proper to sell foods in the market, and improper to become an actress. Even among the very poor, the "good wife and mother" who stayed at home, was adept at housewifely chores, and deferred properly to her husband was the ideal. When a woman did have to take employment, both the woman and the employer agreed that it was merely temporary, until circumstances improved.

Today, in Western industrialized nations, affluence has become possible for many more people than ever before. As a result, the wife in more families has been able to stay at home rearing the socially approved number of children. According to John K. Galbraith (1973:29–44) this affluence is at least in part due to the success with which industry has persuaded women to stay at home and become conspicuous consumers. He cogently points out that even though having a lot of "things" can be burdensome when confronted with their care and cost and renewal, modern industry is based upon the assumption that people constantly wish to acquire objects and will readily replace them, in a short time, if necessary.

Factory and service industries have absorbed much of the labor pool which formerly served as domestic help. As Galbraith (1973:33) states:

> The conversion of women into cryptoservant class was an economic accomplishment of the first importance. Menially employed servants were available only to a minority of the pre-industrial population: the servant-wife is available, democratically, to almost the entire present male population.

In this same chapter, Galbraith goes on to speak about the convenient social virtue which is accorded the woman who acts as consumer caretaker or replacer of goods. He also declares that the idea of women controlling money in our society is a fiction. Rather, women act as the purchasing agents of men, who ultimately hold the power to disperse or withhold resources. Wives of executives, for example, are expected to cook, clean, chauffeur, entertain, dress well, and take responsibility for the children's health, education, and well-being. In doing so, they dispense much money earned by their husbands and acquire many prestigious items, which fulfills the purpose of the industrial society.

Galbraith may be correct in his analysis of the role played by the wife and mother in modern, industrial society, but there have been exceptions. There have always been a small proportion of women who rejected this model in favor of professional accomplishment. This point must be made here because in a developed industrial society much of the back-breaking labor for which women were considered unsuitable has either been eliminated or is done by machinery. There is a far greater variety of careers available. Some women have taken advantage of the educational facilities which for some time now have been open to both men and women. These women were often discouraged by family, friends, and male colleagues. Frequently they were ridiculed and made to feel that they were not considered seriously. Despite this kind of example women themselves have usually preferred the "crypto-servant" role. They were afraid to take the responsibility of fending for themselves. To some of them, marriage was a manipulative process, at which they became as adept as the Tiwi. In the present decade, however, more women than ever before are free to choose their life styles.

Women in Developing Societies

We must finally turn to the status of women in developing societies. These societies have generally been colonial possessions, which have suddenly found themselves independent or have had industrialization forced upon them for other reasons. In any case, the society involved is basically agricultural, with one or a few urban areas. Women in these societies are faced with still other adaptations.

In parts of Africa, male labor is recruited into the towns and industries. This is considered temporary employment, and the wife and children are left in the village to which the men intend to return. Women left in this situation may become very competent in handling both the agricultural problems as well as the affairs of the family. If the husband regularly sends money from the city, his family may be able to live quite well, although his wife may bear a heavier burden of duties and therefore may not be able to place as much land under cultivation. Also, the bonds between husband and wife become more tenuous and she learns to manage without the direction of a husband.

The search for better and easier living conditions often brings whole families into the city. Sometimes these people have in some way been alienated from their land, and can no longer fulfill their needs in the country. In most cases they have been agriculturalists all their lives and possess no other skills; they usually are illiterate in the language used in the city because small villages in rural areas were inhabited by tribal groups who spoke indigenous languages. For example, in Mexico Spanish is the official language of urban areas, whereas people speak Nahuatl or some other indigenous language in the rural villages. For the most part, men are the dominant members of these families. On arrival in the large town, these people often have to find lodging in the poorest areas of town, which do not have the basic necessities of urban life — running water and toilet facilities — let alone paved streets or lighting and such amenities. In some of the large, South American cities one can find such urban slums built on the outskirts of the city.

The job market for unskilled labor in the cities is small. The few jobs that are available tend to be temporary and poor-paying, and it is difficult for men to get jobs and keep them. Conditions for women are often easier, since their skills may be in demand. Boserup (1970: 19) points out that the cities are usually full of men whose wives are not with them, so women can set up stalls to sell cooked food in the market. They also brew beer, do laundry, serve as prostitutes, and work as domestics. Some children also find it easier to earn money than older men. They run errands, shine shoes, sweep stores, vend merchandise on the street, and beg. Thus, the economic position of women and children is often stronger than that of men, and the reversal of economic power may lead to friction and the erosion of male supremacy. Oscar Lewis (1961:XXII) called this type of society a culture of poverty. He (1961:XXVI) describes the culture of poverty in terms of such traits as violence, alcoholism, early introduction to sex, distrust of institutions such as banks, welfare agencies, and so forth. Harris (1972:493–495), among others, objects to the use of the term "culture" because it implies that "once the culture of poverty comes into existence, it tends to perpetuate itself." Harris also regards the traits listed as stereotypes.

If culture is defined as the human adaptive mechanism, then the term "culture of poverty" can be regarded as valid. The traits are, as Lewis explains them, social and psychological adaptation to a life of poverty. The concept that a culture must perpetuate itself is erroneous, for if the condition to which the adaptation is made (in this case poverty) changes, then according to laws of evolution the culture must also change to meet the new conditions or die out. In this book, the culture of poverty will be used as a descriptive classification, with the qualifications stated above. In some societies, laws tend to perpetuate the culture of poverty. For example, in our own society, welfare laws render a family ineligible for assistance if there is a husband resident, even though he may be unemployed. Under these circumstances, the mother and children become the family unit, with other people of varying relationships forming a network around them. This network may be a matrifocal family, which will be discussed in the following chapter.

Status of Women in Developing Societies

The status of the woman in the culture of poverty may be high, depending on how she earns her living and how much she earns. Although some types of work are considered less desirable than others, this ranking may not conform to the ranking given in the society as a whole. For example, certain occupations which are illegal in the larger society rank high in the culture of poverty because they pay well, and also because the individual is in a position where he or she can outwit the oppressive society.

One of the major blocks to understanding the culture of poverty has been the concept that workers are needed, particularly in the service areas, and yet so many people remain unemployed. However, this type of work is not consonant with the goals of the worker. Domestic work, for example, involves very long hours during that part of the day when a woman may urgently need to care for her own children. The salaries paid are uniformly low, perhaps below any legal minimum wage. The nature of the work may be characterized by frequent periods of unemployment, frequent cancellations of agreed days of work, unpaid or no vacations, no fringe benefits. Often a degree of subservience is demanded on the part of the employee. A woman who can brew and dispense her own beer can work from her own home, charge the going rate, and often reap a greater profit with considerably less effort than by getting a legally approved job. The problem is not unemployment as much as under-employment.

Summary

The ways in which women earn their livings, then, influence the status they have in society to some degree. However, there is no one-to-one correlation between a woman's economic contribution and her status. We have seen that a Hadza woman contributes relatively little to her husband's subsistence, but has relatively high status, whereas a Tiwi woman provides the bulk of the wealth but has less independence. The Yoruba woman exhibits a great deal of independence although she works very hard; she may use her earnings in any way she sees fit. Other factors beyond production seem to be involved. How does a society organize itself so as to give or deprive women from their right to self-determination? Perhaps a look at the various types of social organizations will help clarify this question.

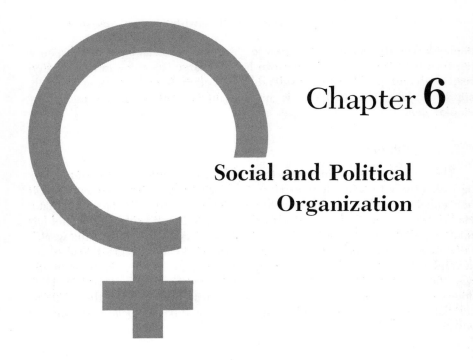

Chapter 6

Social and Political Organization

Function of Sociopolitical Subsystem

The sociopolitical subsystem regulates relationships both within the group as well as outside of it. It functions on two levels: on the level regulating the individual's interaction with society, and on the level regulating interaction between that society and any other society. The first level subsumes all traditions that have to do with marriage, the responsibilities of parents and children toward each other, and the individual's integration into society. The second level subsumes all traditions that govern decision-making for the group as a whole, such as the movement of a pastoral society as seasons change, the movement of an agricultural society which must acquire new land, alignments between one segment of the society against another, and finally, the way in which the society meets contacts from other societies.

The first level, then, is the personal or private sphere where we might expect to find women involved. The second level is the public sphere, where the involvement of women would be true evidence of an egalitarian society. Let us examine the various ways in which societies order their social and political affairs.

Types of Families

Basically, there are two ways of ordering family relationships, the nuclear or the extended family. Western civilization, as well as the Eskimo, opts for the nuclear family. In such societies, health care, rearing and educating children, and care of the aged are all institutionalized. We have hospitals, schools, nurseries, and nursing homes. Moreover, work is done in factories and offices by individuals interacting with other individuals who are not related to them, but are their colleagues. In many other parts of the world the nuclear family is embedded in a larger group.

Other societies do not have such institutions; work is done in a home-like setting, by a group of people united by kinship and marriage. In this case, it makes better sense to extend the kinship unit to more individuals who will share the responsibility of feeding and providing for the young, the ill, and the aged. This is the extended family.

The Extended Family

There are several methods of extending families. All brothers and their wives may live in a group with the husbands' parents, or sisters and their husbands may reside with the wives' parents. A man may have several wives or a woman several husbands. All of these groups contain the nuclear family, which consists of a man, a woman, and their children. However, the residential unit contains more than just two adults and a number of children. Evidence indicates that such groupings are better equipped to satisfy human needs than the relative isolation of the nuclear family. In her book on breast feeding, Dana Raphael (1973) points out that lactation is improved when the young mother is made to feel secure by the presence of other sympathetic and experienced women. We have already discussed the advantages of having many women in residence to share the work. However, the nuclear family has the advantage of greater mobility, which was an important factor during the period of industrial development.

Rules of Residence

In the extended family, the young newlywed couple can reside with, or close to, the parents of either the husband (patrilocality) or the wife (matrilocality). Some societies practice bilocality, where the couple lives part of the time with one set of relatives, and the rest of the time with relatives by marriage (affines). Fortune (1932) reports that the Dobu, a people of the Pacific, spend half a year with each spouse's family. Other societies are not so rigid in their residence rules, and people can live wherever they choose.

Very few people outside of Western civilization choose to live in a new area (neolocally), where neither spouse has kinship relations. Indeed, neolocal residence would be impossible for most people both in terms of the aid and support they would forfeit and in terms of their right to live in a particular place.

Rules of Descent

An individual's right to live in a particular place and to share in the resources of that place are determined by rules of lineality or, more loosely termed, "rules of inheritance." These rules apply even in those societies where there is very little to inherit. Although this may seem paradoxical, it does make sense if we accept the premise that alone each individual is helpless, and that he or she must have group affiliations and support to survive. Every infant born has two groups to which he or she can be assigned, the group of the mother or that of the father. Many societies have rules that stipulate to which group the child is affiliated at birth — with the father's group (patrilineal) or with the mother's group (matrilineal). In many societies the child may be affiliated with kindred composed of members of both groups.

In stable unilineal societies, the rules of residence and inheritance usually complement each other. These societies are both patrilocal and patrilineal or matrilocal and matrilineal. If the society has a discrepancy between residence and affiliation, one can reasonably assume that the society is undergoing culture change.

Most anthropologists agree that rules of residence are determined by the nature of the working group. Where men customarily work in groups, a stable society will be patrilocal and patrilineal as well. The reverse is also true.

Power and Authority of Women

In an earlier chapter, we discussed the fact that women lacked *authority* in most societies. However, in the private sphere, some women wield a good deal of *power*.

It is necessary to distinguish here between power and authority. Power is defined as the ability to make others conform to one's wishes; authority is defined as the legitimization of power by the society. Many women in all societies are powerful due to personality factors or other characteristics. Most likely, any woman has a degree of power commensurate with the network of people with whom she has influence. However, relatively few women have authority, and those who do often find that authority restricted to the domestic or private sphere. The social organization of a society regulates the network of relationships a woman can build. Since such networks are often the measure of a woman's power, we will attempt to describe the various types of social organizations in terms of them.

The nature and people of the residence group had a profound effect on a woman's existence. These factors determined her status, and certainly were concerned with the amount of power a woman could handle.

Patrilocal, Patrilineal Societies

In band societies, rules of residence tend to be rather flexible, and groups tend to be affiliated on the basis of mutual attraction. But some bands do have rigid residence rules, as among the Tiwi. In tribal societies more stringent regulations apply.

The most common form of residence and also the most common form of tracing group membership is by far the patrilocal, patrilineal society. In some societies, the need for such affiliation is obvious — nomadic herders, for example, whose subsistence largely depends on groups of men working together. Why a society that fills its subsistence needs by gathering and occasional hunting should trace descent and residence through the male side of the family is less obvious. It should be noted that although hunting actually provides a smaller amount of food than gathering, it is regarded everywhere as the more important and prestigious activity. This may be in part due to the fact that hunting is less secure, and depends much more upon chance. Also, gathering can be done by women singly, whereas there is usually some arrangement for communal hunting even in those societies which usually hunt individually or in pairs. Another reason for the larger number of patrilocal, patrilineal societies might be that the men form a defensive unit against outsiders.

Isolation of Women in Patrilocal Societies

In these societies, it is recognized that the woman is being removed from her family and that her children will belong to her husband's group. Often the woman's family will be compensated in advance by a gift of bride-wealth for this loss of labor and personnel. Bride-wealth is usually set sufficiently high to require that all the members of the man's kinship group contribute to it. In the same way, the wealth is not held by the woman's parents alone, but is distributed among her kinship group to repay obligations incurred in paying bride wealth for their wives. Under the impact of colonialism, the payment of bride wealth was often forbidden, since many Europeans felt this practice to be similar to slavery. Actually, the woman's lot was made more difficult by abrogating bride-wealth. When both sets of kin had a financial investment in a marriage, they were mutually interested in its success, because returning or forfeiting the bride wealth constituted a hardship. Consequently, a woman could appeal to her relatives by marriage, among whom she lived, if she felt herself excessively abused by her husband or other women in the group.

Marriages are arranged by parents or other kin in most simple societies. The arrangement must be satisfactory to the kinship group of both the man and the woman, before the marriage can take place. Women are valued for their abilities as workers and producers of children. In Samoan society, a woman who has produced children outside of marriage is considered a more desirable wife because she has already proven her reproductive capacity. A woman is also valued because of the affiliation the marriage will create between her group and that of her husband. So far, nothing has been said about the woman as a person, or about her needs and desires. This is simply because, with rare exceptions, a woman is not regarded as having any needs or desires. In *Growing Up in New Guinea* Margaret Mead gives one of the most poignant descriptions of a wedding ceremony. We can visualize the childbride, barely an adult, standing in the boat which will take her to her new residence. She is surrounded by gifts from her family to the groom's family and vice-versa. We see this child as an object who is not personally identified with the ceremonial and whose only feelings are probably bewilderment and fear at leaving her family.

Status of Women in Patrilocal Societies

The conditions under which a childbride lives vary with the society. She may find herself among a group of co-wives, one or more of them from her kinship unit, with whom she can develop associations that are both helpful and pleasant. Or she may find herself the abject slave of a tyrannical mother-in-law or first wife. In such a society, work and responsibility, including child care, are shared among the women. A child calls every woman resident in the group "mother" and every male member of his father's generation "father," because these adults act as parents to the children of the kinship group. A woman's status in such a group rises as her sons grow in age and influence. A resourceful and fortunate woman can form alliances with other women and influence decisions of the entire residence group, particularly when her sons are grown and married. A dramatic example of this change in status occurs in traditional Chinese society (Wolf 1974:158). Upon entering the household as a child, a woman's position in her husband's family remains ambiguous until she has a son. As the youngest wife in residence, she is responsible for doing the most onerous tasks. She has no recourse from ill treatment because she has no kinship group to which to appeal. She was never a member of her father's lineage, nor does she become a full member of her husband's lineage until she provides that group with male heirs. If she is fortunate enough to produce sons, her status improves. Her seniority over younger wives who enter the household relieves her of some unpleasant tasks. Finally, when her sons are grown and begin to bring brides home, she becomes the authority figure, the head of the household, although her formal decisions are limited to the household and do not extend to the public sphere. Among upper class traditional Chinese, the custom of binding women's feet evolved, in order to make it impossible for women to travel great distances from home.

However, there are exceptions, such as the Lovedu, described by Krige and Krige (1943). The Lovedu are residents of South Africa whose subsistence is earned by female agriculture. They have a patrilineal, patrilocal society, but women have an extraordinary amount of power. Sacks (1974:215) has shown that there is no discrimination against women; they participate in all affairs, even those related to the community and religion. There is no sexual double standard; both men and women are compensated when the spouse has been guilty of adultery. Cattle are the measure of wealth in this society, and women are allowed to give and receive cattle. Most unusual is the fact that a woman, usually an older woman, can use cattle as bride-wealth to purchase a "wife." The relationship is not a sexual one, but is based upon the younger woman's productivity in terms of agriculture; the products of her labor redound to the "husband." A widow may inherit from her husband. Often she will marry another woman, not only for the reasons stated above, but also to provide herself with an heir if she is childless. Such marriages are entered into with all the ceremony of a male-female marriage, the object being to legitimize heirs for the woman-husband's lineage.

One cannot, therefore, presume that patrilineality and patrilocality necessarily deprive a woman of high status. Nor can one assume that low status, when it does exist, is permanent. The ambiguous position of a woman is best displayed by the fact that she is an outsider to her husband, but she is mother to her son. The power that a woman wields depends on the closeness of the mother–son bond. Natural networks do not exist with other women since they are often ranked hierarchically and therefore subject to competition with each other. The woman is removed from affiliations that might exist among kinswomen. However, all of this must be modified in terms of particular societies and conditions. As stated earlier, when women have meaningful contacts outside the home, such as women who regularly trade in the market place or who belong to various associations within the society, they are enabled to wield power.

Matrilineal, Matrilocal Societies

In discussing matrilineal, matrilocal societies, Schneider and Gough (1961:7) say:

> . . . it might seem that matrilineal and patrilineal descent groups are precise mirror images of each other, identical in their structure except for the superficial point that in one group membership is obtained through the father; in the other, through the mother. Otherwise, every element is identical. The groups are both defined as decision-making units which hold some activity in common. The roles of men and women are identically defined in both groups, the men having authoritative roles and the women having responsibility for child care.

Schneider goes on to state that in his opinion, the differences are actually greater than appear on the surface, because descent is traced through women, whereas authority is held by men. This conflict leads to structural differences in the two groups.

One of the major structural differences of the matrilocal residence group is that it is permanently composed of related women. The authority figure is not the husband or father, but the mother's brother, who lives elsewhere. It is notable that most matrilineal, matrilocal societies settle in geographically small areas, where distances between villages are quite short. A man is thus enabled to live with his spouse part of the time, and yet attend to affairs at his mother's residence.

Role of the Husband

The role of the husband and father in this type of society is quite different from his role in patrilineal, patrilocal society. For one thing, he does not usually provide for his own children; they receive their right to land, crops, herds, etc. through their mother's brother, who will also provide a wife for them. The father, therefore, is looked upon with affection but is relatively powerless in terms of his relationship with his wife or children. He exercises power and authority over his sister's children, and is treated much more respectfully by them. As noted previously, matrilineal, matrilocal societies occur where women work together, most likely in agricultural societies, although the Navajo, who herd sheep, are a notable exception. Harris (1975) feels that matrilocality corresponds to a situation in which men must be away from the village for long periods of time. The society prescribes particular functions for these men. Sometimes they are required to bring meat to the wife and her family. They often cooperate with the mother's brothers in a communal hunting or building project. Problems of residence also vary. In most matrilineal societies, husbands spend part of their time with their natal group and part of it with their wives.

Often there is a special provision, a men's house, for husbands who sleep over or spend a good deal of time at their wives' homes. All men who spend the night in the village sleep here. This arrangement is particularly common in the matrilocal tribes of Amazonia, South America, where subsistence is based upon the long, boring task of cultivating manioc. Women engage in this labor cooperatively, by sharing jokes, songs, and conversations. Men hunt wild pig and may spend a good amount of time raiding their neighbors. Thus the defense of a matrilocal village becomes a serious problem. While men are supposed to defend the village against raiders, it is doubtful whether they would do so if the raiders were of their own descent group. In order to foster more solidarity and loyalty among the resident males of the villages, they are supposed to sleep in the men's house, where hammocks are strung in order of seniority. The oldest male gets the best sleeping place — close to the fire and away from the door. Often women will bring meals to their men and serve them outside the men's house. In the American southwest, where raiding no longer occurs, men reside with their wives. Basehart (1961:270–279) reports the most unusual residence pattern for the Ashanti of Africa.

Three major household types may be distinguished based upon the following residence patterns: duolocal, where each spouse remains with their own matrilineal relatives; avunculocal [residing with the mother's brother] and patrilocal. In the early years of marriage, residence was predominantly duolocal, but with the passage of time would shift to avunculocal or patrilocal. It is unlikely that the nuclear family of husband, wife, and children was of structural importance in traditional Ashanti.

Avunculocal residence does not necessarily imply sharing the same house, but may refer to living in the same compound or village.

Duolocality

Duolocality is a rather rare form of residence. Husband and wife do not reside together, at least for part of the time, but they maintain residence in their own lineage group. The responsibilities of husband and wife are outlined as follows:

The payment of *tiri nsa* gave the husband exclusive sexual rights in the wife, made him legal father of the woman's children, during the period of the marriage, and obligated the wife to perform economic and domestic services. In turn, the husband was responsible for providing food, clothing, and, if necessary, housing for his wife and children, money for her debts, care in the event of illness, and sexual satisfaction (Basehart 1961:290).

The Ashanti enjoyed a highly developed state as well as a complex economy. Specialization, in terms of occupation, and stratification, in terms of the nobility, the commoners and slaves, existed. There were institutions outside the kinship group which affected the relationships of people to each other. For example, Ashanti women were engaged in raising and selling cash crops. Men were craftsmen, served in public office, and also grew cash crops.

Durability of Marriages

Marriages tend to be brittle among matrilineal, matrilocal societies. Basehart (1961:290) cites that more than half of the Ashanti men over age 40 and women over 35 have been divorced at least once. This figure may run even higher in some societies in the American southwest. Part of the reason may be that there are so few marital obligations between husband and wife that a strong bond is prevented from forming between them. During the period of duolocal residence among the Ashanti, a woman visits her husband's lineage group to bring him food and probably to have sexual relations. Even in those societies where the man permanently lives in the woman's village, the rate of divorce is high and, as opposed to patrilocal societies, can be easily obtained by either sex.

Status of Women in Matrilocal Societies

Basehart (1961:291) tells us that the "crucial relationship in Ashanti kinship was that between mother and child. The bond was one of great strength and intensity for both son and daughter." To this extent, Schneider's statement to the effect that patrilineal systems are mirror images of matrilineages holds true.

However, there are two basic differences: (1) the economic independence of the woman, and (2) the activity of the woman in the public sphere. Both of these factors are interrelated. Since a woman holds the rights to her land and property through her membership in her mother's lineage group, she cannot be alienated from this property. Furthermore, her management of the property is supervised by her brother, rather than her husband. For this reason, her relationship with her husband is of a different nature from that of the woman in a patrilineal society. She can marry for whatever reasons she chooses, and can divorce without fear of losing her subsistence. At the same time, she is brought into contact with the public sphere through her property management and marketing of products of her own manufacture. She may engage in long distance trade, and produce and sell pottery, as is done by some women in the American southwest. Thus she deals with people from outside her community or culture. Apparently, the ability to do these things is consistent with the degree of security felt by the woman in a matrilineal society.

This security is probably based, not only on economic independence, but also on the knowledge that the woman is living among kin. Women work in a group made up of their sisters, their mothers, and their matrilineal kin. Authority is delegated to brothers; the highest authority rests with the oldest living mother's brother, who is not in constant residence, but probably lives at least part of the time with his wife. Therefore, the individual woman has ready access to power.

It should be stated that within matrilineal societies the creativity and business ability of women is never doubted. They are expected to be fine potters, fine weavers, successful marketers.

Viability of Matrilocal vs. Patrilocal Societies

The number of matrilineal, matrilocal societies is relatively small. Although this type of organization allows the individual woman greater security and independence than the patrilocal, patrilineal system, it is evidently not as well adapted for survival. One reason for this is that a patrilocal society is much better organized for defense because the owners live on the territory. Surprise raids, therefore, have less chance of success than they would in a situation where inhabitants have divided loyalties or members are not present at all times.

The Nuclear Family

The nuclear family, with neolocal residence, is characteristic of the modern industrial state. Although there are variations from nation to nation, it can be generally stated that in advanced industrial societies, women may have to sacrifice security in order to achieve a great deal of independence. In agrarian or rural societies, a woman may have neither independence nor security. The typical neolocal residence is isolated from both sets of kin. There is a tendency among recently settled ethnic groups in this country and among lower class groups in England and Germany for married daughters to live close to their parents. This is probably an attempt to mitigate the problems of the isolated wife and mother. There is considerable literature on the troubles of modern marriages, which need not be stressed further. Anthropologically, however, it should be stated that in no other part of the world would such marriages be expected to work.

Mate Selection

Selection of mates seems to be made on the basis of trivial and often transient characteristics. The marriage itself has no built-in, traditional supports such as exist in other societies. There are no kin groups ready to lend a hand to stabilize a marriage. In fact, the assistance of kin may be regarded as "interference." There are no clearly understood patterns of responsibility between husband and wife; each couple must regulate these on their own. Moreover, each partner comes to the marriage from his or her own idiosyncratic family of orientation, so that they may have very different ideas as to what their duties and responsibilities are.

Careers and Children

The woman faces the real problem of choosing between a career and raising children. The mother can seldom rely on kin for child-rearing, but must depend on institutionalized child care, in the form of nurseries and/or baby sitters, instead. These services may be unavailable, undesirable, or too expensive, in which case a woman may have to defer either her career or her children. In addition to these difficulties many women who choose careers over children do so at the expense of feeling guilty. Mothers who work quite often feel that their children are in some way being deprived of proper care. These feelings stem from our society's model of the proper wife and mother as consumer par excellence and as "crypto-servant," to use Galbraith's term. The choice for the woman is further complicated by the fact that status in modern society is often based upon the acquisition of goods, which a family can afford if the mother works.

Bearing children is fraught with insecurity for the modern woman. Until recently, women were supposed to resign from their jobs as soon as they became pregnant. Some male employers are still reluctant to hire and train women because they feel that women will soon marry and leave. Unfortunately, this attitude extends to many college and university personnel who feel that women will only use their professional training until child-rearing takes precedence. Despite their liberated position, most anthropology departments are composed largely of men. Discrimination against women is not admitted, but the tradition that males are the bread-winners and therefore need jobs more than women do lingers. Young women are considered less reliable than men because responsibilities at home may conflict with their class schedules. Sometimes older women are hired because they have established families and are less likely to leave. Also, older women who have working husbands may be willing to accept smaller salaries. Among the 270 departments listed in the 1974–1975 Guide to Departments published by the American Anthropological Association, 43 departments of anthropology and 21 museums in the United States and Canada have no women at all on their faculties.

Pregnancy, Childbirth, and Child-Rearing

Pregnancy and childbirth normally occur in isolation for women. They often must depend for guidance upon male physicians and occasional neighboring relationships. They seldom have access to the everyday model of mothers and sisters going through the same process. Despite a plethora of books and training courses on child-bearing, the very real support of the presence of other women with whom the mother has had meaningful relationships is often missing. Women, particularly those interested in natural childbirth and breast-feeding, have, in the last decade or more, begun to form groups to provide this kind of support. Given the fact that female relatives are often not at hand to give the needed support, young husbands are being trained to stand in for them. Probably this is a better solution than earlier situations in which a woman related only to her doctor, in that it may bring husband and wife closer together. However, since some men fear this obligation, it does place still another burden on the nuclear family which already carries all the responsibility for its own welfare.

The problems of child-rearing are more complicated for the nuclear family than for any other. Young mothers seldom have experienced mothers to rely on for practical advice. They therefore rely again on the pediatrician, how-to books, and each other. The fact that these young mothers were themselves reared by inexperienced mothers tends to aggravate the problem. Each nuclear family sets its own pattern of expected child behavior. Wide variations exist in this area. Some babies are fed on rigid schedules and toilet trained at six months, while some households are extremely permissive and children are fed on demand; there are no efforts at toilet training until the child is several years old (Henry 1971). Children themselves are quick to take advantage of the lack of traditional patterns with arguments such as, "Everybody else has one," or "Everyone else does it."

The Empty Nest Syndrome

Once the children are sent off to school and the woman is no longer needed in the home on a full-time basis, her problems become more acute. Many have never received the training that would make them valuable in industrial society. Husbands sometimes perceive a wife's return to work as a derogation of their abilities to provide for their families and a threat to their masculinity. Part of being a good wife and mother is being able to advance the family interests socially, and often a good deal of a woman's time and energy is expected to be devoted to volunteer work or women's organizations. Whatever the woman does with her time, it is rarely accorded the same respect as whatever a man does. Having fulfilled herself as a mother, she is now expected to go off stage gracefully, to disappear. Out of frustration, some women become compulsive drinkers; a few take to sexual promiscuity.

The Older Woman

The older woman in modern society suffers the greatest hardships. In most other societies, her status would be highest at this point in her life. Marriages of children are no longer arranged by parents. A mature woman does not become overly involved in the lives of her married sons and daughters, or modern American society would view her as "interfering." Women entering the job market at this point in their lives find almost insurmountable obstacles due to arbitrary retirement rules and training requirements. Since statistics show that males tend to die earlier than females a woman is faced with many years of widowhood. Although her financial needs may be met, her need for identity and security usually is not.

Power and the Nuclear Family

In terms of power networks, the woman in the nuclear family has none. She may find some support among neighbors, or members of volunteer groups, but these groups usually have defined goals and tend to have transient personnel. They may be incapable of fulfilling the woman's needs and are not regarded by men as a possible source of censure.

However, despite all the handicaps stated above, the individual woman in modern Western civilization has a greater capacity for self-determination than ever before. This will be discussed more fully in a later chapter. There are many living examples of women who have successfully surmounted the barriers created by society. Admittedly, the cost has been high, and the effort great, but they do serve as a model for other women.

Considering the lack of institutionalized supports for marriage, the divorce rate in Western society is low as compared to the divorce rate in matrilineal societies. This may be due in part to the stigma associated with divorce in some circles, and also to the nature of divorce proceedings in some areas. Another factor in keeping the divorce rate relatively low is that the family unit tends to fill many needs (economic, social, and psychological) which would, in other societies, be filled by people outside the nuclear family. On one hand, this factor makes the nuclear family harder to dissolve. On the other hand, undue stress is placed upon the individuals in such a family, which may result in the breakup of a marriage. Such a break is all the more traumatic when no alternative people or institutions are available to replace the nuclear family unit. Despite the fact that marriages fail, divorced people tend to remarry with great regularity. Most people prefer to believe that a marriage failed because of the idiosyncrasies of one or both partners, rather than accept the idea that modern marriage imposes too great a burden on the individual, in that one cannot be all things to all people.

The Matrifocal Family

Of all the forms of the family, the one which is most controversial and least understood is the matrifocal family. This type of family structure is found primarily among the urban poor, in what Oscar Lewis (1961:XX) has called "the culture of poverty." The basic unit in such a family is the mother and her children.

This has led many people to regard such a family as immoral. The children are perceived as illegitimate and are said to lack a proper father image. Particularly in societies such as our own, where many members of the culture of poverty subsist on public welfare systems, the matrifocal family is viewed as an aberrant form of the "normal" family, a debased form of marriage, and generally immoral. Stack (1974:113–128) has documented the living arrangements of a group of black women and has concluded that the basic unit of the matrifocal family consists of the mother and children.

Unemployment or underemployment of males makes the middle class, neolocal, nuclear family maladaptive. The family unit, then, extends to kin and close friends (see Aschenbrener 1974).

Stack (1974) rejects the use of the term "matrifocal family" because of its perjorative implications. She points out that the family in this case is really made up of a network of people who may sleep in different houses, and take their meals in still other houses, but which does have continuity over time and "elastic boundaries" (Stack 1974:115). The network expands as some members are added and contracts as others leave.

Substandard housing with frequent condemnations and evictions, changes in earnings and employment, and births and deaths all contribute to the frequency of change in residence patterns. But, contrary to popular opinion, children are recognized by their fathers and, more important, father's kin contribute considerably to the care of the child. Alliances usually exist between a woman, her children, her mother, her mother's sisters, and resident males, including brothers of both generations of women and "friends" who may be fathers of some of the children. The formation of nuclear families is deterred because it would remove the contributions of those who do marry; also, it is consciously recognized that the chances of such a family succeeding are very slim.

Stack documented eleven changes of residence for her chief informant, from birth to age twenty-one and a half; however, each change involved primarily the same related groups of mothers and children, in different combinations, with the addition or loss of friends. For example, Stack (1974:117–118) shows that the informant, named Ruby, was born into a household made up of her mother and maternal grandparents. Ruby and her mother had to move into their own quarters in order to qualify for welfare. Shortly thereafter, Ruby's mother gave birth to a son, and moved back into her parents' home. When her grandparents separated, Ruby accompanied her grandmother to the home of her maternal aunt and uncle. Ruby's mother continued to live with her father. Ruby remained in this household for many years, although her grandmother remarried and subsequently died. For one year, Ruby set up a household with the father of her second child, but when this set-up ended she and her children rejoined her mother, her mother's husband, and several half-siblings. Another abortive attempt to build a nuclear family ensued, and Ruby moved into her maternal aunt and uncle's house, which was next door to the house occupied by Ruby's mother. Still another change came when her aunt moved out because of family quarrels.

Although there is considerable movement here, the people remain the same. Maintaining a permanent nuclear family is difficult for economic reasons. Men who would support such households too often lose their jobs and become a financial drain upon their wives. Such a network is not limited to kin, but includes male and female friends.

However, the child does have a good deal of contact with men. As a matter of fact, children in this type of environment usually have more exposure to men than those who come from typical middle-class suburban households. Both sets of grandparents, even if not resident in the home, often contribute to child care. Uncles are also available, since young males are encouraged to remain resident even after they have formed a relationship with a particular young woman. In addition, the children's fathers remain on good terms with their mother. Stack says (1974:127):

> A mother generally regards her children's father as a friend of the family whom she can recruit for help, rather than as a father failing his parental duties. Although many fathers voluntarily help out with their children, many fathers cannot be depended upon as a steady source of help.

Employment for black men is fraught with vicissitude. Their salaries are often inadequate to support a family, and jobs are likely to be seasonal or in other ways temporary. Nevertheless, the fathers' families do recognize and welcome all their children and whenever possible help both financially and in day-to-day care.

Another significant factor in these domestic networks is the readiness of the current father in residence to assume social parenthood of the mother's other children. Stack emphasizes the positive aspects of such a situation, given the economic conditions under which it exists.

In terms of every-day living, this type of structure makes it possible for a woman to leave her children in the care of someone who knows the children and will be responsible for them while she works; often this person is a grandmother or an aunt. There are never great distances between these people's households. Their residences may be next to each other or on the same street. The fact that people pool their resources is significant in stretching the substandard wages. For three basic reasons, the nuclear family unit is ill-equipped to meet the daily needs of children. These are: (1) women are more employable than men; (2) women with dependent children are denied financial aid if there is a male head of the household; and (3) hours are long and jobs insecure. The elastic domestic network described by Stack (1974:128) is more adaptive:

> I have particularly emphasized those strategies that women can employ to maximize their independence, acquire and maintain domestic authority, limit (but positively evaluate) the role of husband and father, and strengthen ties with kin. The last of these maximizing relationships in the domestic network helps to account for patterns of black family life among the urban poor more adequately than the concepts of nuclear or matrifocal family. When economic resources are greatly limited, people need help from as many others as possible. This requires expanding their kin networks, increasing the number of people they hope to be able to count on. On the one hand, female members of a network may act to break up a relationship that has become a drain on their resources. On the other hand, a man is expected to contribute to his own kin network, and it is assumed that he should not dissipate his services and finances to a marital relationship. At the same time, a woman will continue to seek aid from the man who has fathered her children, thus building up her network's resources. She also expects something of his kin, especially his mother and sisters. Women continually activate these lines to bring kin and friends into the network of exchange and obligation.

Although Stack's work was with urban black, poor people, similar networks pertain among Mexican and Puerto Rican urban poor. The concept of a domestic network rather than a nuclear family must be seen as an adaptation to urban poverty. Some aspects of this structure are applicable to other areas of life. Some people find that communal living solves the problem of child-rearing for mothers who desire careers. The Kibbutz in Israel and the factory-nursery in the Soviet Union are institutionalized attempts to free women for employment and yet provide satisfactory child care.

If women are to be freed to enter the public sphere through careers of various kinds, arrangements for child care will have to be devised both on a public and private level. It would seem that most societies today are actively experimenting along these lines.

Women Seek Balance between Functions

Two themes have run throughout this discussion of the sociopolitical sub-system and its implications for women. The first is that in all matters pertaining to the family, women have had to strive to maintain a balance between their needs and the needs of society. Rearing children is the one constant, since every culture assumes that this is the function of the female. Children represent continuity for the society, and are often the only means of gaining recognition for the mothers. The power women have in a society is often measured by how successful they are in rearing their children in spite of harsh economic and social conditions. They must forge such strong bonds with children that loyalties to the mother continue into adulthood. In some societies, adulthood for the child brings high status for the mother. In other societies, it means economic and physical aid for the mother. Thus, raising children has been the primary, constant theme for women in all societies. The second theme is the power women have outside the domestic sphere, and how this is affected by their necessary domestic demands.

Women and Political Control

In most societies women exercise their power in the domestic or private sphere. West African women are one notable exception. They generally hold higher status and tend to be active in the public sphere. In an earlier discussion, we learned that Yoruba women were active in the market network. Another example is given by Kuper (1965:485) in her discussion of the Swazi people:

> The homestead of the *ingewenyama* (the king) is organized on principles similar to those of other polygynists, but has certain significant additions reflecting the main stages of his selection (as frequently happens); he must live in the same homestead as his mother, the future *indlovukati*, while the queen regent (the "mother" for the deceased king) maintains the old capital. After he is installed, he and his

mother establish the new capital, sanctified with material from the old. The rulers remain together until the king takes his first ten queens, when he builds his own residence some distance away. His mother remains in charge of the capital, the largest homestead in the country; his homestead is second in size.

In Swaziland, women — at least the queens — have not only power but real political authority as well. Kuper (1965:498) states that the king is chosen by the rank of his mother, and that the king and his mother symbolize the Swazi state.

> Honors are fairly evenly distributed between them, and though the king, as the male, is dominant in legal and executive activities, she — the source of his selection — exercises complementary rights.

Kuper also reports that conflict between the two rulers is recognized *by the community* to be dangerous to the national security of the community. Laws have been passed for use in this event, which indicates that the Queen's decisions are of real significance to the community.

Still another instance of the autonomy of west Africa women are the Igbo of southeast Nigeria. Uchendu (1965:87) describes them thus:

> The African woman regarded as a chattel of her husband, who has made a bridewealth payment on her account, is not an Igbo woman who enjoys a high socio-economic and legal status. She can leave her husband at will, abandon him if he becomes a thief, and summon him to a tribunal where she will get a fair hearing. She marries in her own right and manages her trading capital and her profits as she sees fit. Though women are not the normal instrument through which land rights are passed, and though their virilocal residence after marriage makes it impossible for them to play some important social and ritual roles in their natal village, yet they can have leaseholds, take titles, and practice medicine.

By such standards, it seems that the modern American woman either does not have or, more likely, does not use the political power she possesses. American women have won the right to vote, but have for the most part voted with their husbands. They have failed to change policy significantly or to be elected in great numbers to decision-making offices. In the United States, the numbers of women elected to Congress are insignificant in comparison to the size of the female voting population. However, this is not the only measure of authority. Women have also largely been excluded from appointed positions in advisory capacities, although there have been some exceptions: for example, Frances Perkins was appointed Secretary of Labor by Franklin D. Roosevelt. Women were appointed most often to offices that were considered more "naturally" the woman's sphere, such as consumer affairs. More meaningful appointments in the Department of State or Department of Defense continue to be filled by men. Even Eleanor Roosevelt, whose contribution to the public sphere was great, accomplished her ends indirectly, by influencing her husband.

It is not possible to assign the blame for this state of affairs to anyone. It is true that men have difficulty in visualizing women in positions of authority. Women, on the other hand, have too often failed to grasp or demand opportunities to wield authority, agreeing that such positions belong to the male sphere.

Some developing nations — Ceylon, India, and Israel — have placed women in positions of authority. Human resources, in terms of educated, capable, knowledgeable people, are valuable in such societies and consequently, no person's assets are wasted, regardless of sex. It should not surprise us that women in such positions have shown themselves to be no more or less capable than men. Women are products of their societies, just as men are, and often reflect similar attitudes.

Chapter 7

Women and Ritual

Most societies discriminate against women in matters concerned with ritual. In fact, in attempting to find a theory to explain the status of women, Sanday (1973) concluded that their contribution to the economy of the society was a necessary but not sufficient concomitant of status. Her research indicated that control over resources was based upon religious and/or magical factors, and that the status of women was often a function of the religion of the society. She (1973:1698) states:

> A belief system emphasizing maternity and fertility as a sacred function can also be seen as the legitimization of sex status which develops because of ecological and economic factors. Furthermore, there is ample evidence in the ethnographic material discussed above, that a change in female status is associated with a change in the productive system. Where this has occurred, as with the Ibo, it is interesting to note that sex antagonism develops or increases. Perhaps sex antagonism develops in the absence of a belief system which legitimizes and sanctions the power of women. Sex antagonism might be reduced in such societies when a belief system develops in which female power is attributed to the natural functions of women. Clearly, this is another area for future investigation.

Function of the Belief System

The belief system of any society has the function of legitimizing and rationalizing both the economic and the social order of a given society, such as in tribes and theocratic states. It also functions as the political organization.

Most societies do discriminate against women, and in particular prohibit their participation in the public sphere. The public sphere involves those decisions and activities which affect the community as a whole; the private sphere is concerned with individual households.

In some societies, the belief system constitutes the entirety of the public sphere. In some bands and tribes, leadership of the community may be vested in an individual who also acts as the religious leader. In others, particularly the age-grading societies of east Africa, community decisions are made by elders who have achieved their position by passing through a series of rituals marking each age grade. Gibbs (1965:157) states:

> The Jie religion and age group system are fused into one integrated institution. Traditionally, the Jie had no chiefs, and their society was, and largely still is, organized, not in terms of political functionaries or of a centralized political structure, but in terms of communal rituals carried out at territorial levels.

Where religion is the society's organizing principle, and hence the only public sphere, a woman's power will be confined to the domestic or private sphere, and she will be completely excluded from the public sphere. Even where the society has a larger and more complex public sphere, elements of discrimination against women will be retained in the belief and ritual system, due to the cumulative nature of culture. Therefore, findings such as Sanday's may relate to an effect rather than to a cause.

Change in Ideologies

Among the three subsystems which comprise the system of culture, the so-called ideological subsystem is under the least pressure for change. In fact, it functions to stabilize the society; consequently, although it does change, such changes are often slight and tend to be slow in coming.

Ritual and belief systems will accommodate new ideas, such as those resulting from environmental or historic changes, by synthesizing them with their old beliefs. Conscious missionary attempts to change the belief system of a given people often accomplish no more than this. The belief system of a society is a reflection of the other internal subsystems of that society, and efforts to change one subsystem without concomitantly changing the other subsystems are often dramatically unsuccessful. People who become members of the new belief system are sometimes completely cut off from other members of the society in which they live (Turnbull 1968; Lewis 1964).

Certainly, in simpler societies, one would expect to find large areas in the belief system which deal directly with the "problem" of women. As stated earlier, the women who become wives and mothers in some societies are aliens, often intentionally brought over from potentially hostile groups. The ambivalence toward these outsiders who are so essential to the reproductivity of the society is often manifest.

Menstrual Taboos

One biological universal that cannot be ignored is menstruation among women. It is, therefore, not surprising to find that many societies impose restrictions upon women during their menses (Bock 1967:213). Most of these restrictions have to do with preventing menstruating women from coming into contact with men and all their activities and possessions. Perhaps this is in recognition of the fact that this biological function crucially separates men and women. Or maybe it serves as a reminder that women are potentially dangerous. As Audrey Richard (1956:19) states:

> The universality of menstrual taboos and the fear of the girl's first period struck earlier anthropologists such as Crawley and Frazer so forcibly that they overcame what must have been very strong Victorian reticenses on the subject. Blood appears to be the object of a set of emotionally tinged ideas in all human societies. It stands for death, murder, life-giving force or kinship. Menstrual blood, with its mysterious periodicity, is considered especially terrifying and disturbing, to judge from what we know of primitive ritual.

There is an enormous variety of ways in which menstruating women are secluded; however, a few examples will be used to demonstrate the general principle.

Netting (1969:1044) provides one description:

> Certain granaries may not be entered by women, and their dangerous state during menstruation prohibits them from preparing food for their husbands or coming in contact with his medicines.

These relatively minor proscriptions may occur in a society in which the women have much independence, due to their roles in patrilineal kin groups and also their economic importance, although Netting (1969:1037) states:

> With a relatively unimportant sexual division of labor, and limited marital and economic control, husbands are able to achieve little domestic authority over their wives. There are some indications that male distinctness and dominance are asserted chiefly, though not entirely successfully, in symbolic terms through sexsegregated rites and ritual injunctions.

Among the people of Wogeo, New Guinea, whose subsistence is based on fishing and the cultivation of taro, the following rules apply:

> A girl does not become regular immediately, and several months may elapse before she has a second period. The only thing out of the ordinary, then, is that the mother cooks her a bowl of curry and advises her to lie near the fire; otherwise she now starts taking the precautions that all menstruating women are expected to observe. First, to make her condition known to all, she replaces her white or colored skirt with one dyed black or dark brown. After that, the keynote of her behavior is

avoidance. She does not appear to be embarrassed and is allowed to speak freely and join in conversation, but she has to refrain from physical contact with other people. Equally, other people are expected to refrain from physical contact with her — that is why she advertises her condition with the dun-colored skirt. It is agreed that one menstruating female is unlikely to contaminate another, but they still keep their distance. She does not touch anyone else or anyone else's belongings; when leaving or entering the house, she passes through a hole in the floor or wall, not the doorway. When obliged to visit the cultivations, she stays in her own gardens. When hungry, she cooks for herself; when thirsty, she sucks liquid through a straw; when eating, she holds the food with a fork; and when itchy, she takes a scratcher (Hogbin 1970:136).

Another people from New Guinea, the Mae Enga, live in scattered homesteads which range over the territory belonging to the partriclan. For a livelihood, they cultivate yams and raise pigs and fowl. In this group, women do not live in the same houses as their husbands, but reside with their unmarried daughters and infant sons in a house built near the men's house. The men of the patrilineage live in a large house central to the women's houses. There is strong hostility between the sexes. According to Meggitt (1964:210), men believe that every ejaculation decreases their vitality. As a consequence, they will have intercourse only as often as necessary to beget children and only after performing magic to prevent the female from weakening them or otherwise making them ill. Needless to say, the sexual act is performed without foreplay, and leaves the men in a condition of anxiety rather than contentment. Meggitt further states that after intercourse occurs, men will not enter their gardens lest the aura of the female blight their crops. Men rarely discuss sexual matters even among themselves and would be embarrassed to discuss such things in mixed company. Meggitt (1964:207) reports:

It is not surprising that men refer to a woman during her menstrual period as "she with the evil eyes" and require her to remain in seclusion. In some localities she retires to a small hut used only for this purpose; in others she stays in the rear cubicle of her house, the room that a man never enters. Everywhere she withdraws from the sight of men for four days from the onset of her menses.

During this time the woman has her own fire and may prepare food for herself alone. She can collect food at night, but may harvest only mature "female" crops such as sweet potato, setaria, or crucifer, those which women normally cultivate. Should she enter a plot containing "male" (-tended) plants such as taro, ginger, or sugar-cane, these would die. Similarly, she must not walk among any young plants lest they wilt and those who eat them fall ill. She may feed pigs for these are, therefore, "female," but not dogs or cassowaries, as these are "male" and would lose their condition. She must not eat game, for this, too, is "male" and the hunter concerned would never again be successful.

One the fifth morning the woman cleanses herself before emerging from seclusion. Because an unmarried woman is by definition, chaste, she is less dangerous than a married woman and need take fewer precautions. She spits on white clay, recites a spell taught her by her mother, and draws a line from navel to vulva and an arc under each eye. A married woman, however, also receives from her husband (through a daughter or sister) a package of leaves (*Evodia sp*) which he has collected and bespelled. She bites off the ends of the leaves before placing them in the gable of her house, an action intended to neutralize the effects of blood remaining in her uterus when next her husband copulates with her. Meanwhile, she hides in the forest, the soft moss used as menstrual pads; the moss is not simply thrown away lest a pig eat it and die, and men then eat the contaminated pork.

The fact that the Mae Enga presume that unmarried women are chaste and thus allow them to use simplified precautions, may also mean that they realize that the unmarried women among them are daughters and sisters, and consider them less dangerous than the outsiders who became wives. Mead (1935:26) reports that the Arapesh also have menstrual huts for the women who reach menarche among their affines. A girl usually reaches menarche among her consanguineal kin at home. Meggitt (1964:218) states the case succinctly:

Typically, then, a man's wife and his mother come from those clans which are perennial enemies of his own clan and which are responsible for most of the deaths of his clansmen.

A fruitful problem for research would be to determine whether menstrual taboos occur more frequently and/or more stringently among people who consciously "marry their enemies," such as the Mae Enga and the Sarakatsani of Greece, than among people who contract marriages among friendly groups.

Richards points out that among the Bemba, a matrilocal, matrilineal society, where the in-marrying male is honored because he brings fertility to the woman, there are still menstrual taboos. A woman may not touch the household fire during her periods, but must have a small fire of her own apart from the others. There are heavy penalties upon a woman who permits even the accidental showing of menstrual blood. She may not wash in the stream with the other women at this time, and of course, intercourse is forbidden. Apparently, in many societies this distinguishing feature of womanhood is much feared.

The closer women come to approximating male roles, the higher the status accorded them by society. A woman who performs essential tasks and contributes heavily to the subsistence economy may enjoy fairly high status, but once she enters the public sphere as a trader or diviner or any other professional specialty, her position will almost always be higher still. This concept clashes with Lévi-Strauss's (1969) ideal of men being more closely allied to nature, i.e. "raw," whereas women are more closely allied to culture, i.e. "cooked." Women are accepted to the degree that they engage in typically male activities and are rejected and feared for their natural processes, such as menstruation. Thus the opposite of Lévi-Strauss's position, as proposed by

Ortner (1974), seems true: women, being more subject to natural cycles, should be regarded as "raw," whereas men, who spend most of their time and energy culturally manipulating nature, should be regarded as "cooked."

Childbearing

It is this natural menstrual cycle, uniquely a woman's function, which makes childbearing possible. No society can survive without the birth of children, and in many societies, childbearing is woman's only legitimate duty. Even people such as the Mae Enga, who fear their women, must risk contact with them in order to achieve the desired progeny. What, then, is the status of the pregnant woman? How does the society reward a woman who is obviously fulfilling her obligation?

Childbirth, in itself, can sometimes be quite dangerous for people lacking medical help. The Aztecs recognized this when they reserved one of their heavens for soldiers who died in battle and women who died in childbirth. As we have seen from time immemorial, the supernatural has been invoked to aid in childbirth. In addition to the danger to the mother, a very real danger to the infant exists; the infant death rate in primitive societies is phenomenally high. Many deaths take place in the first weeks after birth, but the first several years of the baby's life are fraught with danger.

While nursing, a baby is totally dependent upon its mother's milk. This means that the nutrition of the mother is extremely important to the child's well-being. In areas where famine is endemic, or where there are periodic food scarcities, the mother's ability to nurse is jeopardized. Also, nursing a baby promotes immunity to disease through the action of the mother's anti-bodies as well as nutrition. Successful nursing, then, is of paramount importance to the health of babies. Raphael (1973) and others have shown that feelings of security and comfort are vital to the mother's capacity to nurse. She needs the support of people around her — her husband, her co-wives, her sisters-in-law — or whoever makes up the household. In some of the societies we examined, this kind of relationship is difficult to achieve. However, in most societies, women who are past childbearing age, are called upon to help the pregnant woman and to assist at the birth of the child. Each society regards pregnancy as a special status.

Some groups establish a relationship between intercourse and pregnancy, and some do not. Mead (1935:48–56) tells us that the Arapesh believe that the child in the womb must be nurtured by both father and mother. Mead states:

> The Arapesh distinguish two kinds of sex activity: play, which is all sex-activity that is not known to have induced the growth of a child, and work, purposive sex-activity directed towards making a particular child, toward feeding it and shaping it during the first weeks in the mother's womb. Here the father's task is

equal to the mother's; the child is a product of a father's semen and mother's blood, combined in equal amounts at the start, to form a new human being.

Mead goes on to tell us that after the mother's breasts show the characteristic swelling and discoloration of pregnancy, all intercourse stops. The mother is no longer permitted to eat certain foods, such as ell, frog, or bandicoot, as well as coconuts or sago from a holy place.

The father cannot be present at the birth; the child must be delivered outside the village because the blood associated with childbirth is believed to be a pollutant. The mother is supported in her ordeal by several older women who act as midwives. When mother and child return to the village, both mother and father lie beside the newborn child. During the first day they both fast. They may not smoke or drink water. A series of small rituals are performed during the day to aid them in caring for the baby. The father's brother's wives are in charge of the materials needed for such rituals. The Arapesh believe that the birth of the first child is especially dangerous to the father. He must remain in seclusion for five days, must eat all food with a spoon, use a stick to scratch himself, and abstain from tobacco. Meanwhile, a small leaf house which is decorated with red flowers and herbs, is built near a pool of water. The new father retreats to this hut. He drinks from the pool after cleaning his mouth on a large, white ring which is placed at the bottom of the pool. Next he bathes and recaptures the white ring, which he returns to his sponsor. Now he is regarded as having successfully created a child.

Among the Aborigines of western Australia, Kaberry (1939:42) has found ignorance of the male role in paternity. Here it is believed that a spirit-child enters a woman, but the man claims social paternity. The mother must observe food taboos because it is believed that what she eats will affect the child. The mother spends no time in confinement during or after pregnancy. Birth takes place away from the camp, and the mother is accompanied by older women who chant particular songs to help in a difficult birth. After delivery, the mother and child stay away from the father for five days. Food taboos must be observed for a year. Socially, the child becomes part of the father's lineage, even though no connection is made between any physical activity on the part of the father and the birth of the child.

Evans-Pritchard (1974:22) notes that the Azande have food taboos for pregnant women; they cannot eat red pig, waterbuck, or eggs and must eat from new pots. After the birth of a child, the woman stays indoors for two or three days until the afterbirth has fallen. Then a fire of special wood is built in the doorway of the house. The midwife holds the baby over this fire, and later over a fire built in the middle of the path to the house. Porridge is made, part of which is consumed by the women, and part of which is given to small boys. When an Azande woman first becomes pregnant, her husband consults an oracle to find out whether or not the child is his.

Among the Mundugamur (Mead 1935:135), children are neither desired nor regarded fondly. Mead tells us that the husband views the woman's pregnancy as an imposition, because now he must observe certain taboos. At birth, the parents need not let the child live. They discuss this option a great deal during the pregnancy, and usually decide to let the child live if it is a girl, and to kill it if it is a boy, because girls belong to the father's patrilineage and are necessary in order to trade for brides for the men. Often the children are nursed by a wet-nurse, rather than by the mother. Birth takes place in the forest with little fuss. It it is not his child, the man has the option of taking his case before the prince and receiving compensation from the biological father, or killing the child. As a woman's delivery date approaches, her husband again consults an oracle who names a midwife to help at the birth. The oracle also designates where the birth should take place. If the woman's mother is available, she too presides at the birth of the child.

Among the Bemba, one of the women who helped in the initiation rite of the mother acts as midwife. Since the Bemba believe that each child is a reincarnation of an ancestor, it is up to the midwife to name which ancestor has returned in the child. In most societies, despite the degree to which women are feared or considered outsiders, older women — usually kinswomen of the husband if the couple reside patrilocally — come to help at the birth of a child. Birth rarely occurs in the home, and pregnancy is almost always surrounded by food and other taboos. In India, where the young bride is received so coldly in her husband's home, she is often allowed to return to her family for the later months of pregnancy and childbirth. Among people who accept bride-wealth for their daughters, the full portion must be paid upon the birth of a child.

Among some of the Amazonian tribes in South America, the tradition of *couvade* is observed when a child is born. The father takes to his hammock and obeys stringent food taboos. He may not hunt or smoke for a given period of time. The rationalization for this custom is the belief that the mother provides the child with its body, but the father provides the soul, and is therefore weakened by the birth. The people believe that the father's actions and behavior after the birth of the child can affect the child's health and well-being as well as its life chances.

Apparently, the process of childbirth is surrounded by two types of rituals: one is meant to safeguard the delivery and health of the child, the other is intended to incorporate the father as legitimate progenitor of the child. Where kinship is traced through the male line of descent, this is especially important because the son becomes a member of his father's patrilineage and thus adds to its numbers and strength. It is essential that the father, even where his biological role is not understood, be made part of the process of child creation. This can be achieved through ritual.

The Men's House

Another way in which ritual is used to reinforce the social order is through the use of the men's house. Many tribal societies have a large house, usually in the center of the community, where ritual paraphernalia is stored. It serves as a meeting place for men and, in some societies, as a dormitory where they sleep. Among other things, women bring cooked meals to the men's house. Here men discuss trading expeditions and the everyday business of living, plan raids, and rehearse and cast the various ritual performances. The men's house combines secular and religious functions, and all decision-making for the society as a whole takes place in this area. It constitutes the entire public sphere of society and serves as a repository for folklore and wisdom. Men's houses may be built by the group as a whole or at the instigation of a particular individual.

The men's house represents a social construct, in that it is used to acquire prestige and for other purely cultural purposes. It is also indicative of the separation between men and women in the society.

Women are strictly forbidden to enter the men's house. All the ritual and the paraphernalia connected with the ritual must never be seen or handled by women or uninitiated young men. The men's house symbolizes the dichotomy between males and females in society. It can be used for many purposes — to house male visitors or to house young bachelors — but its main function is to serve as the place where all men can find male companionship and discuss male concerns. To the best of present knowledge, there is not any similar vehicle for women.

Mead (1949) discusses the paraphernalia in the men's houses of the Pacific. All contain flutes, masks, and bull-roarers (pieces of wood on string, which emit a roaring noise when spun). The bull-roarer is usually used to announce the start of a ritual during which no women or uninitiated males dare to approach the vicinity of the men's house. If a woman did make such an attempt, her punishment might be a gang-rape or death.

Mead (1949:211) also reports that when Iatmul men are preparing for a headhunting expedition they sleep in the men's house in order to avoid sexual contamination by their wives. In many societies, the men's house is used as a hotel or club when men need to avoid female contamination. Mead (1935:43) also describes how the Arapesh men's society is concerned with the worship of a supernatural monster, the *tamberan*, part of whose function is social control. If a man has acted in shameful fashion by, for example, creating a public scene with his wife or a young relative, he will be visited, during the night, by men playing the sacred flutes which represent the voice of the tamberan. The offending man and his family will be driven off the premises, and his home will be broken into and littered. The man will then go live with relatives in another village, and will return only after he has offered a pig in sacrifice to clear his name in the village.

Hogbin (1970) states:

> In the majority of villages, the most imposing building which, if the terrain permits, stands in the center, is the men's club. Usually this building is about 20 feet long by 12 feet broad and thus larger than the average dwelling. It is also better put together and has thicker thatch which projects and so conceals the walls

below. The floor rests on stout hardwood piles, 8 to 9 feet high permitting gatherings to be held below. The absence of a club in a few settlements is to be accounted for by the fact that as yet, sufficient food has not been accumulated for the feasts that must accompany the construction of a replacement.

The club serves as a meeting ground, a dormitory, and a store for sacred objects. Here the males gather late in the afternoons to smoke cigarettes, chew betel, chat, and receive visitors. Sometimes they yell an order to the women to bring the evening meal across. Provided a nocturnal fishing expedition has not been arranged, the young householders return to the dwelling, but the youths and older men stay on to sleep. The ceremonial objects are lodged on a shelf beneath the bones of famous ancestors.

The men's house or club, then, is the sanctuary of the men's world. It is not surprising that men should need an area freed from any danger of female intrusion, when the society's women come from potentially hostile groups and are perceived to be alien. Male activities are planned and enacted in the men's house. It provides not only a place to plan raids or defenses against raids, but supernatural protection for the group. The supernatural consists of the men's deities and must be kept secret lest the women learn of them, and enact counter-magic. The men's house is still with us in the form of all-male clubs and various secret societies which are restricted to men, but which may have women's auxilliaries, provided the women's activities are supervised by a male member of the club. In large cities, these organizations may be anachronistic, but in small towns many transactions are concluded in such clubs. Men view membership in the club as a road to power in the community, as, indeed, it often is. In most societies, membership in men's clubs and rights to entrance in the men's house, are reserved for the initiated, who are recruited among young boys of the lineage. As earlier stated, young children, regardless of sex, reside with and are cared for by their mothers. Girls continue to live with their mothers until marriage, but boys must be made into men and this is one of the prime functions of the men's society.

Male Puberty Rituals

Puberty rituals are among the "rites of passage" defined as marking the changes of an individual's status in the community. Van Gennep (1960) has delineated three stages of any rite of passage: isolation, education, and reentry into the community in a new status. Among most simple societies, the education accompanying the puberty ceremonial is the only formal education available to the individual. According to Van Gennep, education refers not only to the education of the individual entering a new status, but also to the education of kin and neighbors, who must recognize the individual's new status and treat that person accordingly.

Some societies have puberty rituals for both girls and boys; others have them only for one sex or the other. By far, ceremonies for boys are most prevalent. This may be related to the fact that there is no critical biological moment that marks the passage from childhood to adulthood for men. Or, it may be indicative of the need to separate the young boy from his feminine associations and thrust him in the male role, to inherit the male responsibilities of the society. In any case, most cultures find it necessary to make a formal and complex statement, through ritual, when they initiate and incorporate boys into the body of male society (Young 1965). A brief summary of the major stages of male puberty ceremonies has already been given, although a great deal of variation exists. How long the isolation lasts, what is taught, how courage is tested, and finally, how the reentry into society is manifested are dealt with in various ways.

Hogbin (1970:100–124) gives an account of the ritual for the people of Wogeo. Here, initiation takes place in several stages over a period of years. The men of Wogeo articulate that the ceremonial is held in order to make certain that a boy will grow up to be a man. In the first ceremony, the ears of a four- or five-year-old boy are pierced by men who enter the house in which the boys and their mothers hide. The boys have their eyes bandaged with barkcloth and are pushed outside roughly. There, while boards are banged together to make noise, each child has the lobe and top of his ear pierced by a bone. Hogbin reports that all the small boys scream with terror. The children are told that they have been bitten by monsters (*nibek*), and then they return to their mothers. At this point, the men light a fire and proceed to cook and eat the food offerings.

The second part of the initiation occurs when boys are about ten years old. Parents daub them with red ochre and lead them to the foot of the ladder of the clubhouse. Each boy's sponsor descends the ladder, pushes the mother aside, slaps the boy's shoulders in order to rid him of the remains of his mother's influence, and carries him upstairs. Again, most of the initiates howl with terror. The men spend the night with the boys in the clubhouse. In the morning, a few men paint their bodies grotesquely, and make loud noises; they drag the boys to the beach, where they are shown the flutes and hear them played. Each boy's sponsor takes his charge into the sea and scrubs him. The boys have their ankles and wrists pulled and are removed from the water by waiting relatives who twist spearblades in their hair. These actions are believed to make the boys grow. After they return to the clubhouse, the boys are initiated into the mysteries. They are told that there are no real monsters, only men who impersonate them, and that the boys themselves will eventually be taught to do this. The fact that this must be kept secret from the women is stressed. The men state that they are aware that women would laugh and poke fun at them if they knew.

The third part of the puberty ritual occurs when a boy is judged ready for sexual intercourse. At this time, he must have his tongue scarified, a practice which, it is believed, will enable him to play the flutes. Hogbin (1970:114) like this to the boy's first artificial menstruation. The tongue is chosen for scarification because this is the area where the boy absorbed the most contamination from his mother, in nursing and eating food prepared by her. The scarification is produced by scraping the tongue with sandpaperlike leaves until the tongue bleeds. The boys are now taught how to induce artificial menstruation (described earlier).

The final phase of the ritual comes about when the young man is ready for marriage. He is again bathed in the sea, and pulled ashore by a spear entangled in his hair. His hair is then confined in a wicker cone. As it grows, the wicker cone is replaced by larger ones until the hair is about ten inches long, at which time it is trimmed to fit the cone. A feast follows, for the young man is now considered totally grown and ready to assume the responsibilities of adulthood.

Female Puberty Ritual

Puberty ritual for women occurs less frequently, but just as elaborately. Attempts to account for the presence of female puberty rituals in some cultures and not in others has led to a number of theories.

Brown (1963:837) notes that female puberty rituals occur primarily in areas where the woman does not leave her home after marriage — that is, in matrilocal societies — or in areas where women play the major role in providing subsistence. Kloos (1969:898) agrees with this idea and points out that in a community where women have been raised and will continue to live as adults such a change in status must be marked.

The participants understand that the purposes of the ritual are different from those of the male ritual. There is no question here of making women; women grow into womanhood naturally. However, they must be taught proper conduct for women in their society. Since female puberty rites are restricted to women and most field anthropologists have been men, a full description of women's rituals is rare. We are fortunate, therefore, to have Audrey Richards' (1956) account of the Chisungu rite among the Bemba people of Africa. This ceremony lasted 23 days.

A girl who has her first period must wait until there are several more in the same situation so that the ritual can be performed for several girls at a time. Marriage cannot take place before the Chisungu rite is completed; the bridegroom pays the mistress of ceremonies and sometimes participates in it.

During this ritual the girls act out, with props, some of the things they will have to do as grown women. For example, the girls crawl a little way with a bundle of boughs on their backs, in imitation of the way they will be carrying firewood when they marry. They learn many dances, some of which symbolize gestures of respect toward older women. They also make models of everyday objects such as hoes and water pots. The songs they learn have morals. Richards mentions one which admonishes the girls never to speak about their husbands' adulterous conduct. Much time is spent instructing the girls not to wean their babies too soon, not to gossip, not to be lazy, and similar directions for being a proper Bemba wife and mother. The high point of the ceremony occurs on the seventeenth evening, when the bridegrooms of the girls in the ceremony enter the house. Each bridegroom aims an arrow at the spot above the head of his bride as she sits against the wall and each girl is presented with a bundle of firewood carried by the bridegroom's sister. Meat, beads and red dye are enclosed in the bundle. In the last part of the ceremony, the girls, adorned in their new beads painted with red dye, sit on mats beside their bridegrooms and receive gifts of coins and bracelets from their kinsmen.

Comparison between Male and Female Puberty Rituals

Young has done a study of initiation ceremonies which is pertinent to any comparison of male and female puberty rituals. After a discussion of alternative explanations for the male puberty ritual, Young (1965:41) states:

> The central hypothesis of this study is that dramatization of status changes in a group are most elaborate when the solidarity of the group is great — that is, when there is a great deal of cooperation among the members for the purpose of creating and maintaining a stable definition of the situation. This hypothesis is applied specifically to the potential disruption of consensus and solidarity in a group of men when boys are taken into it. The dramatization of sex role-initiation is functionally necessary for maintaining the solidarity of the men. Such ritual-ization calls attention to the boy's change in status and gives him access to the intimate communication of the group. In this new social sector, the boy quickly consolidates his role and the stability of the community's age-sex status clas-sification is preserved.

In a similar vein, Young analyzes female puberty rituals as serving the same purpose, integrating the girl into a solidary group of women. Young (1965:109) claims:

> Girls grow up in the domestic establishment and are adequately socialized for work and marriage by the time they reach early adolescence. But in communities where corporate families are typical, the girls must also learn to take part in the tightly organized group of women that dominates every-day affairs. Regardless of any rule of residence that may take her to another such group, a girl must learn to submit to the authority of the elder women, to do her part of the work, and ultimately to contribute to the ongoing unit while maintaining a certain autonomy in her own hut and among her own children.

The Chisungu ceremony demonstrates how this deference for older women is dramatized. On the seventh day of the ceremony, the girls are permitted for the first time to play the adult role of offering food, by offering baskets of seeds to the older women. The girls are required to obey the commands of the mistress of ceremonies and of the older women who take part in the ritual. The solidarity of the group of women is displayed when the girls give gifts to the older women. On the tenth day the girls gather around a tree which symbolizes fertility and has rings of white beads hanging from it. The girls must bit off these rings and pass them to the mistress of ceremony. Small clay models which the girls have made and decorated are also presented to her. She is shown great deference. On the eighteenth day, each girl kills and plucks a chicken which is cooked along with porridge and served in a communal feast in which both the initiates and the older women take part.

Young (1965:109) points out that girls are initiated into the domestic or private sphere. Boys are initiated into the community at large or the public sphere.

> To facilitate this role-learning, the women of the household arrange a dramatization of the transition from girlhood to pre-adulthood, and the more institutionalized the family, the more elaborate the ceremony. However, because the unit of solidarity is smaller, the ceremonies are rarely as elaborate as those for boys. Similarly, they are less likely to involve the whole community.

Another significant distinction is that male puberty rites rigidly, and sometimes forcefully, exclude women. Women's puberty rituals often include men. Although there are times when the girls remain hidden from view, the impression that women are being socialized into a world in which men play an important role persists, whereas boys are viewed as being prepared to live in a male world. Ritual, then, may largely be seen as reinforcing the role of men in the public sphere and the role of women in the private sphere.

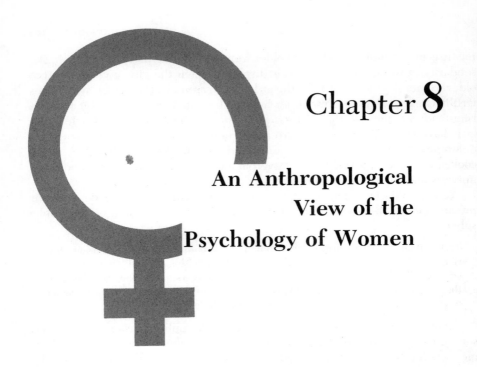

Chapter 8

An Anthropological
View of the
Psychology of Women

In most societies there are constructs of ideal personalities for men as well as women. There also tend to be modal personalities for both sexes. Much research has been devoted to eliciting the causes for these differing ideal personalities. As D'Andrade (1966) states, psychologists tend to look for such patterning in the individual; anthropologists tend to look for it in the culture.

> Psychology tends to consider sex differences as differences in personal characteristics. Anthropology, on the other hand, generally conceives of sex differences as social and cultural institutions (D'Andrade 1966).

Feedback between Culture and Personality

The relationship between culture and personality seems to be a feedback system in which the personality of the individual interacts with the culture. Culture sets and reinforces "normal" behavior, and even the pattern for deviance. In his discussion of the Dobu, Fortune (1932) points out that a generous, good-natured man who lacks suspicion of his fellows is considered to be akin to the village idiot.

It is more questionable whether individuals can influence particular cultures through their own personalities. There is no question that some individuals do move societies in given directions. However, are these individuals not also creatures of the culture? Anthropologists give little credence to the

84

"great man" theory of cultural change and cultural achievement. They generally agree that culture is a process that moves under its own momentum and is articulated through individuals who happen to be at the right place at the right time. Yet certain individuals in anthropological literature have moved their cultures; for example, Handsome Lake, the Iroquois prophet, or Wovoka, the Paiute who founded the Ghost Dance religion, undoubtedly came to prominence due to the cultural conditions of their time, but nevertheless they managed to influence the course of history for their people as a result of their strong personalities.

Although genetic and hormonal differences do exist between men and women, it is not yet known precisely how these affect personality. The pervasive sentiments that boys are more aggressive than girls and that girls are more nurturent than boys persist, and it is thought that these traits may be inherent sexual characteristics.

Barry, Bacon, and Child (1957) reported that in 110 nonliterate cultures, 82 percent encouraged girls to become nurturent, 87 percent encouraged boys to achieve more, and 85 percent encouraged boys to be self-reliant. This being the case, it would be surprising if there were no measurable personality differences between adult men and women in these areas. Williams states that the female children born to women who had been treated with progestin, a synthetic androgen to prevent miscarriage, exhibited a tendency toward what Money calls "tomboyism." Williams (in press) lists six characteristics of girls so affected:

1. a liking for vigorous outdoor activity and boys' sports
2. self-assertiveness and competitiveness with boys, not including aggressiveness
3. preference for utility in clothing, hair style, etc. rather than female adornment
4. little enthusiasm for doll-play or baby-sitting
5. achievement and career seen as more important than romance and marriage
6. no special affinity for lesbianism

William states that Money (1965) found that a large precentage of these girls had unusually high IQs. Other investigators have found that girls born to mothers who took a female hormone, progesterone, during pregnancy also tend to have high IQs. An interesting proposition, which might be tested, is that women who took medication during their pregnancies to prevent miscarriage apparently wanted children, and therefore these children may have received much more of the parent's time and attention. This extra stimulation and interaction may be the cause of higher IQ scores rather than the hormones.

Another area in which hormones play a part in a woman's life is the menstrual cycle. Williams (in press) states:

> The entire cycle is controlled by an elaborate feedback system which, though ultimately regulated by the hypothalamus, is essentially a function of hormones produced by the pituitary gland and the ovaries. The hypothalamus monitors the level of these hormones in the blood.

This cyclic alternation of hormone levels is popularly supposed to cause serious fluctuation in mood and ability among menstruating women. Williams (in press) points out:

It is almost certain that the various symptoms associated with menstruation have a basis in physical factors; the view that such problems are "all in the mind" can no longer be seriously held by anyone. On the other hand, as with most human characteristics, emotions and attitudes affect the woman's perception of what is happening to her, and the manifest result is an interaction between the soma and the psyche. Knowledgeable women today, especially those who are feminists, look with concern upon any over-emphasis of the role of woman's biology in the totality of her life; they know that such emphasis has too often been used to limit arbitrarily her participation in the whole spectrum of society's interests.

Mead's Seminal Work on Personality

The characteristics that define male versus female personalities are not cross-culturally universal. Mead (1935) has demonstrated this neatly for the Pacific. She showed that the personalities of men and women in a particular culture were more similar than the personalities of men from different cultures. Mead studied three cultures in the Sepik River of New Guinea: the Arapesh, the Mundugumor, and the Tchambuli.

Mead describes the Arapesh as an agricultural people who live in villages that are "clustered" into localities for which people are named. When an Arapesh man goes to his garden or other lands, he will make himself known to the ancestral ghosts who, it is believed, own the land. In addition to this bond with the past, the Arapesh also have ties with the present — men cultivate several plots of ground, each one in cooperation with a different set of relatives. The people in these gardening groups change from time to time, but the fundamental cooperation continues. Mead (1935:37) states that an individual may be a guest while working some gardens, or a host while working others, depending on ownership and inheritance rules. Since the land is poor, plots which yield inadequate harvests are worked less frequently than those which show greater yields and thus the membership of each gardening group changes often. Both men and women work in the gardens and tend the pigs. In this society there is no formal political leadership. Mead (1935:34) reports:

It is a society where a man conceives responsibility, leadership, public appearance, and the assumption of arrogance as onerous duties from which he is only too glad to escape in middle years, as soon as his eldest child attains puberty.

This society does have male rituals which exclude women; however, this is because the Arapesh view such ritual knowledge as dangerous to women and small children, and men take the burden upon themselves in order to spare the women. Mead (1935:34) characterized Arapesh society as follows:

Arapesh life is organized about the central plot of the way men and women, physiologically different and possessed of differing potencies, unite in a common adventure that is primarily maternal, cherishing and oriented away from the self and toward the needs of the next generation. It is a culture in which men and women do different things for the same reason, in which men are not expected to respond to one set of motivations and women to another, in which — if men are given more authority — it is because authority is a necessary evil that someone, and that one, the freer partner, must carry.

Mead (1935:259) finds that both Arapesh men and women are trained to be cooperative and responsive to the needs of others. Aggression is not valued in either sex. Despite the possibility that aggressiveness may be a natural part of maleness, the Arapesh, by devaluing this characteristic, have not made it part of the personality of their men. The existence of societies such as the Semai and the Arapesh brings into question the biological imperative toward aggression which some authorities claim. Humans are so much a creation of their culture that biological imperatives, if they exist at all, are often overridden by cultural factors. Although the Arapesh practice a division of labor and exclude women from ritual, they have fostered a single personality type, that of the nurturing adult.

The Mundugumor live along the Yuat River which is a tributary of the Sepik River. Until recently, the tribe practiced head-hunting and cannibalism. There are no village clusters; rather, each man builds a compound containing his own house, a house for each of his wives, and a house for his adolescent sons. Residences are scattered, not for ecological or technological reasons, but as a result of the incessant quarreling among the tribe's people. Mead (1935:171) states:

> There is no place where a group of men can sit down together except upon the rare occasions when a ceremony is on foot. . . . But feasts are oases in a life that is riddled with suspicion and distrust.

The social organization of the Mundugumor is called a *rope*. A rope consists of a man, his daughters and their sons, and his daughters' sons' daughters. The alternative rope consists of a woman, her sons and their daughters, and her sons' daughters' sons. It is clear that even within a single household there are divisions of loyalty between brothers and sisters who belong to different ropes. Mead also describes the condition between co-wives in this polygynous society as one of "fiercely competitive enmity."

Unlike the Arapesh, the Mundugumor live in a very fertile area. This makes the general level of hostility more difficult to understand. Their land contains palm trees, areca nuts, and sago palms. The men cultivate tobacco, which they use for trade with other groups along the river. They also fish and grow yams in gardens. In addition, men are responsible for cutting down the sago palms in order to allow the sago-grub, a much prized item of diet, to flourish. According to Mead, women do all the other subsistence work. The hostility engendered within this society is not due to conditions of economic scarcity; rather, it carries down to the birth process itself. Neither Mundugumor men nor women feel a strong attachment to their offspring because children impose restrictions upon their freedom. As a result, infanticide is commonplace. Even in this practice enmity arises between husband and wife: the man favors the survival of female infants because they will become members of his rope, whereas the woman prefers the survival of male infants for the same reason.

Mead (1935:259) describes the Mundugumor personality as "ruthless, aggressive, and positively-sexed" with a minimum of the nurturing qualities of the Arapesh. However, the Mundugumor personality is not unique. Chagnon (1968) describes similar personalities among the Yạnomamö of the Amazon jungle, whom he appropriately calls the "Fierce People." It is notable that persistent raiding and warfare have left their mark on the personalities of both the Mundugumor and the Yạnomamö and neither one can sustain peaceful relationships for any length of time, even among themselves. In each case the people are suspicious and resentful of each other, and frequently move into new areas to avoid old enemies. This constant hostility interferes with daily life.

The Mundugumor woman is as violent, temperamental, and aggressive as the Mundugumor man. She routinely climbs coconut palms. In other societies, this chore is relegated to men or young boys, because it is regarded as too dangerous and difficult for women.

The third group of people described in Mead's study are the Tchambuli, who live on a lake separated by two waterways from the Sepik River. Their subsistence is based mainly upon the sago palm and fishing. Canoes are used to implement trade for sugar cane and sago. Although the Tchambuli practiced head-hunting at one time, they never exhibited the combative spirit of their neighbors, the Mundugumor. Mead reports that a young male must kill a human being before he can be initiated. The Tchambuli bought slaves or captives from other groups for this purpose. The Tchambuli do have a highly ornate men's house and participate in much ritual. It is the women who fish, trade, and weave.

In this society the personalities of men and women differ from each other more than in either of the other two societies discussed. Here the men are regarded as temperamental, and spend their days creating works of art — dancing, carving, and painting. Their personalities are the reverse of those considered ideal by Western society. The women, on the other hand, are thought to be more capable, practical, and mature. In fact, the women provide the subsistence and trade. Mead (1935:266) states:

> While there is reason to believe that not every Tchambuli woman is born with a dominating, organizing, administrative temperament, actively sexed and willing to initiate sex relations, possessive, definite, robust, practical and impersonal in outlook, still most Tchambuli girls grow up to display these traits. And while there is definite evidence to show that all Tchambuli men are not, by native endowment, the delicate, responsive actors of a play staged for the women's benefit, still most Tchambuli boys manifest this coquettish play-acting personality most of the time.

Are There Feminine and Masculine Personalities?

Having compared sex and personality in these three societies, Mead (1935:260) concludes:

> The material suggests that we may say that many, if not all of the personality traits which we have called masculine or feminine are as lightly linked to sex as are the clothing, the manners, and the form of head dress that a society at a given period assigns to either sex. When we consider the behavior of the typical Arapesh man or woman as contrasted with the behavior of the typical Mundugumor man or woman, the evidence is overwhelmingly in favor of the strength of social conditioning. In no other way can we account for the almost complete uniformity with which the Arapesh children develop into contented, passive, secure persons while the Mundugumor children develop as characteristically into violent, aggressive, insecure persons. Only to the impact of the whole of the integrated culture upon the growing child can we lay the formation of the contrasting types. There is no other explanation of race, or diet, or selection that can be adduced to explain them. We are forced to conclude that human nature is almost unbelievably malleable, responding accurately and contrastingly to contrasting cultural conditions.

Although Mead's work was done in the 1930s, much of it is still valid. Modern research tends to show, however, that there are parameters of human temperament and that human nature is fairly constant. Still, environments and cultural determinants play a large role in establishing the behavior and/or the form that the individual exhibits.

Genes, for example, may determine a normal range of stature; however, the stature of the individual, whether human or animal, is subject to modification by factors of nutrition and disease. Culture plays such an important role in determining the personality of the individual that even if it could be shown that hormonal and glandular activities were responsible for causing certain responses, these responses would still be modified by culture. In an emotional display of anger, for example, we know that the adrenal glands secrete adrenalin which causes physiological changes in the pulse rate, blood pressure, and blood flow. However, culture determines how the individual will handle his anger — through violence or sulking. The problem can best be observed in the simple societies studied by Mead, because these societies are more homogeneous than our own. In Western civilization there is a great variety in the description of masculinity and femininity, due to class and subcultural differences. Too often, when psychologists and sociologists attempt to test for masculine or feminine characteristics, they apply norms that are accurate only for one segment of the society.

Classification of Personalities

Gough (1952) set up a scale of measurement for femininity which had among its criteria: (1) acceptance of traditional roles and hobbies; (2) acceptance of clean, white-collar work; (3) social sensitivity; (4) timidity in both social and physical situations; (5) compassion and sympathy; (6) lack of interest in the abstract political and social world; (7) lack of braggadocio and hyperbole; (8) presence of pettiness and irritability, and (9) presence of niceness and acquiescence. In former times, these were considered the standards of femininity for middle-class Western civilization. According to these criteria, many modern women would be diagnosed as excessively masculine. Only a few examples of recent studies in which psychologists place middle-class value judgments upon the differing personal characteristics of men and women can be cited: Adams (1964); Ames and Ilg (1964); Beller (1962); Beller and Neubauer (1963); Borgatta and Stimson (1963); Hall (1964); are typical, and perhaps special mention should be made of the Honzik and McKee study (1962).

How Roles Are Learned

Most psychologists recognize that gender role is actually quite well established by the time the child enters nursery school. In the Crandall and Rabson (1960) study two groups of children were the subjects — the first group consisted of three- to five-year olds; the second group contained six- to eight-year-olds. The children were given two puzzles to work on and were permitted to finish only one. They were then asked to choose between working further on the completed or the uncompleted puzzle. The following factors were also observed and rated: achievement efforts in free play; seeking help from peers and adults; seeking approval from peers and adults; and withdrawal from threatening situations. As part of the conclusions, Crandall and Rabson noted that there were no significant differences between boys' and girls' behavior at nursery school age, but in the six- to eight-year-old group significant differences in all variables existed. Girls asked for help and sought approval from adults rather than from peers and girls also withdrew from threats more often than boys. The responses to this test seem to indicate that gender role learning occurs during the three to eight year age bracket.

If we assume that gender roles are learned, we should try to find out *how* these patterns of behavior are learned. Most psychological testing in our own culture tends to show that three-year-olds already know their gender (Kohlberg 1966). Throughout their growing years, this knowledge is reinforced by the institutions and persons who have access to the child. Tuddenham (1951) reports on a study in which 1,000 first-, third-, and fifth-grade school children were asked to nominate their classmates according to certain pairs of traits (good at games, not good at games, etc.). The results showed that certain traits for boys elicited a favorable response in all grades: these were leadership, daring, and being good at games. Girls' responses were more variable, however. In first grade, "acting like a little lady" was the key to popularity, but by fifth grade this was no longer an important characteristic.

Woman's Role in Enculturation

Chodorow (1974) makes an important contribution to the understanding of gender behavior development in both males and females. She points out that in modern Western society, both boys and girls are encultured, or socialized, by women, usually the natural mother. Even in cases where a surrogate must be used, a woman is usually fills the position. Chodorow shows that women in all cultures tend to identify with their daughters.

Writing in psychoanalytic terms, Chodorow states that women grow up "without establishing adequate ego boundaries, or a firm sense of self." This means that a woman is closely bound to her own mother and does not establish firm boundaries between her daughter and herself. In many ways, a mother perceives her daughter as an embodiment of herself, and perceives herself as an extension of her mother. A mother often knows first hand the problems which will beset her daughter later in life and she tends to prepare her for them, even unconsciously. Out of her own experience, she knows what is considered "proper behavior" for women, and sets an example which she encourages her daughter to emulate. The daughter does not consciously have to separate herself from her mother and the feminine world in which her early years are spent.

Male Identification

On the other hand, after an early identification with mother, a boy is made to understand that he must behave differently from his mother. Fortunate boys find an acceptable male model and make the transition into manhood without trauma. In Western civilization some boys have a problem with this kind of identification because their father, who would be the natural model, is not home as much as their mother. And even when he is, the father presents a fallacious view of manhood to his son because he is at leisure. He attempts to teach the boy masculine leisure activities such as playing ball or fishing. He is seldom able to have his son watch him at work, and the child cannot grasp the significance of his work until he is quite grown. In simple societies, young boys are encouraged to watch their fathers at work, where the product is tangible, the work is visible, and the male attitudes are clear.

For us, too often the product is intangible, the work is invisible, and the father is unavailable. Since separation from his mother is necessary, the boy usually finds his way into a peer group long before his sister has felt the need to socialize outside the family. He must make a traumatic break with the world of women in order to become a man, whereas a girl is a small woman to start with. Young children often show this differentiation in their play. When a small boy and girl play house, the girl, who plays the mother, often pushes the boy, who plays the father, out of the house, telling him he has to go to work. Thereupon the little girl plays at cleaning, cooking, and tending doll babies. The little boy, having imitated the motions of the father driving off in his car, has no further role and is left to his own resources. By the time "mother" announces that dinner is ready, the little boy has wandered out of the game.

An important fact here is that during her growing-up process, the little girl learns to relate to people by identifying with her mother. Since a little boy is taught to relate to males rather than his mother, Chodorow (1974:66) suggests that a condition of psychological defensiveness and insecurity is created in men which does not exist in women. The male drive for achievement may be an attempt at compensation.

Flexible Ego Boundaries of Women

Psychologically, the female personality is molded by bearing and raising children. A woman has more flexible ego boundaries due to the strong relationship between mothers and daughters. Out of this strong relationship comes her ability to relate to people as a whole. The gentle and nurturing qualities of women are based in their procreative activities, but not limited to them. These traits pass on a continuum from mother to daughter, with each culture perpetuating its own definition of femininity. This does not imply, however, that this definition has remained unchanged. Through identification with their daughters, many mothers consciously try to correct what they perceive to be failings in their own mothers' methods of child-rearing. A mother who is dissatisfied with her own role, for example, may be determined to have her daughter, who is a projection of herself, live another sort of life. This is not an unusual situation. Smith (1939), in a study of children aged eight to fifteen, found that both sexes initially credited their own sex with having more of the desirable traits listed in the test. Boys of all ages rated themselves high in possession of these positive traits, but as the girls' ages increased, they tended to equate femininity with more of the undesirable traits listed. Women who think they possess undesirable characteristics would be moved to correct these traits in their daughters.

SILHOUETTES

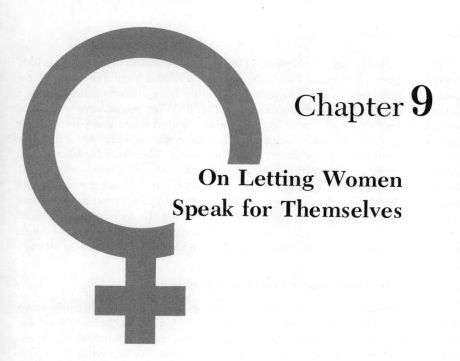

Chapter 9

On Letting Women Speak for Themselves

What is it like to be a woman in societies other than our own? We have already mentioned attitudes, described ceremonials, and referred to customs that affect women in various societies. In this section we will try to round out the picture by allowing women to speak of their lives as they remember them.

Representatives of Simple Societies Are Not Replicas of the Past

For the nonanthropologist, a problem that is obvious, but often overlooked, must be clarified. The anthropologist is seldom the first member of Western society to come in contact with a group of people. Most often, the anthropologist follows on the heels of the military, the administrator, the missionary, and the industrialist. Western society has spread both its personnel and its materials so widely that it is relatively impossible to find a people who have not been contacted, either directly or indirectly. The Tasadays, a group found in the Philippines in 1972, are an exceptional case, although these people constitute a mere remnant of what must at one time have been a much larger population.

The Westernization of the World

These women have lived in societies which have been undergoing change. This does not make their stories invalid in terms of ethnography, however, because all cultures change through time.

Much of the change they describe is the result of Westernization. It would, then, be an error to regard their lives as typical of the lives of women in the same society before European contact. Not only have attitudes and behavior changed, but expectations have changed as well. What might have seemed a satisfying life aboriginally, may appear unduly limited when compared to the lifestyles seen in movies and magazines. The changes brought about by modern equipment and techniques have been enormous. The introduction of the automatic tortilla press in Mexico, for example, has saved much time and effort; however, it has deprived women of a feeling of pride in making well-shaped tortillas by hand. The drudgery of grinding corn with a *mano* on a *metate* has been replaced by the almost social event of visiting the local mill on a daily basis. Communication systems have brought the people of the most isolated areas into contact with urban areas, which are modeled on Western societies.

The Good and Bad of Modernization

Modernization is often desirable because it effects improved health care, better diet, and easier working conditions. However, such changes may also bring with them destruction of a culture, disease, and malnutrition. The replacement of raw meat by a European diet has caused the Eskimo to lose certain essential vitamins and minerals, which has led to a high incidence of tuberculosis. The Western notion of bottle-feeding and early weaning of infants has led to a substantial rise in infant malnutrition and mortality throughout parts of Africa, particularly in those areas where an adequate adult diet is seldom found.

In sum, then, the women speaking in this book are not the embodiment of women in aboriginal societies as they existed in a pristine state. They are women whose lives have been changed and influenced by Western civilization. Many recognize this consciously and comment upon it. Others seem less aware of the historical context in which they live.

Another caveat is related to the imposition of Western values by the anthropologist or other observer upon the position of women.

The Etic and Emic Views

There are two ways in which any role can be observed: There is the etic view (the outsider's objective evaluation of the role) or the emic view (subjective evaluation of the role by the person being observed). These two views are often diametrically opposed to each other, but are not mutually exclusive. The best results are obtained by viewing the subject from both aspects. For example, the observer may perceive women to be a particularly depressed and exploited segment of a society, yet these same women may view themselves as being quite well treated, relative to others. To avoid this kind of misinterpretation, both the emic and the etic views will be presented whenever possible.

Anthropologists and other people who come into contact with other cultures are enabled to present both views by the use of tape recordings, which allow people to speak for themselves. In some cases, only an interpreter is needed to translate the tapes into whatever European language the investigator is using. Autobiographic material is valuable, but even more valuable is information derived from a member of a culture who has been trained as an ethnographer. As education becomes more widespread, such ethnographies should become more numerous.

Unfortunately, not all the silhouettes presented are autobiographical. The technique of tape recording is too new to be ubiquitous. However, wherever a woman's story must be related by the anthropologist, every effort will be made to select direct quotations and to present an even-handed evaluation free from both the "noble savage" and "cruel Barbarian" concepts.

Ordering the Life Histories

Any attempt to order the biographical material to be presented in terms of band, tribe, state, or in terms of "primitive" or simple versus complex societies, has been eroded by the factor of Westernization mentioned above. Is an Eskimo who lives in a wooden house, wears Western clothing, buys food in the grocery store, still an Eskimo? One can argue well for either side of the question. Still, some sort of classification must be imposed, if only to point up similarities and differences between groups. For this reason, four major groupings have been devised.

Indigenous Societies

Indigenous societies are those which have had contact with Western civilization, but have largely remained in the area they inhabited aboriginally. Or, if they have moved, they now consider their present location as home. Primarily, this first category is based upon the fact that the people view themselves as a group, separate and apart from the larger society in which they move. The question of the Eskimo is answered in that an Eskimo is an Eskimo as long as he or she feels he is an Eskimo and/or is perceived to be an Eskimo by members of the larger culture.

Peasant Societies

The second major category refers to a subculture within a larger culture. These are rural agriculturalists who grow food for their own subsistence as well as cash crops for the market. They should not be compared to, or confused with, agrarian industries in Western society. The latter are large, mechanical enterprises which employ labor in the same way other industries employ it. In some areas, the peasant speaks a different language from that of the larger society. In Mexico, for example, Spanish is the national language, but many peasants speak Nahuatl, Maya, Otomi, or any one of a dozen Indian tongues. The peasant is more closely tied to the outside world than the member of an indigenous society. Income derives largely from the world price of commodities and crafts. Taxes must be paid to the state, the state provides certain amenities such as education, health services, and defense against external aggression. Going to market often involves visiting the nearest large town or city in which what Robert Redfield (1955) called the "great tradition" of Western or modern society prevails over the "little tradition" of the peasant society (Redfield 1955). Peasants may be remnants of indigenous people who remain on their land and interact with the state, or they may be a class of people within a modern state. In any event, they are small agriculturalists who maintain a common tradition within the boundaries of a larger state society.

The Culture of Poverty

The third category has been given its name by Oscar Lewis (1961). He referred particularly to peasants who either left or were deprived of their land, and subsequently moved into the larger, urban area where they form the lowest class socially as well as economically. Their adaptive strategies in this new environment are quite different from their former patterns. Slum areas — whether in Mexico, Harlem, or South Africa — share enough common traits to constitute a separate culture. These people basically lack the technological and educational skills necessary to exploit the economy successfully. Thus, they are relegated to the worst housing, the poorest health care, food, and clothing. Often women and children must work because the income of the major wage earner is inadequate to care for all. Children may learn more readily how to manipulate the new environment, and thus they reverse the traditional patterns of esteem, since the older generation cannot adapt as readily to the new culture. Under such harsh conditions, frustration easily gives way to violence, alcoholism, and drugs. The structuring of welfare laws often makes desertion of families by fathers necessary. The culture of poverty is the strategy of staying alive under desperate conditions. Although the Ik of East Africa are not an urbanized people, and therefore technically not members of the culture of poverty, they have been included in this section because they, too, have been forced to give up their traditional form of subsistence — hunting and gathering. Due to the nationalization and politicalization of Africa, they have been forcibly and permanently settled on land which has suffered from a long drought. They, too, find it impossible to subsist, and have shown the characteristic effects of such deprivation. Violence, cruelty, and frustration pervades, but still there are a few who strive to remain human under inhuman conditions.

As has been stated earlier, not all anthropologists accept Lewis's concept of a culture of poverty. It is subject to misinterpretation and can be used against poor people everywhere to infer that their particular way of life constitutes a pathology. There is danger in the use of the term "culture" since this may indicate a tradition passed from generation to generation with little hope for amelioration even when economic conditions are altered.

The author has taken all these objections into consideration and, combined with her firm conviction that the "culture of poverty" can be eradicated with the addition of income, she uses this category to describe the populations who have had to adapt to conditions of want. They are subject to experiences which are quite outside the ken of middle-class people. The life experiences of women in such conditions should be brought to the attention of a wider public, so that they may broaden understanding of the condition and lead to some remedial action.

Modern Societies

The final category is that of modern society, including one on the women of Liu Ling in the People's Republic of Red China and four silhouettes of women in our own society, and the varieties of responses it provokes. In the United States, as in few other cultures, there are many alternative life styles possible for women. In earlier generations, few women explored these alternatives. It is worthwhile to compare life styles of those who took the traditional path with those who did not. It is also interesting to look at the young women who today are making the kinds of choices our society permits.

Why These Case Studies

Most people in modern American society have had little contact with societies radically different from our own, and where there has been such contact, it has often been on a superficial level. Anthropologists have found that exposure to such cultures is a vital element in gaining an understanding of, and an appreciation for, the varieties of the human condition. These case studies are the most expedient method of providing the reader with something similar to the field experience of the anthropologist. They are an introduction to the diversity of human experience. Each case study has been chosen for specific reasons.

Pitseolak, the Eskimo woman, was chosen because her life began in the traditional Eskimo society and continued into modern times. It was also selected because Pitseolak is an unusual and talented woman.

Bessie Longhair's story is also told because she experienced the traditional and the modern elements of society, but, in addition, it is an example of the strength and independence of Navajo women, and perhaps of many women brought up in a matrilineal society.

The silhouette about the women of the Ituri Forest provides a glimpse into the world of the foraging societies, a type of society few nonanthropologists have observed.

The Mundurucu women give us the comparison between traditional societies and modern ones. The effects of Westernization are evident here. Another unusual feature of this group is that Mundurucu women are considered the less conservative of the two sexes, and it is they who press for change.

Both the Puerto Rican village women and the Sarakatsani women of Greece are used to demonstrate the subjugation of women in many peasant societies. The Zapotec women traders provide a contrast to show that subjugation is not universal in peasant societies, and also to demonstrate the important role women play in such a society.

Carolina, the woman from the favela, was chosen to illustrate the degrading conditions of poverty and how an unusual woman was capable of rising above them.

The stories of Consuelo of Mexico City and Soledad of Puerto Rico and New York are more typical of women who live in the culture of poverty. Their stories were told to underline both similarities and differences between them. Consuelo and Soledad both use their bodies as a means of survival, but Consuelo is plagued by guilt and recrimination and Soledad is more outspoken about her position and seems much more guilt-free.

In the category of modern women, an attempt was made to present as diverse a picture as possible within the bounds of available material. Chinese women are an example of people with whom we have had little contact during a time of rapid cultural change. They represent a society which some admire, others deplore, but of which we know relatively little.

The women of Fun City were chosen to portray life in one of the newer types of communities developed in the United States, the retirement village. Also, these women are examples of middle-class, older women who lived prior to the articulation of changes in the goals of women.

The studies of Linda and Carol are examples of the various possibilities open to young women today.

Annie Robinson was chosen to represent a woman on the threshold of upward mobility in our society. She also represents a black woman striving toward the life style some white women are rejecting.

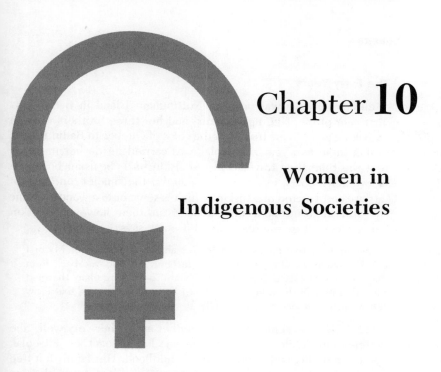

Chapter 10

Women in Indigenous Societies

1. PITSEOLAK, THE ESKIMO ARTIST

The Eskimo World

On the southern coast of Baffin Island, high in the arctic area of the New World, lies the town of Cape Dorset. Until as recently as 1950, Eskimos living on Baffin Island still spent their winters in igloos and their summers in skin tents. Through the long winter, people were widely dispersed in small groups, consisting of one or two nuclear families; they fished and hunted sea mammals. During the short, Arctic summer, they gathered in larger groups near the shores of the sea.

Today Cape Dorset is a town with a permanent population who live in clapboard bungalows, buy food at the local traders, and have their own church. Many of the residents of Cape Dorset earn some part of their subsistence by painting, drawing, and carving works of folk art which have a considerable market in Canada and the United States. One of the artists who works with colored crayons and paint is Pitseolak (Eber 1971). She is about 73 years old and has lived both the traditional and modern life.

My name is Pitseolak, the Eskimo word for sea pigeon. When I see the pitseolaks over the sea, I say, "There go those lovely birds — that's me, flying." I have lost the time when I was born, but I am old now — my sons say maybe I am 70. When Ashoona, my husband died, my sons were not even married. Now they are married and having their children.

The Early Years

Pitseolak tells us that she was born on Nottingham Island in Baffin Bay. During her first year of life, she, her parents, and her three brothers were in the process of making an arduous trek from the coast of Quebec to Baffin Island. This journey took them two years. Pitseolak was carried inside her mother's parka. Much of the time they traveled in a sealskin boat. Sealskin boats are called *umiaks*, women's boats, as opposed to *kayaks*, the smaller, one-person boat. The boats are constructed of sealskin, which is sewn onto a wooden frame by women who work in groups on a single boat. Even, then, however, sealskin boats were being replaced by wooden ones. Pitseolak says:

> But even in my childhood these sealskin boats were already disappearing. My first memory of life is when we stopped in Lake Harbour, on our way back from Frobisher Bay to Cape Dorset to buy a wooden boat. There were many there. It was while my father bought the wooden boat that I first saw houses and that I saw the first white man. I was scared. (Eber 1971)

Pitseolak relates that she remembers her mother and father very well. She claims she was one of five children who were always happy together. Pitseolak recalls the apparent mobility and freedom of her childhood. Her family felt free to wander from camp to camp, joining with larger groups when it was pleasant to do so, and leaving when this was desirable. Her father hunted with bow and arrow. She remembers bad winters when there was hunger, but has no recollection of starvation. Pitseolak tells us that women in those days tatooed their faces as a form of decoration. They used a needle and caribou thread soaked in oil and soot from the oil lamps to make the marks. The thread was pulled through the skin, causing swelling and pain, and eventually healed to form the scar, which is the tattoo. When asked about shamans, Pitseolak becomes a bit defensive. She tells us that her father used to tell stories about how he was once almost killed by a powerful shaman (Eber 1971):

> My father was a very good hunter and that is why the shaman tried to kill him — he was jealous. I don't know very much about shamans — I don't like to think about them — but my family and my mother's family all believed in shamans because we had heard so many stories. They were Eskimos just like other people, but they had these strange powers. They had power over the hunt. They could bring the animals, and they had the power to kill.

Later on she says:

> I don't know much about shamans because I don't like to think about them.

Pitseolak is also ambivalent about the relationship among people. On the one hand she says:

> It was always most joyful when people come together in Cape Dorset. Every year we would make three trips to Cape Dorset with the dog team. In those days, a lot

of people and families would spend a long summer in Cape Dorset and then, before the weather got cold, they would look for new camps inland. We used to be happy together. There would be dances at the bay (Hudson's Bay) residence and at the warehouse (the trading company's warehouse).

Earlier she states:

When a shaman was jealous or hated another Eskimo, he would try to kill him, and sometimes, I think, if an Eskimo had an enemy, he would go to a shaman friend and ask him to kill this man who hated him.

As far as Pitseolak's life as a child growing up to be a woman:

When we were children, we played lots of make-believe. We used to play igloo, we used to play dog-team. We played a game in which other children would run after you; if they catch you, they would pretend to eat your eyes.

She relates a typical Eskimo legend that was told to her by her father. It involves a poor, blind man who invokes his spirit guardian, the loon. The loon takes the man on his back and dives under the water three times, finally restoring the man's vision. In gratitude, the man gives the loon his dearest possession, a necklace which the bird wears in the form of white feathers scattered on his neck and breast. Pitseolak's childhood thus recalled, she goes on:

There were no teenagers in those days. The young people got married so early they didn't have time to make any trouble.

Marriage and Childbirth

When Pitseolak's father died, her husband's father came to get her on a dog sled. She and her husband, Ashoona, had been childhood friends, and he had told Pitseolak's brothers that he would marry her. They were married that summer in Cape Dorset by an Anglican clergyman. Many people had gathered in Cape Dorset to see the arrival of the ship bringing supplies to the Hudson's Bay trading post. Ashoona, however, was an inland hunter, and so they soon left Cape Dorset for other areas. Pitseolak tells us that because Ashoona was such a good hunter:

He brought me beautiful skins — all kinds of seal and caribou. Many women used to be jealous of me because I had such lovely clothes.

Before the birth of her first child, Pitseolak and Ashoona were camping with Ashoona's two brothers and their families. They stayed in this camp for about a year. About the birth of her first child, Pitseolak says:

When Namoonie, my first son, was born, three women held me. It was like that in the old times — there were always women who helped. Afterwards they would make magic wishes for the child — that a boy should be a good hunter; that a girl should have long hair, and that the child should do well at whatever he was doing.

She reports that she had 17 children, one each year, but many of them died in infancy. In accordance with the Eskimo tradition, two of her sons were adopted by other Eskimos. If one family has few or no children, they will "adopt," (feed and care for) children from a family with many children. In return, the children are expected to help with the household chores. Only five of Pitseolak's 17 children are still living. Pitseolak says:

> Among those who are living, I have only one daughter, Nawpachee. Except for Kaka who lives in camp in the old way, they all live here in Cape Dorset, and now I live with Kumwartok and his wife.

The effects of Westernization were felt early in Pitseolak's married life:

> On Akudluk Island, where Namoonie was born, there was good hunting. There were no caribou but there were polar bear, walrus, and seal. But I did not care for Akudluk — my relatives were all around Cape Dorset and it was too hard to get the white men's food from the bay. We hade no tea, only meat, After a year we went back to Cape Dorset for a short time, and then to Ikirasaq.

We are told that many people settled in the camp at Ikirasaq. The precise number is unknown because:

> In those days we didn't bother counting people. Here, however, Ashoona became restive because he was primarily a hunter and he didn't like to live with other people.

Pitseolak says that her family moved as often as 10 times a year. They moved both in summer and winter. Pitseolak disliked the summer because of the big mosquitoes, In the Arctic, the summer is too short to allow the ice to melt down to the earth level. As a consequence, stagnant pools of water are formed above the permafrost, and mosquitoes have a fertile breeding ground.

Women's Work

Pitseolak's housing varied — sometimes igloos, sometimes *kaamuks* (tent-huts), and sometimes the summer tents. She claims to know little about the building of an igloo because that was "men's work." Women made the large, summer tents that accommodated two families by scraping the skins and covering them with moss to prevent them from drying out, and sewing them together. Speaking of the activities of her early years, Pitseolak says:

> In the old days I was never done with the sewing. There were the tents and the kayaks and there were all the clothes which were made from the different skins — seal, caribou and walrus. From skins we also made cups for drinking and buckets for carrying water. And when we caught geese we used to make brooms for cleaning from the wings which we bound together. If we had enough brooms, we would throw the wings away.
>
> As soon as I was finished sewing one thing, I was always sewing another.

Sometimes when I was very busy with the sewing, my husband would help me. He used to help me with parkas.

She describes the method used to prepare skins for sewing and how clothing was worn:

Before we started living in one place as we do now, we used to walk very long distances and the boots would wear out quickly. I was never finished with making *mukluks*. I also would make new soles and sew them on the worn boots. For boots we used only sealskin and once the skin was cleaned, we would chew it so that the mukluks would be soft. It was hard to do, but it worked well.

Pitseolak says that she is now too old and her eyesight too poor to do much sewing:

But every year I still make sealskin pants for Kaka (her son). Like his father, Kaka does not want to live with other people and he stays in camp. Like his father, Kaka is a very good hunter and every year he gets the most beautiful skins from a special seal — the *Kasigiak*. The skins are lovely and dark and he brings them to me and I must make these pants.

She discusses the hard work and danger of the hunting life, and the interdependence of men and dogs for the dog team. Ashoona, her husband, was so skillful as a hunter that his dogs always had meat, even in winter. She thinks there are fewer animals available now because the ski-mobiles, which she calls "skidoos," make noise and frighten them away.

Speaking of food, Pitseolak says:

I can't remember the first time I tasted the white man's food, but I do remember one incident. At the time they were building the Hudson's Bay post's big warehouse and I was just a little girl. I remember watching people unload the supply boat and I was crying very hard. They gave me a pilot biscuit and I really liked it.

I like the white man's food, but I think the old food was better for Eskimos. In the old days we had more food from animals and we didn't get sick so much. We ate the food raw. We used to eat seal, whale, caribou, ducks and ptarmigan all raw, though we used to cook the goose, and cooked goose is very good. We also used to cook the polar bear, though some people ate it raw.

We had fruit in the summer. We used to pick the berries on the tundra, and something else we ate was dulse."

Speaking of life in camp:

Sometimes in the winter it was boring in the igloo but we never stayed inside much. We had warmer clothes in those days and it used to be fun when it was windy. . . . Very often in those days when we felt happy in camp, Ashoona and I would play the accordion. My favorite brother once gave me an accordion and we both could play. The little children would come and dance. Kaka used to dance lot. Ashoona used to like to juggle. He could keep three small stones in the air and sometimes, just for two seconds, I could keep three stones up there too.

Pitseolak speaks of other games played in camp, and of traveling through the light nights to Dorset to sell skins. Her family always made a trip to see the supply ship bring provisions to the trading post.

Ashoona died during the epidemic in Cape Dorset. Pitseolak says there was no doctor available, so they never knew exactly what the sickness was, but many people died at that time.

Widowhood

After the death of Ashoona, Pitseolak and her family were very poor. The sons tried to hunt but were evidently too young to be successful. Pitseolak was poor "until Sowmik and the government houses come." Sowmik is the Eskimo name for Jim Houston, a government agent working with the Eskimo. Houston started a cooperative in Cape Dorset which supplies Eskimos with raw materials so that they can paint pictures, or do stone or ivory sculpture, or make clothing which can then be sold in the States. The Eskimos are paid for their work.

Pitseolak comments:

> I bought some paper myself and I think I made four small drawings. I think I drew little monsters. I meant the drawings to be animals, but they turned out to be funny-looking because I had never done drawings before. I took these drawings to Jim's office. I was scared to go there at first, but he gave me the money — I think it was $20.

Since that time, Pitseolak has been living in government housing in Cape Dorset and supporting herself by drawing. Dorothy Eber was impressed by Pitseolak's artistic ability and, after she had known her for some time, she asked Pitseolak to tell her story on tapes, which were then translated into English by a young, bilingual Eskimo woman.

Overview

Pitseolak's life is, in many ways, more similar to that of women in Western civilization than any other women's stories. She came from a nuclear family — father, mother, and children, and only lived for part of the time within larger groups. Perhaps time has softened her recollections, but she does not seem to have found cause for great distress as a woman. Woman's work and man's work were quite clearly differentiated. She performed her duties and took pride in doing them well. When her tasks overwhelmed her, her husband helped her. Pitseolak remarks that when the men left the camp for long periods of time, they left a shotgun with the women. However, Pitseolak admits that although she tried she was never able to use it well. This remark is made in a matter-of-fact tone, as though a woman could not be expected to shoot well. She and her husband seem to have had a complementary relationship, where neither one overwhelmed the other. Nevertheless, when it was necessary to choose a place of residence, Pitseolak had to give up the companionship of the village and move to various camp sites where her husband was able to hunt. She does not seem to find this degrading or very unpleasant. She takes pride in her family and recalls the happy times they shared. In her old age, she still takes great pride in her handiwork and in her ability to earn money for herself. She explains:

> To make prints is not easy. You must think first and this is hard to do. But I am happy doing the prints. After my husband died, I felt very alone and unwanted; making prints is what made me the happiest since he died. I am going to keep on doing them until they tell me to stop. If no one tells me to stop, I shall make them as long as I am well. If I can, I'll make them even after I am dead.

This appears to be the kind of statement that would be made by a competent, secure, and independent woman, the kind of statement any professional woman in our society might make. There is neither self-pity nor immodest pride, but there is a sense of reality here, which could only be gained through the process of living a useful and productive life and finding emotional support from parents and husband. This is, of course, much easier to do in a society in which traditional values are maintained. Whatever may be the Western view of the Eskimo woman trudging behind her husband over the ice while carrying her baby, or sitting in an igloo chewing hides for mukluks, the Eskimo woman seems to have derived security and satisfaction from these activities.

The harsh, rigorous environment of the Arctic has room for neither the incompetent nor the malcontent. Work is divided between men and women, old and young. Each must be able to pull his or her own weight, although the human principle of cooperation in need does prevail. Pitseolak bore her children with the aid of other women. When her sewing reached proportions she was incapable of handling, her husband came to the rescue. In normal circumstances, Pitseolak was concerned with providing those services which her culture assigns to women.

Pitseolak's story is that of an individual, and a unique one. She has become a successful artist, something which is not true of every Eskimo woman. Anthropologists such as Norman Chance (1966) and Ernestine Friedl (1975) give a very different picture of the life of an Eskimo woman. Chance (1966:96) describes the results of a special study of identity change and personality adjustment among Eskimo as follows:

> Briefly, the results showed, however, that the Kaktovik women tended to have many more symptoms of emotional difficulty than the men, which probably reflected the greater stress placed on most of the women as a result of their loss of many traditional roles without adequate replacement, and the problems associated with their slower rate of acculturation as contrasted with that of the men.

He also states that the most common symptoms of Kaktovik women were those relating to feelings of inadequacy and tension. Perhaps Pitseolak is a rare woman, whose talent has made her inner security possible.

2. BESSIE YELLOWHAIR, NAVAJO WOMAN

The Navajo World

The Navajo of the American southwest are among the most numerous, and the wealthiest, indigenous Americans. They number about 130,000 people, and their average per capita income is about 1,000 dollars a year (Halsell 1973:29). The Navajo are part of the Athabaskan speakers who came into the New World from Asia. Although many Athabaskan speakers now live in northwestern Canada, the Navajo migrated into the southwestern area of the United States in about 1500 A.D., where they came into contact with Hopi, Pima, and Papago Indians, among others. The Navajo quickly acquired the horse, which was made available through European contact, but their most important acquisition was sheep. From 1846 to 1860, the Navajo indulged in sheepherding.

The United States government fought its "Indian Wars" to bring "peace and stability" to the Indian lands. Kit Carson implemented the scorched earth policy on Navajo land to force the people into an area of 40 square miles near Fort Sumner, New Mexico. Nearly 2,000 Indians died, and finally, in 1868, the Navajo were permitted to return to their land, which was declared a reservation.

The Navajo are particularly interesting to anthropologists because they are matrilineal although animal-herding people usually trace their descent patrilineally. This is not the equivalent of matriarchy; men continue to hold authority, but uncles, specifically the mother's brothers, have jurisdiction over the children. Many anthropologists think that the Navajo borrowed their descent system from the Hopi.

Spanning Two Worlds

The biography of Bessie Yellowhair is unusual because it is told by Grace Halsell, who not only lived with Bessie and other members of her family, but succeeded so well in empathizing with the Navajo that she found the return to her own world painful.

Bessie works as a clerk in a hospital run by Project Hope. She is relatively well-off in that she owns and drives a pickup truck, and lives in a house with her sister and brother-in-law. But she makes the trip back to her family *hogan*, the traditional house, at least once a week. She has been brought up in the traditional way and bridges a very real gap between her parents and the modern world.

Grace Halsell (1973) describes the world of the Navajo as a silent one in which all the noises necessary to modern life simply do not exist. The land is arid, and only fit for grazing sheep. The vista is overshadowed by the great mountains of the American southwest. The Navajo seeks to fit into nature rather than bend nature to human needs. The traditional dwelling is a *hogan*, a semisubterranean earth hut, with earthen floors. The furnishings are simple — primarily sheepskin used to sleep on and moved to the side of the hogan during the day. Food is cooked over the fire or on a wood stove. The traditional diet consists of simple meals of mutton, Navajo fry-bread, and quantities of coffee. The general lack of electricity means there are no telephones or television. Many modern customs have not yet become part of the Navajo traditions. For example, the Navajo still do not greet or welcome strangers who enter the hogan. This traditional custom of ignoring the newcomer used to extend even to children. A visitor is never stared at or questioned; that would be rude. The visitor is made welcome by the fact that the family goes about its business, and prepares food and a place to sleep for all. Halsell (1973:67) says:

> Only people with furniture that has to be dusted and beds that must be made, with things, worry about being accepted. People who sleep on dirt floors will move over a couple of feet and there is room for you.

The first government school for Navajo, a boarding school, was built in 1883 at Fort Defiance. White ethnocentrism was so entrenched at that time that day schools were considered useless because the child would spend only six hours a day in school and the rest of the time would be spent with his "barbarian" parents. Children were forbidden to speak Navajo at school and were often severely punished for any attempt to display their heritage. Long hair had to be cut short, European style clothing had to be worn. Stories about children being severely beaten, handcuffed, and maltreated abound. When these poor, tormented children returned to their families at the end of the school year, their parents preserved silence until the child felt secure enough to speak. According to one informant, sometimes this silence, which was a gift of peace, was maintained for weeks, until equilibrium could be restored. It bore no resemblance to the European silence meaning ostracism or "shunning." Today there are schools on the reservations, and children are transported to them every day by school buses. Some Navajo feel that this arrangement is even more painful because every day means a fresh break with the traditional home and new exposure to modern society with its strange ways and noisy contexts.

Traditional Marriage and Childbirth

Bessie Longhair's mother's marriage was arranged by her uncle. The husband's family gave eight horses, some jewelry, and some money as bridewealth. Bessie relates her earliest memories:

> All of us were born in the *hogan*. There was another baby between Mary and me, but at the time I didn't know mother was pregnant; she kept moving around. One night she had a miscarriage. In the morning when I got up, I found some blood. . . . my father was away. My mother had to do it all by herself.

Bessie remembers her sister Mary's birth. She was sent to fetch her grandmother. Both grandparents came, along with many other people. Grandfather brought the "ritual priest" in. People dug a small hole and tied a rope from a stake to the ceiling. Bessie remembers her mother holding the rope, sitting over the hole and thus delivering the baby. The actual delivery was assisted by many people. The new baby was wrapped in sheepskin. Bessie's mother continued about her household tasks later in the day. Bessie recalls that at the birth of one of her brothers, neither father nor grandparents were available, and her mother took care of the delivery herself.

Menarche

Bessie recalls her first menstrual period as a time of joy. Her mother provided a sing-ceremonial for her. In such a ceremonial, a specialist is called in who makes a painting on the floor with corn pollen and colored sand. This specialist then chants a particular song — in this case the "Blessing Way" — which is a prayer for the health, fertility, and well-being of the person involved. The ceremony is attended by many relatives and friends. In the old days, soon after this event, the girl's uncle made arrangements for her marriage.

Work

The Yellowhair family earn their basic livelihood as sheep herders. Grace Halsell (1973) reports:

> I have seen Bake Yellowhair come riding in at sundown, herding the sheep into the corral, and his wife, Harriet, in her long calico skirt, sitting down in the dirt of the corral like some mother hen with her chickens. Linda and her brother Bert join their mother. I watch them silently greet all of those who are present, for a Navajo knows each sheep just as an Anglo knows people.

The land on which the sheep graze is tribally owned, but each family has the use of a specific parcel of land assigned to it. This makes overgrazing a problem. The Navajo particularly resented a livestock reduction program carried out by the United States government in the 1930s, in which sheep were shot and left to rot. This condition appalled the Navajo because sheep represent not only wealth, but also a personal, emotional attachment. However, the program was successful in cutting the Navajo herds down to half the earlier number. From the Navajo point of view, this represented a 50 percent reduction in their aggregate wealth. The Navajo do not find more fluid forms of wealth, such as cash, as convenient.

Although there are banking facilities in the large town, it is difficult for most Navajos to get to town on a regular basis. Riding a horse takes a very long time and few have cars. The roads are poor and often fail to connect strategic points on the reservation. Consequently, Navajo women keep their wealth in the typical silver and turquoise jewelry, which they can pawn or sell to the local trader in time of need.

Clothing and Jewelry

Bessie tells us that the bright blue turquoise is considered "male," whereas the softer green-tinged turquoise is "female." The typical Navajo woman's costume is not really traditional in the ethnographic sense of the word. Rather, it consists of jackets of velvet or cotton and long, cotton calico skirts. These styles were prevalent among the wives of army men at Fort Sumner and were adopted in the 1860s as proper attire for women.

Bessie's Youth

Halsell never tells us how old Bessie is, but we do learn that she went to boarding school, where she learned basic skills. Yet her first job did not require her to use those skills. Bessie states that it is customary for California house-wives to advertise in the "Navajo Times" for domestic help. Such jobs demand that the girl stay for a year. Her bus fare is paid for and as compensation she gets room and board, and 25 dollars a week. Bessie recalls hitching rides from her hogan to Holbrook, getting lost at the bus terminal in Los Angeles, and losing her meager possessions there. She remembers being frightened by the noise and the crowds in Los Angeles and, finally, by the terrifying sense of solitude among people who made no effort to know her as a person but only viewed her impersonally, as the Indian maid. She worked hard, and claims to have been hungry much of the time. One aspect of her stay which greatly impressed her, was the lavish use of water and electricity. Bessie, who lived in an area where water had to be laboriously carried from a distance, was accustomed to bathing with a cupful of water. In her job, washing machines were used daily to clean the children's clothing. Her deepest impression was that her employers seemed to regard their possessions in higher esteem than their children.

When we go into the master bedroom with its king-sized bed, Mrs. Morton emphasizes a rule: "The kids are never allowed in our room." Her words sadden and confuse me. In the Navajo family, one puts others — not himself — first, that the parents love one another by working and providing and sacrificing for their children, and since they love their children, the young are always close to their parents.

During the year, Bessie never received any wages, and she finally returned. In typical Navajo manner, her welcome was silent. Bessie says:

I wasn't worried about getting it (the money) into my hands, but I was worried about maybe she wasn't getting it to my mother. And I'm not sure whether she ever did send the money, because my mother never said anything about getting the money. Up to this day, my mother and I have never discussed the money that I earned; the only important thing was that I got back.

Bessie and Tradition

Despite or perhaps because of her boarding school experience and her travels in the Anglo world, Bessie is ambivalent toward traditional Navajo Sings. The gods who are prayed to include several female deities. Changing Woman is the primary myth figure. It is she who taught the people to grow corn. Salt Woman brought the gift of salt, and Spider Woman taught the technique of weaving. The Navajo find it rather silly that the "Anglos" worship only a Father and Son. She does believe in witches, and finds the male Gods of Christianity too alien. Although she drives a distance to attend a Sing and joins others in the frame house where a feast is laid out, she sits outside the hogan when the actual ceremony takes place. Here, her attitudes toward men, life, children, and the future, unfold.

Bessie is having an affair with Calvin, another Navajo. She has no guilt feelings about sex outside marriage. She states that Navajos do not forbid sex, but have rigorous incest laws; Bessie cannot even touch a man of her mother's or father's clan. These people are considered brothers.

When asked whether she uses contraceptives, Bessie replies: "No, I don't believe in that. I want to be natural." She goes on to say that Calvin wants to marry her, but she does not feel ready for marriage yet. She is hoping to get a scholarship so that she can go back and get more education. She admits to being a strong person.

> Navajo women *are* strong. In your society, you take your father's name, but we always take the name of our mother's clan. If you get pregnant and are not married, you worry about your child not having a name — you might worry so much you kill the child, but if I am pregnant, my child will have my clan name whether I am married or not.
>
> And then Navajo women have always been owners of property. I got my first sheep when I was five years old. I have always had my bit of grazing land.

Bessie tells us that traditionally, after marriage, the man goes to live with his wife's family:

> If the couple don't get along, then it is the man who must leave, and the woman keeps everything: the house, the sheep, the blankets. Also, a Navajo woman can always earn money by weaving a rug. The woman, not the man, always has this handy source of income.

Halsell says:

Bessie seems to have "found" herself already: to have taken a hold of her identity. Navajo women like Bessie are adaptable. Though she believes in witches and never goes to beauty parlors or wears make-up, she is tuned in to Anglo styles and thought patterns. A woman can conform without loss of identity, but a man must constantly prove his masculinity or be branded a "failure."

Navajo Women's Independence

Aunt Zonie is an example of an independent Navajo woman. Halsell spends some time with her. She is an elderly widow who lives alone. Once, when they arrived at Aunt Zonie's hogan, they found that someone, probably one of her nieces, had visited while they were gone. Two mattresses were left, which completely filled the small, round hogan. Typically, Halsell offered to drive to the nearest neighbor to get help in moving the mattresses out. Aunt Zonie, however, resisted, and after putting away their groceries, and getting water (which involved a twenty-mile drive to the windmill to fill a water barrel), Aunt Zonie, with Halsell's help, wrestled the two mattresses onto a wheelbarrow and moved them into the barn. The independence of this act is characteristic of Aunt Zonie and other Navajo women. Aunt Zonie's mother died when she was very young. She was sent to boarding school at Fort Defiance and the Indian School in Albuquerque. At twenty, her uncle arranged her marriage, although she would have preferred not to marry. She describes the ceremony and the ensuing marriage as follows:

> My uncle killed two sheep, and many relatives came, and my husband's mother came from Ganado: she was dressed in a beautiful long, velvet dress, with much silver and turquoise jewelry loaned to her by her relatives. We went into my uncle's hogan and he talked to us about who each of us was, about our past and our families, and how we must be true, be good to one another. He fed us the holy corn mush from his fingers, placing it on our tongues.
>
> My uncle had prepared a special hogan for us, and we stayed there two days. I had no problems. I knew how to cook; I had my own grinding stone for corn.

Aunt Zonie spoke of how her husband taught her how to rope cattle and sheep. They both searched the woods near a lake for herbs, piñon nuts, and plants to be used for special purposes. Aunt Zonie states that Indians never pick flowers for the sheer beauty of them because they are sacred to those who know how to use them. In speaking of her foraging expeditions with her late husband, she says he killed game, deer, and rabbits, and they gathered only as much wild greens and piñon nuts as they needed.

Town Life

As much as she loved the simple, outdoor life she shared with her husband, Aunt Zonie also seems to relish trips to the trading post at Fort Defiance. These trips were usually infrequent, until Halsell came to visit, with her car. She visits the trader who acts as an informal post office for messages left for people in his area. The trip to town is also an occasion for Aunt Zonie to indulge her taste for Anglo food — hamburgers, apple pie, and malted milk. Now that her husband is dead, she feels no need to remarry. She will pay someone to tote her wood and water. Steeped in the past, deeply-rooted in Navajo tradition, she can securely enjoy the modern world and the unusual things it has to offer.

Navajo Women's Perspective

The traditional way of Navajo life has given them internal strengths which our own culture may well emulate. The quiet of the hogan is made possible by the fact that the Navajo values silence. Since their space is so limited, with so many people in the small confines of a hogan, they can ill afford the constant babble and noise of the traditional Anglo home. They have learned to move about carefully and purposefully, without ever stepping over a reclining body. Since they cannot have the kind of privacy enjoyed by those who live in houses with many rooms, they give each other privacy by being careful never to stare or look others directly in the eye.

Perhaps most importantly, since each hogan is relatively isolated and roads and transportation are poor, the people have learned to truly relish opportunities to be together. They will travel many miles to see and speak with friends and relatives. Yet, they know that most of their time will be spent within the small circle of the nuclear family. They have learned to preserve these relationships through reservation of speech and gesture. They practice economy of words.

The Navajo woman has always been "liberated." She has had to be. She cannot be deprived of her land and resources by any man. Yet, she must also have the strength to cope with solitude and isolation from conveniences of all sorts. She must be able to deal with emergencies alone. Although she values the kindness and companionship of a good husband, she is also well aware of the fact that she can live independently.

3. WOMEN OF THE ITURI FOREST

The Ituri Forest

The Ituri Forest is located in the Congo region of sub-Saharan Africa. It is a vast expanse of rain forest, constantly humid and set in semidarkness. Little direct sunlight penetrates the deep growth of trees, and violent rainstorms assault the area. There is no silence, only the constant sounds of animals and birds who make their home in the area.

The Mbuti

The Mbuti, a pygmy people, whose height rarely exceeds four and a half feet, make their home in the forest also. They have inhabited the forest for thousands of years. Their existence was acknowledged by Egyptians of the Fourth Dynasty, and by Homer and Aristotle, as well. In Pompeii there are mosaics showing pygmies and the huts they built in the forest.

The Mbuti have been visited by anthropologists such as Patrick Putnam; Father Schebesta; and Colin Turnbull. This silhouette is based upon the work of Colin Turnbull, who loves the Mbuti and feels at home with them. Fortunately, among the Mbuti, the lives of women and men are not hidden behind walls of privacy. They live in small bands which move in and out of the forest from time to time. Their possessions are few, their moves quite frequent, and their quarrels and reconciliations are matters of common knowledge to those who share their camp. Their "private lives" are public to their camping companions, and their ceremonials are not kept secret from those whom they accept as part of their group.

The Mbuti and the Bantu

The Ituri Forest edges had been cleared and settled by the Bantu when Father Schebesta visited the area in the 1920s. In examining the work of Schebesta (1938–1950), the anthropologist is faced with the difficulty implicit in documenting the emic views of a people. According to the Bantus, the Mbuti were a servant, or quasi-slave, class. They were debased people with no culture of their own. Hired as servants on the Bantu plantations, the Mbuti were unreliable and often went off into the forest when they were most needed on the farms. The Bantu made every effort to integrate the Mbuti into their own society, in a special class, of course. They even held ritual puberty ceremonies for the Mbuti boys, in the hopes that they would be converted into more reliable workers and more dutiful servants.

Turnbull found that the Mbuti had a very different idea about their relationship to the Bantu. The Mbuti regarded themselves as people of the forest which they considered their home. Here they hunted and collected honey, and above all, indulged in the *Molimo* ceremony in praise of the god of the forest who protected them. Occasionally they felt the need for tobacco or iron for their hunting equipment. Then, they visited their friends, the Bantu, bearing gifts of meat and honey. As guests of the Bantu, they did their best to conform to their hosts' desires, doing such farm and domestic tasks as were set out for them. In this way they were assured gifts of tobacco, corn, and metal. After a time, however, even such pleasant visits became onerous; the forest called, the Bantu villages became too noisy, and the ceremonials became too demanding. So, the Mbuti returned to the forest from whence they came, to visit again another time when the mood was upon them.

This discrepancy between Father Schebesta and Colin Turnbull's report is not due to a difference in quality between the two anthropologists, but rather to the fact that Father Schebesta lived with the Bantu, while Colin Turnbull lived with the Mbuti.

Life in the Forest

As hunters and gatherers, the Mbuti live in camps in the forest. Each nuclear family in the band has a hut of its own, which is built by the women of the family. It consists of a wicker frame over which layers upon layers of broad leaves are placed, which make the shelter impervious to rain. They participate in communal hunting forays using nets and spears. Women and children take part in the hunt, and act as beaters to drive the game toward the nets. This is one of the few substantiated accounts of women taking part in hunting. Gathering is done on an individual basis or in small groups.

Religious ceremonials are important, but simple. The prime belief is in a single god of the forest who protects and cares for his special people, the Mbuti. When Turnbull came to visit the Mbuti in 1954, they were encamped in a Bantu village. They attracted his attention by their behavior at a Bantu-held initiation ritual for Mbuti boys. He gathered with the other men around the campfire in the evening to hear the singing, especially the voice of the *Molimo*.

Culture Change

Two years later when Turnbull returned, he found many changes. The former medical aid station set up by Patrick Putnam had become a little town to which the Mbuti often came to buy food, tobacco, and palm wine with the money they earned from working either at the local motel or at the animal station. Moreover, the colonial government has been encouraging Mbuti to clear and settle down on plantations like their neighbors, the Bantu. The group with whom Turnbull had shared an initiation ceremonial three years before was now largely settled in plantations around Camp Putnam. This band consisted of people related through blood or marital ties. The particular band with whom Turnbull associated was composed of two large families.

Death in the Village

The band was hit by two misfortunes, the death of a child and the death of a much loved, old woman. Little ceremony or grief was shown over the child's death; she was buried in the style of the local Bantu. The Mbuti themselves largely paid only token respect. The women of the group departed from the funeral even before the body was interred. However, the death of Balekimito, mother of Ekianga, one of the leaders of the group, seemed to evoke much sorrow. The already middle-aged and powerful sons and daughters the old lady had left behind began to cry and show their grief in ways that were not so much directed by tradition, but rather dictated by their strong emotions. Turnbull (1961:49) states:

> For the moment it seemed that the pygmies faced with the death of an old and well-loved and respected person such as this old lady, had nothing to cling to, and I was genuinely afraid that some of them would come to harm.

Back to the Forest

These deaths precipitated the movement of the Mbuti from their plantation homes back to the forest, their true home. Immediately after the funeral, the people were on the move. The funeral itself was held by Bantus who sought the source of the evil magic in witchcraft. The Mbuti took no part in this; they went about their business gathering their possessions for the return to the forest. Turnbull (1961:53) states:

> In the forest, people cannot carry loads on their heads as they do in open country because of overhanging branches and frequent obstacles that have to be climbed over or crawled under.

Women carry loads on their backs with a tump-line across their foreheads. Men let the tump-line lie across their chests. In families where polygamy is practiced, co-wives help each other in balancing these loads on their backs. In traveling back to the forest, men and women go in separate groups. The women leave earlier because they will take longer, since they carry the bundles and will stop to gather mushrooms and other edibles on the way. Just before they entered the forest, they stopped to wash in a nearby stream, seemingly to rid themselves of the pollution of village life and to purify themselves for acceptance into their forest home.

Division of Labor

The men arrived at the camp first. They had already killed an antelope and selected the camp site when the women came along, carrying babies and loads. The women immediately set to work cutting branches and leaves to build their new homes. Some of the men helped by running to an area about one-half hour away from the camp site to collect the leaves the women would need for construction. People built their houses close to friends, co-wives, or relatives. In some cases, men helped in the construction process itself, but usually the work was swiftly and completely done by the women. The thatching is often imperfect, and when it rains, water may trickle in through a gap in the leaves, but it is the women's responsibility to fix such leaks. The simple furniture, chairs, tables, and beds are made of sticks, which are adequate but not very comfortable. The direction in which the door of the house faces, and the positions of the house are changed often to conform to new friendships or animosities.

The Molimo Ceremony

The first night, a *molimo* ceremony was held. First, the men took a log or an ember from every house in the camp to build the central campfire. Later, one of the men went from house to house, placing a snare before each door. The women in the hut put an offering of food, usually mushrooms or bananas, into the snare. The man would then empty the snare into the basket. This was food for the molimo. Before the ceremony itself, the men closed the paths leading into and out of the village. Then they gathered around the fire. Women were excluded and had to remain within their huts. The men joined together around the fire to sing the molimo songs. They were not allowed to sleep that night, but must sing and eat continually. During the singing, the men's voices were echoed in a hollow trumpeting, which came from the forest itself. This is the voice of the molimo. As the night passed, the molimo, never visible, circled the camp, trumpeting its sounds ever closer to the fire. Occasionally the molimo made animal sounds at which the men looked toward the huts where the women and children stayed. As soon as it was ascertained that women and children were not in view, two young men carrying the molimo on their shoulders, danced into the clearing where the men continued to sing around the fire. One man balanced the end of the molimo on his shoulder. Another held the other end and blew into it, making the trumpeting sounds. The molimo, after all, was a discarded length of metal drainpipe. The men said they preferred this new molimo to the older, carved wooden ones because it lasted longer. The physical entity of the molimo was less important than its symbolic significance as the voice of the forest. The molimo is dipped in water before it is carried into camp; it must drink. After its ritual appearance in camp, the molimo is carried back to its hiding place in the forest. This is the awesome ritual, which the women may not see.

The molimo ceremony can go on for several days. The men become increasingly sleepy in the morning. At daybreak, women get up, and go down to the river to bathe and collect water. On their return to camp, they prepare the family meal. Sitting outside their huts, they put plantains in the ashes on the fire to roast, or stewed mushrooms with whatever meat is left. Little girls take care of younger children, bring twigs to stoke the fire and watch the pots to be sure they do not spill. As the little girls do such chores, the younger women take time to apply a body paint which consists of black paste. Friends help each other to adorn inaccessible parts of their bodies. When a communal hunt is planned, women prepare for it by making sure their baskets and tump-lines are in good condition to carry home the meat. Often a communal dance precedes the hunt. Both men and women participate in such a dance. The procedure for the communal hunt is that each man takes his own net and spreads it on an area which is customarily his. Women and children leave camp earlier, carrying baskets in which they will transport the meat and also mushrooms and greens that they have foraged along the way. A hunting fire is built outside the camp as an offering of their most precious gift, fire, to the forest.

Sharing the Hunt

Women usually take part in the division of the meat brought home by the hunters. The distribution is usually in terms of relationship — so much to the wife's family, so much to the sister, brother, and so on. Often the women use the opportunity to remind the hunter of services and kindnesses they have performed for his family, hoping to maximize their share. After the distribution, the women cook the meat, adding mushrooms and other plants they have gathered.

Women's Work

The women also have the task of making clothes of bark cloth. Using tools of elephant tusk, the men pound at the strip of bark removed from the tree to make the actual cloth, but the women decorate it with vegetable dyes. This work is almost always done outside the hut; women work in pairs or trios. Bark cloth aprons as well as belts to hold them are made.

The hut is considered the woman's property. Turnbull (1961:132) explains:

This is one of the strongest points a woman has in arguments with her husband. I have seen a woman who has failed to get anywhere in a matrimonial dispute simply turn around and start methodically pulling all the leaves off of the hut. Usually her husband stops her halfway.

Perhaps it is for this reason that Turnbull (1961:154) says:

> The woman is not discriminated against in Ba Mbuti society as she is in some African societies. She has a full and important role to play. There is relatively little specialization according to sex. Even the hunt is a joint effort. A man is not ashamed to pick mushrooms and nuts if he finds them, or to wash and clean a baby. A woman is free to take part in the discussions of men, if she has something relevant to say. In fact, it was the apparent, absolute dominance of the male in the *molimo* that had seemed to be the exception.

Female Puberty Ceremony

The female puberty ceremony is called an *elima* and is celebrated at the first menstrual period. The girl who has reached maturity retires to a special hut where she spends about a month with friends whom she has invited to join her. An older woman, a specialist in the tradition, also joins the girls. Unfortunately Turnbull could not be present to learn what transpires within the special hut, but he could hear the girls singing songs which strongly resembled the molimo songs. That night the singing around the fire included groups of girls singing, clapping, and dancing. After they retired into the hut, the men continued to sing for a while. After men and women had both retired, the molimo was brought into camp. For about an hour, groups of young men wearing leafy branches in their belts and carrying long branches, dashed about, striking the huts and even damaging some. At last all the men emerged from their huts, gathered around the fire which blazed with new fuel, and loudly sang their songs. Finally, the molimo was surrounded by the leaf-clad young men and retired to the forest.

After the evening meal on the following day, the early singing was again joined by the girls and the old woman who had been in a special hut all day. This time the girls had painted their bodies and wore vines and feathers in their hair. They danced compactly around the men, forcing them to sit closer to their fire. Instead of retiring, as was customary the girls built a fire at the edge of the men's group. The old woman and a childless, young married woman were in the circle. The men's group and the women's group began to sing the molimo songs together. The young married woman who seemed to have been a sponsor of this ceremony suddenly began to drum the distinctive rhythm of the molimo. She and the old woman began to dance, leading the girls into the center of the men's group. The women danced and sang while the men stood and clapped for them. After about half an hour, the old woman danced in such a way as to drive the girls back from the fire, until she occupied the central area alone. She danced toward the fire and then backed away from it. She was joined by the sponsor. They circled the fire, dancing on opposite sides of the fire, on the hot ashes. The sponsor finally withdrew.

The Molimo Legend

The dramatic enactment of a Mbuti legend followed. The old woman danced right into the molimo fire and scattered the logs and embers in all directions. The men quickly gathered up the embers of the fire, singing the molimo songs loudly. When the fire had been rebuilt, the men entered into an erotic dance, moving backward and forward toward the fire and away. This part of the ceremony was repeated twice more — the old woman scattering the fire, the men rebuilding it. The legend is that once the women "owned" the molimo, but the men stole it from them and have since forbidden them to see it.

The men continued to sing, and the old woman came forth alone with a long roll of twine. She tied a loop of the twine around each man's neck. As she did so, the man stopped singing. The men agreed that the old woman had tied them up, tied up the molimo, and the hunt. One of the men offered food and cigarettes as a gift to the woman to untie them. As each man was released, he again began to sing. The old woman took the food and tobacco and returned to another camp, where she had relatives.

The Move Back to the Village

The final phase of the ceremony, the *elima*, was the subject of discussion for the next few days. The issue of whether to hold it in the camp in the forest or to move back to the village and hold it there was in question. The more traditional people wanted to hold it in the forest, but one cunning old gentleman thought it should be moved to the village where tourists might come to see the dancing and spare some money or tobacco for the band. It was settled by sending the elima group into the village in charge of an older woman. The rest of the camp stayed in the forest. The people in the forest would complete the molimo and bring it into the village on the final night. Perhaps the Bantu, who believed that the molimo was a mourning ceremonial, would give the Mbuti food enough for a final funeral feast.

Turnbull (1961:186) relates that the Pygmies, as opposed to their Bantu neighbors, recognize the coming of menstrual blood as a symbol of life rather than one of defilement. Most unusual among the peoples of the world, the Pygmies encourage intercourse during a menstrual period in the belief that this strengthens the possibility of conception. Thus, the first menstrual period is a time of pride and joy, a promise of fertility. In the house of the elima, as in the Chisungu ceremony, the girls learn the art of motherhood, the etiquette of wifehood, and the songs of the adult women. Pygmy men and boys come from all the neighboring groups to pay their respects and to sing with the girls. The house of the elima must have an adult male and an adult female in residence to protect the girls, chaperone them, and see that their needs are taken care of. In this particular elima, a bachelor and a widow accompanied the girls back to the village. In the evenings the girls gathered outside their house to dance and cast their eyes about for likely suitors. They often made their preferences known by their dance, and any man who was offended or teased by the girls was likely to be the target of their next attack. Turnbull writes:

> At any time of the day the girls were likely to emerge from the elima house armed with long fito whips. . . . Any males, young or old, and particularly those who had shown annoyance at being teased, were liable to be chased and whipped by the eager, young furies.

The object of the chase was to whip a particular man, who then was under obligation to visit the elima house. Once he visited, he did not have to do anything further, although he would generally be teased and scorned if he did not. The girls also whipped at old men and young boys, which may have been meant as a compliment. In any case, since most of the eligible young men came from other villages, the girls and their whips ranged far and wide over the countryside, raiding neighboring plantations. They were allowed liberties that would be unimaginable under other circumstances. Turnbull describes one raid in which a pitched battle was fought. The men fired slices of banana skin from taut bows; the girls, using baskets as shields, closed in to get at their targets with the whips. Both sides threw stones and, at one point, the girls threw logs taken from burning fires. Each man so assaulted had to preserve his self-respect and pick up the challenge to visit the elima house. The girls, after a while, felt they had attained their objectives and returned to their own village singing their elima songs.

Return to the Forest

Soon it was felt that too much time had already been taken from the hunt and that the women were having entirely too much fun, so it was time to return to the forest. One night the women of the band gathered outside the elima house. The girls emerged one by one, each one with her body painted in unique designs. They joined their mothers and sisters outside the house and sang the songs of grown women. This emergence marked the beginning of the last week of the elima. During this week, the boys who want to enter the elima house must fight their way through the mothers standing guard outside. Any boy who is considered undesirable will surely be denied access, for the women are armed with all sorts of sticks, stones, and other weapons. Once inside, the boy often has to fight the girls themselves, especially if he has not been invited. The boys and girls flirt, sleep together, and may even have intercourse. Turnbull remarks that there are certain restrictions on intercourse and that he has never known a girl to become pregnant during the elima ceremony. At any rate, young boys and girls can come to know each other intimately before any formal engagement or marriage takes place. Often such affairs end with the betrothal of several of the girls.

For the Mbuti, the elima ceremony ended when the girls joined the older women in singing the songs of the adults. But for the sake of the Bantu villages, the affair was protracted so that the villagers could provide a suitable feast as they would for puberty ceremonials in their own style. To assure this ending, the girls, on the last day of the elima, took a purifying bath in the river, oiled their skin, and danced in the way of the villagers.

Turnbull writes about various betrothals which did not come to fruition during the elima ceremony, because the wrong suitor courted the right girl, and so on. There is also a misunderstanding between the Bantu and Mbuti villagers. The Bantu feel that any proper elima must end with marriage ceremonies. The Mbuti, however, consider the elima merely as a statement of maturity rite of passage, with marriage coming about only when and if the principals desire it.

Marriage, among the Mbuti, is necessary to achieve adulthood. Turnbull (1961:206) says:

> To them a woman is more than a mere producer of wealth; she is an essential partner in the economy. Without a wife a man cannot hunt; he has no hearth. He has nobody to build his house, gather fruits and vegetables and hunt for him.

Status of Mbuti Women

The status of women in this society is, at best, ambivalent. From the amount of consciously imitated ritual, in order to please the Bantu or get extra gifts from them, one wonders how much of the status of women has also been adopted from the Bantu tradition. If the women know so well the songs of the molimo, why are they secluded when it enters the village? What is the significance of the old woman stamping out the molimo fire, while the men revive it?

Certainly the women in such a society do not seem bound by any tradition of subjugation to their husbands. Marriages are contracted on the basis of mutual admiration more often than in most traditional societies. And yet, women do not have the options here that they enjoy even among the Navajo. A woman needs a husband just as surely as a man needs a wife. This fulfillment is important in making marriage secure. A Mbuti woman knows her role in life and is neither mistreated nor demeaned if she goes along the traditional ways. But there is little chance for her to do anything else. So it may well have been in earlier times with all human societies. One cannot speak here of women or men having authority. Leadership in a Pygmy band constantly shifts and is transient. Some older people are respected for their wisdom, some are feared as witches;

some wives are highly regarded by their husbands while others are not. The society itself sets no rigid categories, no heritable positions of leadership. The band operates as well as it can to maximize the gifts of the forest. The women are part of the band — practical, realistic, and yet capable of enjoying to the fullest whatever opportunities come their way. They live in a perilous balance with the neighboring Bantu, who can very easily drive them out of their beloved forest forever, should they provoke such action. Both women and men remain people of the forest.

4. MUNDURUCU WOMEN IN TWO SETTINGS

The Mundurucu of the Amazon jungle in Brazil present a valuable source of information about the status of women in a horticultural society and also about the reaction of women toward culture change. Yolanda and Robert Murphy (1974) were able to study the Mundurucu under nearly aboriginal conditions, as well as in new villages created through contact with traders and Catholic missions. Yolanda was able to establish rapport with the women. The results of their study present a new variation on the theme of woman's status.

The Mundurucu

Originally the Mundurucu were a hunting and horticultural people. Their first contact with Brazilians occurred in 1770, when they were extending their area of control in the jungle through warfare. They were known as fierce and successful warriors. After they were pacified by the Brazilians, the colonists used them to pacify other tribes and to help the Brazilians gain control over the jungle area. In the course of this relationship, the Mundurucu developed strong ties to Brazilian traders and familiarity with industrial goods. Their number has been much reduced by disease, the usual consequence of contact between two peoples who do not share the same immunities. From 1952 to 1953, when the Murphys did their field work, Mundurucu were living in two kinds of situations: in the small villages of the savannah which were similar to the traditional Mundurucu villages; and in isolated families living close to the river, where rubber trees grew wild and were tapped for sale to Brazilian rubber traders. We shall first describe the savannah village, noting the status and position of women there, and then go on to the changed conditions of the rubber tappers' families.

In the Aboriginal Village

Murphy and Murphy (1974:55) describe the Mundurucu savannah village as consisting of four dwelling houses and a men's house. Each of the dwellings is fully enclosed, and has only a front and back door. The men's house, however, is fully exposed and built like a lean-to. Near the men's house, in a small, tightly-enclosed building the sacred trumpets are stored. These trumpets may never be seen by the women. The village is circular, with an open plaza in the center, and surrounded by an open area about 40 feet wide, where garbage is dumped and where people go to relieve themselves. Murphy and Murphy (1974:58) report that this area, as well as the immediate savannah and gallery forests leading down to the river, are frequented mostly by women. The women draw water, gather firewood, do the laundry, and bathe in the river; they also do their gardening within a radius of about two miles of the village. The men's range goes far beyond these boundaries. They travel ten miles or more to hunt or to tap the rubber trees during the dry season. They also travel to meet the rubber traders.

Subsistence

Subsistence is based primarily upon gardening and hunting and, to a lesser extent, upon fishing and collecting wild foods. Although the men work to clear the gardens, the women do the rest of the gardening and, most important, food processing. The basic food, which is used at every meal, is farinha, a product made from the tubers of bitter manioc. Bitter manioc contains prussic acid which can cause discomfort or severe illness, if not removed. The Murphys (1974) describe two processes by which this can be done. The method most frequently used is also the most laborious, but it provides more of the essential starch. The tubers, usually about a foot long, are carried by the women to the village farinha-making shed, where they are peeled. The next, and by far the most unpleasant job, involves grating the tubers on a sheet of metal in which holes have been punched, and which leads into a trough. The wet pulp is then soaked in water in a large, metal basin. The process requires a great deal of water, and women are constantly carrying water from the stream for this part of the process. Next the pulp is put through a wicker squeezer called a *tipiti*, where it is sieved. The larger remaining pieces are broken up with a mortar and pestle. Finally they are toasted; this dries the mash into a flour, and also removes any remaining trace of prussic acid. The basins, scrapers, and oven used for this process are communally owned and used by household groups who cooperate to make farinha approximately every ten days. In order to use the equipment efficiently, the various tasks are all done by different women at about the same time. Some peel, some grate, some bring water, some squeeze the tipiti. The roughest work, the grating, is usually done by several women taking turns. Murphy and Murphy (1974:127) tell us that in their village, it took about two days to make a supply of farinha sufficient to last for ten days. Since there were four households in the village, the farinha shed was in use nearly every day. In addition to the farinha, women spin cotton, make hammocks, do the rudimentary housework, repair clothing, and, when new houses are con-structed, make the clay floors and bring thatch for the roof. Villages move about every ten years since the soil is depleted in about that time.

Men hunt, build houses, clear the gardens, and seasonally tap the wild rubber trees. The only tasks in which men and women work together (Murphy and Murphy 1974:130) are garden clearing, house building and fishing.

Social Units

The domestic units, the houses, are ideally inhabited by a group of women who are related to each other, either mothers and their daughters, or sisters and their young daughters, and boys up to age 13. At the time of the Murphys' field work, one house was inhabited by the chief and his wife, the chief's son and his wife, and the chief's wife's daughters by her previous marriages. One of these daughters was married and brought her husband into the household. The chief's position was anomalous. He had moved into his wife's residence, but thereupon took another wife, whom he attempted to bring into his first wife's residence; however, she would not allow this. Since most of the village people were related to her, they backed her in her position and forced the chief to send his new wife back to live with his father, where she promptly added to his disgrace by having affairs with the local men of that village. House number two contained 25 inhabitants — three sisters and their husbands and children. The children of one of the sisters remained in the household, although their mother had died. House number three was based upon a core of three men who were parallel cousins. The principal woman of the house had a sister and maternal uncle who lived in house number two. House number four contained a principal woman and two of her three children, and two stepchildren and their families, including the children of one stepchild who was dead.

The Mundurucu ideally exhibit a matrilocal form of residence, although this is not universal. The houses are inhabited by groups of related women. The men who are married into the group, come to the houses in the morning for breakfast; sometimes they come at night for sexual intercourse, but more frequently this is done by slipping away from the group to a tryst in the forest, or near the river. Otherwise, the men spend their time with other men in the *Eksa*, or men's house. Their wives bring the evening meal to them here, and their sleeping hammocks are also slung here. This focuses on the central integrative social organization of the Mundurucu. Formerly, most anthropologists agreed that matrilocality was an outgrowth of the need for women to work together at some cooperative project. The manufacture of farinha seems to answer this purpose, since this process recurs at regular intervals and involves the pooled labor of the entire female population of the household. More recently, however, Harris (1975) has suggested that matrilocality occurs in those societies in which men are absent for long periods of time. Here, again, the Mundurucu seem to qualify because prior to Brazilian pacification, men were still used as jungle scouts and raiders as the Brazilians made their way through the Amazon. These expeditions often lasted for as long as a year. Harris' point is that such prolonged absence by men would leave patrilocal villages in the care of women whose loyalties might be in doubt since they were not bound by ties of kinship. Whatever the reason, the Mundurucu do reside matrilocally; however, their kinship organization is complicated by the fact that they inherit membership in their clans and moieties patrilineally, from their fathers. The moieties simply mean that everyone in the society belongs to one of the two groups, the Whites or the Reds. Membership in one group necessitates marrying into the other group; for example, a Red woman must marry a White man. The clan units, formed within the moieties, further restrict marriage in that it is necessary to marry outside one's clan. Clan members are supposed to feel closely related and obligated to each other. Since both moieties and clan membership are reckoned through the father, the Mundurucu may be said to be patrilineal and matrilocal. This type of kinship was unknown before the Mundurucu, and such dissonance, where it occurs, usually reveals culture change. In fact, the Mundurucu have gone through three historically known changes — from independent hunters and gatherers to the intensive manioc flour producers where the men were involved with long scouting raids and hunting expeditions, to neolocal living in rubber tapping communities (Murphy 1956). Kinship here seems to be an adaptive strategy for whatever subsistence mode is currently in use.

Murphy and Murphy (1974:77) note that this type of kinship provides a "unique type of integration." Men are likely to have clan brothers in many different villages, which makes it easy for them to travel among villages. This diffuse kinship also effectively stifles intervillage raiding. At the same time, clans are prevented from fighting other clans because members of those clans may be coresident in a number of villages, and neighborliness and friendship are equally important as kinship. Yet, despite the fact that in this society the women live in strong kinship units, whereas the men are scattered through the villages and have no spatial power base, the men possess power and authority.

Mundurucu Myth

This is seen in the myth concerning the sacred trumpets, which reside adjacent to the men's house. It is believed that at one time in the distant past women owned the trumpets, and they used them to placate the gods and to bring all good things, such as good health, subsistence, and luck to the Mundurucu. However, the trumpets had to be fed regularly, and the women could only provide them with a drink made from sweet manioc, but the trumpets demanded meat, which the women could not supply since they did not hunt (Murphy and Murphy 1974:89). The men did not like the idea of the women having the trumpets because the women neglected their husbands and their housework to play them. Therefore, when the women attempted to force the men into the houses while they played the trumpets, the men threatened to forego hunting. Through agreement, then, the men took the trumpets from the women and have forever since confined women to their houses when the trumpets are played.

The Murphys (1974:91) have a unique interpretation of this myth. For them it does not indicate the fact that men have authority over women so much as it indicates that this authority is based on factors other than biological inferiority.

> We could not find a shred of evidence to indicate that men think that women are inherently, biologically, and irredeemably inferior or submissive. Indeed, the whole key to the myth is that once women did exercise dominance, and that they had to be overthrown in a primal revolution. Women, as people, are not inferior, for otherwise the rebellion of the males would have been unnecessary. Only their status is inferior, and this is so only because the men managed to shear them of their power in the remote past.

Threat and Force

Women who behave in ways considered threatening or unwomanly are punished in the same way as women who have looked at the sacred trumpets. The standard punishment is gang-rape. Any woman who dares go alone into the forest or to the river is considered fair game for sexual attack. Indeed, Murphy and Murphy (1974:108) relate a story of a girl who ran away from the mission school and was gang-raped. Murphy and Murphy (1974:108) state:

> Here, the concern was not with promiscuity or spying on men's secrets. Nor were the Mundurucu upholding the rights of the missionaries to educate their children, for at best they are unenthusiastic about losing their young to the school. The girl's sole crime was the flaunting of male authority and the pursuit of her own inclinations.

In actuality, according to the Murphys, men are not able to use all of their authority effectively. Women will seldom be seen out alone. Gossip and other methods of informal social control are used among women to correct other women's wayward behavior before it comes to the attention of the men.

Status of Mundurucu Women and Female Power

However this may be, in Mundurucu society, as in so many others, the behavior of women is modest and deferential to men. Murphy and Murphy (1974:106) state:

> Back seat status is standard for younger women; they sit in the rear, walk in the rear of a file, eat after the men do. A woman is retiring in other ways as well. If something amuses her, she is supposed to cover her mouth when she laughs. An open mouth is like an open vagina to the Mundurucu men. And a proper woman does not look directly at a man, nor would she ever engage his eyes. This is considered to be a rank and blatant invitation by the men, and of course, by the women, as well. . . . .By the same reasoning, men and women do not touch, except as a tentative prelude to sex.

In the everyday context in the village, women live out their lives in the company of their mothers, sisters, and daughters. They form a solidary group which can and does often protect individual members, and formulate policy regarding many private matters, However, this is done, not so much as a matter of authority, but rather as an outcome of "real politics." For example, the oldest woman of a household is usually the head of the household. She informally organizes the production of farinha. As both the older woman and head of a household, she can and does make demands on younger sons-in-law, which they cannot very well refuse, since they lack the solidarity of a united male clan or the prestige of age. The Murphys (1974:132) make the point that the leadership of the older woman is not exercised through the despotism of the traditional Chinese mother-in-law, but rather through the informal guidance of a group of related women who have always worked together.

Nevertheless, when excess farinha is produced for sale, the men deal directly with the trader, while the women stand by and instruct the men as to what they want from the trader. When the men sell rubber to the trader, however, the women take no part in the transaction.

Resentments of Mundurucu Women

In daily life, Mundurucu women live separate lives from their men. They see them regularly but infrequently. Marriages occur gradually and dissolve frequently. Women have definite antagonisms to men for a number of reasons. They resent the fact that the women's labor is constant drudgery and the men do nothing to help them. They resent the existence of the men's house and the fact that men live apart from them. They are cognizant of the Brazilian nuclear family and prefer it. They resent the fact that they cannot refuse coitus to their husbands and consequently they are almost always pregnant, since they have no safe and secure method of contraception. But most of all, they resent the threat of gang-rape.

> . . . It should be stated here that Mundurucu women are not servile toward men in either a real or a symbolic sense. The men are regarded as exploitive and dominant; not as superior.

Although women are excluded from the rituals and theoretically should have no knowledge of the sacred trumpets or of their significance, the Murphys found that they did, indeed, know all about these secret matters and counted them of little importance. The Murphys (1974:140) characterize the women of the Mundurucu as secular and pragmatic in their orientation. Although, they state:

> They knew all about its ritual and paraphernalia though none would admit peeking, and they were neither mystified nor cowed. It is as if they had investigated the secret sources of the men's power — and had found absolutely nothing.

It is also true that the women have a degree of autonomy in a matrilocal setting that they may not otherwise have. A woman and her children are fed by being members of a household, not by the largesse of any male. As a consequence, marriages are brittle.

Marriage among the Mundurucu

The most important function of marriage, besides the obvious fact of procreation, is the creation of bonds among the clans and between moities. Marriage among the Mundurucu is celebrated neither by secular nor ritual events. A young man, seeking to marry, will drift into a village where he will undoubtedly have clan brothers. He will hang his hammock in the men's house. If he wants to marry an eligible girl, he will present her with the product of his hunt. If she accepts it, they are married and will continue to be married until he no longer brings her meat. Sexual activity will take place either in the wife's hammock after the rest of the household is asleep, or in the forest or other outdoor situations. A marriage may dissolve if a man finds his wife's family uncongenial, or if the family finds the man lazy, or for any number of personal reasons. As with marriage, divorce is not marked by any great changes. The man simply goes to his own or another village. The woman and her children remain within the household. The only real disdadvantage that a woman without a husband suffers is that she will not derive any trade goods through the male activity of rubber tapping. This is critical because, as stated above, much of the paraphernalia of the farinha shed is metal which can only be obtained through the rubber trader. In addition, the Mundurucu have taken to wearing cheap Western clothing in preference to their former nudity. Trade goods carry a prestige value beyond their actual value; therefore, women prefer to marry men who will, at least in the dry season, tap rubber trees.

Moving to the New Villages

In fact, women are in the vanguard encouraging men to take up rubber tapping on a full-time basis. Etically, the Murphys see the traditional village as providing the women with a greater power base, promoting female solidarity, and providing needed services such as baby-minding and cooperative farinha-making. Emically, Mundurucu women do not value these advantages compared to the isolated neolocal nuclear family which exists where rubber tappers live. Men who become full-time tappers live in either small villages or isolated homesteads along the river. The village is not arranged in a circle. It consists of anywhere from two to a dozen adobe houses, and its population ranges from 12 to 100 people (Murphy and Murphy 1974:184). The greatest difference between such small villages and the traditional savannah village is the absence of a men's house. Originally, such settlements were encouraged, not only by rubber traders, but also by the Catholic mission in the area. It was the Catholic mission that was instrumental in prohibiting the men's house and promoting nuclear family units. But there is more to it than that. The mission and the traders became sources of needed and desired goods.

> The Mundurucu men really only wanted knives, guns, axes and the like, but as is always the case in culture change, they got very much more. Their desires started them down a road, along which their women have relentlessly pushed them, that has seen the disappearance of the men's house and a good deal of the social organization that went with it (Murphy and Murphy 1974:185).

In the new rubber tapping villages, nuclear families work individual gardens. Young boys and their fathers, as well as the women, do gardening. The traditional division of labor has fallen apart. Murphy and Murphy (1974:192) explain:

> Nowhere is this change in the division of labor more striking than in *farinha*-making. The farinha shed in our Cururu River village had most of the same equipment as had the one in Cabrua. There was a long trough, the oven, the toasting pan, large metal basin and tipiti, but there was also a hand-operated mechanical grater. This instrument, bought through the mission, was a relatively primitive affair by modern standards, but it helped accomplish a sexual revolution. The most onerous and time-consuming of all manioc processing chores became reduced to a simple task in which the man turns a crank and the woman drops the peeled tubers into a hopper — but the man, indeed, does turn the crank.

Men in the river villages also cooperate in peeling the tubers and in carrying water from the river for washing the pulp and loading the tipiti. Quite simply, all the functions which had traditionally been done by a household of women — the functions which gave them solidarity and a power base — are here performed by the nuclear family. The same individuals, primarily the men, are the rubber tappers, who each day make a short incision in the rubber tree, hang a cup to collect the sap, return later in the day to collect the cups, and pour liquid over a pole revolving over a fire. This ball, so formed, is either taken down river to the traders, or is sold at the mission.

The Murphys, as is true with many anthropologists, have a preference for the traditional savannah village. They feel that here the women are, for practical purposes, virtually autonomous. They live in a situation which lends itself to mutual support, and it is expected that women and their children will remain fixed in the village, while the men come and go. Women need not look to any man for subsistence; they can let the men play their games in the *eksa* while they, the women, go about the serious and practical tasks involved with living. In the rubber tappers' villages, women are dependent upon their husbands for subsistence, help, and support. There is no ready group of women to rely on. Women no longer live with their mothers and sisters, surrounded by other women with whom they have grown up. In all fairness, the choice between the savannah village and the rubber tapper's riverline village is a matter of choice for the Mundurucu women.

Mundurucu Women's Preference

Murphy and Murphy (1974:201) state:

> The answer here is quite unequivocal; with but few exceptions they prefer the nuclear family arrangements of the new communities. They do so because trade goods are more readily available, and they prefer their men to help them. On one level, this is exactly what the women want — they seek aid and relief in the drudge work of manioc growing and processing. . . . Why do women want to lock men into marriage and the family? Here we should stress that whatever we may think, the relative status of women to be in the traditional as opposed to the new communities, the Mundurucu women think it is better in the latter. And although there may have been little absolute improvement in their situation, the gap between them and the men is perceived by them to have narrowed. The women may not have been elevated, but the men surely have been reduced.

In the opening chapter of the Murphys' ethnography, the typical day of a Mundurucu woman is described: she rises early, takes care of her baby, works in the farinha shed and in the garden, then prepares dinner for her husband at the men's house. Finally:

> Borai listened for a very short while (to insect sounds) before tiredness overtook her. Her last thought before drifting into full sleep was a hope that her husband would not decide to pay a night visit. A woman's day had ended (Murphy and Murphy 1974:20).

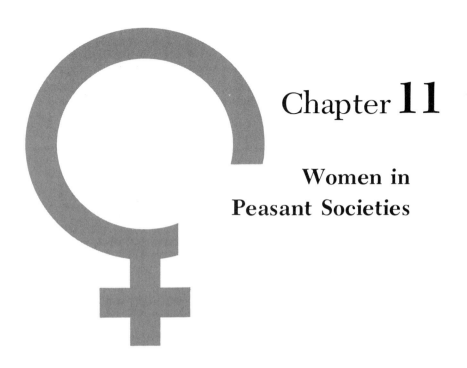

Chapter 11

Women in Peasant Societies

1. PEASANT WOMAN FROM PUERTO RICO

The study of woman's status in a peasant community brings with it special problems, because a peasant community is part of a larger community, a state. It is, therefore, difficult to separate those behavioral traits which are universal to peasantry from those traits which are particular to the individual state. The study of peasant life in Puerto Rico illustrates this problem. This study was done by Carlos Buitrago-Ortiz (1973) in the barrio of Esperanza, part of the city of Arecibo, which is situated west of San Juan. Buitrago-Ortiz is Puerto Rican, and thus adds the knowledge of the native to that of the trained anthropologist.

The Locale

Arecibo, like much of Puerto Rico, is rapidly becoming modern, urbanized, and industrial. The barrio of Esperanza, however, remains largely rural. In order to understand Puerto Rico, one must first understand that it had been a Spanish possession for several hundred years. The people are Spanish-speaking, and hold their Spanish culture in great respect. Some of the attitudes of the people may be traced to this tradition. It is difficult to determine from where particular patterns of behavior stem: for example, the exaggerated paternalism and concern for the "honor" of the women. The Puerto Rican

134

people are themselves a blend of New and Old World peoples. Puerto Rico was aboriginally settled by several waves of Indian people, including the Arawaks and the Caribs. Spanish colonialization produced a blend of the two races, to which Africans were added, who were brought by the Spanish to work the sugar plantations. Today, the population is a kaleidoscope in terms of racial characteristics, but is bound firmly together by a common Spanish heritage.

Relations with the United States

Another factor which makes Puerto Rico unusual is its proximity to, and relationship with, the United States. Although the United States has vigorously denied that it is a colonial power, there is little in the ambiguous status of Puerto Rico to differentiate it from colonies of other European nations. For example, Puerto Ricans are allowed free and unimpaired entrance into and exit from the mainland. Puerto Rico has delegations at the political conventions of both major political parties, but they do not have the right to vote. They have served in the armies of the United States, but have no representatives in the American Congress. These injustices are perhaps compensated for by the large economic incentives the United States has given to Puerto Rico in that industries which set up operations in Puerto Rico are granted tax relief. For our purposes, however, the important thing is the ease of mobility between Puerto Rico and the United States. Many families and hosts of individuals have come to the United States to make their fortunes. Such people will be the topic of another chapter. For present purposes it should be noted that many Puerto Ricans who do migrate come from rural barrios like Esperanza.

The Barrio

The term *barrio* may be defined as a district or section of a larger town or city. Esperanza is about five or six miles from Aricibo and is a wholly agricultural district. The crops grown may be divided between cash crops, sugar cane and tobacco, and subsistence crops, corn, sweet potatoes, yams, and plantains. Most farms also have several domestic animals: cows, some pigs, chickens, turkeys, and pigeons. Before the automobile became readily available, most farm families also owned a horse. Many still do and use it for trips to local stores. In most cases, the women are in charge of the domestic animals. Milk, eggs, and pork are consumed within the household and seldom sold.

Buitrago-Ortiz set out to study the family in a peasant community and found that economic or occupational factors provided the framework for the family.

> In communities like Esperanza, the economic pattern is particularly closely related to other areas of family life. There is a definition of "being a man" that begins, in a sense, with some sort of economic autonomy and leadership. "being a man" is not an abstract definition; it is a social role deeply embedded in the context of family life. A man must head a family to be a man; he must be married.

Division of Labor

Buitrago-Ortiz goes on to state that in families of Hispanic and Mediterranean origin, certain spheres of activity are reserved for men. The man is the link between the domestic world and the outside world. It is the man who establishes patron-client relationships with townspeople. It is he who arranges for credit at the local store. He may have a particular dealer to whom he sells his tobacco or cane. One of the forms through which a peasant will try to manipulate such relationships is the institution of *compadrazgo*, which centers around various rites of passage of his children — baptism, confirmation, marriage — when the peasant will invite his patrons to act as godparents. Although the ritual centers on the child, the important relationship is the tie between parents and godparents. Each is formally bound to treat the other with great respect, to grant favors, and generally to give preferential treatment. In this way the peasant hopes to make the patron-client relationship more enduring. The male role, then, is concretely defined in terms of economic provider. He is the conduit through which all his wife's associations outside the immediate family are passed. He mediates between home and community. Through compadrazgo, he spreads a network of relationships which bind both husband and wife. This is expressed by the peasants themselves in terms of *arriba* and *abajo*. According to Buitrago-Ortiz (1973:27), arriba means *up;* it refers to the kitchen, the backyard, and the bedrooms, which are the provinces of the wife. Abajo literally means *down*, and refers to the fact that the man is supposed to be outside in his fields, barn, or veranda. It is not seemly for a woman to stroll about the village or to be seen too frequently outside her household. In the same way, it is unseemly for a man to be unable to support his family and it would probably be an unparalleled catastrophe for a man to help his wife with her work. This raises some problems inherent in the economic situation of Puerto Rico. Not all men have enough land to feed their families. There is heavy migration of young men to the United States where they hope to earn enough money to buy land in Puerto Rico and marry. But in times of stress — when a crop fails, the world price of sugar or tobacco declines — the small landholder will feel the pinch immediately. In such cases, fathers of families may have to go to the mainland to work until they accumulate enough money to make another start. This means that despite the strong, cultural division of labor, there will, in fact, be some women — usually poorer women — who will be the heads of their households for certain periods of time. These women will, of necessity, behave in ways that are not traditional and will be most ill-at-ease when doing so. Of a sample of 50 households in Esperanza, Buitrago Ortiz found only three headed by women. Let us examine the context in which women are expected to live, and then we shall examine particular women and how they live within these constraints.

Childhood

A woman is supposed to confine her activities to her kitchen, her backyard, and her bedroom. As children, little girls are kept close to their mothers. They go to school when they are older, but since the girl is seen as a natural sexual magnet for boys, she is guarded carefully by her brothers. As in most Hispanic cultures, the strongest barriers are raised against possible incest. Father-daughter relationships are marked by a lack of physical contact such as kissing or hugging. There is also the rule of complete respect in that the daughter must defer to her father's judgment in all things and obey his commands. Sexual jokes and sexual talk, in general, are forbidden in the presence of both male and female children. Education is not considered as important for girls as knowledge of domestic crafts such as cooking, sewing, and so on.

Marriage

When a girl has matured, not only sexually, but also in terms of her domestic skills, she is ready for marriage. The opportunity to meet men occurs during religious vigils at church and at parties. A man is considered ready for marriage when he has a small piece of land or a job, and preferably a house. Until he acquires these, his status is still that of a boy. The young man and woman who are attracted to each other at church or social events may declare their intentions toward each other, but this has no validity until the young man speaks to and receives the consent of the girl's father. Even in the event that the father approves the courtship, he still has the responsibility of guarding his daughter's sexuality. The young man is expected to take the initiative in the courtship, but the father of the girl stipulates which evenings the young man may visit, how long he may stay, and usually arranges to have an adult chaperone the courting couple. After the marriage takes place, and only then, does the father relax his control over his daughter. That same control, however, is then exercised by the husband. Women are regarded as extremely weak, both emotionally and mentally. This weakness does not apply to the amount of physical labor they are supposed to do or to the number of children they should bear. Father, brothers, and later, husbands, are constantly on guard lest their daughters, sisters, and wives yield to temptation and have extramarital sexual relationships. The husband is always in charge of financial matters, since women are not considered capable of taking care of them.

Maturity

As a woman ages, she is not perceived as having acquired wisdom, nor is she regarded as any more capable of taking charge of her own affairs. Gradually her guardianship is transferred from husband to son. Sons regard their mothers in a semireligious manner. She is the person from whom one can onfidently expect love and loyalty. Sons deeply respect their mothers and tend to idolize them. At the same time, they are fiercely protective of their mother's name and reputation. To speak ill of a man's mother leads to a fight to the death.

Isolation of Women

There is a double standard evident in Esperanza, as in many Latin-influenced areas. This is reinforced by traditions which keep the women house-bound to an extent seldom found in other areas. There are very few opportunities for women to hold jobs in Esperanza. One woman who does have a job is the wife of a chronic invalid who receives a pension. Even though the woman works all day while her husband is busy taking care of his horses, his cocks, or visiting local politicians, she is still responsible for running the household. The wife's mother and the couple's daughter actually do most of the housework, but when the husband is displeased by anything, he complains to his wife and she must straighten the matter out. Many men boast that they have never set foot in their own kitchens; that is the woman's domain. The husband's meals are served in the dining room. Later, the wife eats in the kitchen.

Even the marketing, which is done by the men, is deposited on the veranda for the wife to bring into the kitchen. In Esperanza, women do not shop or go to market. This double standard also prevails in such matters as recreation. Women are permitted and indeed expected to attend church functions, vigils held in private homes, and parties given by both biological and fictive kin. But every Sunday the men of Esperanza gather at the country store where beer is sold and a juke box is available. From about ten o'clock in the morning until six or seven in the evening, men gather here to drink and chat. Some buying and selling of horses also takes place. This is a context from which women are strictly excluded. Even the wife of the owner of the country store does not appear on Sunday.

Sexual Differences

The behavior of both sexes is markedly different in other ways as well. Men customarily meet at the cafe in the evenings. Here they exercise a form of social control over their neighbors by goading them to display their manhood in such ways as fighting or drinking. The air is heavy with boasts and loud taunts. Women, on the other hand, meet either in their homes or at acceptable social functions, where gossip is the method of social control. Two women gossiping in a corner avoid talking about each other, but do discuss other women who are not there. They also give and receive information about the behavior of men. Thus, any event, no matter how insignificant, becomes public knowledge throughout the community. The men share it openly in public places, and the women share it privately.

This dichotomy between males and females is stated by Buitrago-Ortiz (1973:75) as follows:

When people say "women's affairs" they mean the domestic sphere; when they say "men's affairs" they mean outside the domestic sphere. Going out alone, especially on holidays and at night, drinking, going to cock fights, going into town of Arecibo alone, are men's things. In the sexual sphere, this can be translated in the following way: a man who has an affair outside the house is very smart, very macho (male), but a woman who does it is simply a *puta*, prostitute. A wife tends to ignore and tolerate a husband who has an affair unless he becomes irresponsible toward her and the children. The man never tells his wife about these adventures; to confess anything would be an unmanly thing to do.

The extremes of this dichotomy between the world of men and the world of women are exemplified by the treatment of utensils and room space. Buitrago-Ortiz (1973:28) reports:

Most men state that they never went into the kitchen as that was not the place of a man, but of a woman. Most of them said that they just sat down at the dining table and ate what the women had prepared. In many cases, they would not even sit at the dining table, if they were working on the farm (the wife carried food to them) or they would sit in the living-dining room, but not at the table. The women never touched men's belongings (or tools) and in all the time we spent in Esperanza we never saw even one woman take anything from the "masculine space.

From the descriptions given above it is not surprising to find that although there is no legal or customary prohibition against a woman becoming the head of a household, this is a very rare condition. Even as a widow, a woman with grown children is expected to make her home with one of them.

Buitrago-Ortiz contrasts his work with that of Oscar Lewis, who worked in Esmerelda, a barrio of San Juan, in which the women had more freedom of movement and responsibility. The women of Esperanza, on the other hand, have their spheres so narrowly defined, are so closely guarded, and have so little opportunity to exercise choice or make decisions that they appear to lack the dimensions necessary to define them as human beings. We get no picture of what they think, how they feel about their lives, or what they aspire to; we merely get a one-dimensional schedule of daily activities which involve no more than a routine of chores.

A Day with Dolores

Dolores, an upper middle-class woman, begins her day at 6:30 AM by preparing breakfast for the family and feeding the domestic animals. At 8 o'clock Dolores brings coffee to her husband who is at work. From 8:30 to 11:30 she is alone and tends to her household chores. At noon she has lunch with her husband, either in the field or at home. By 1 o'clock she is washing the lunch dishes, and at 2 o'clock she again brings coffee to her husband. The children return from school at 4:30. She sets the boys to work taking care of the horse and cows. The girls help their mother in the kitchen, where they begin to prepare the evening meal. When Miguel, the husband, returns from the field, his dinner is served to him at the dining table, by Dolores and her daughter. He then goes into the living room to rest. Now Dolores feeds the rest of the family at the table; she has already eaten in the kitchen. After dinner Dolores and her daughters wash the dishes and clean the kitchen. By 7 o'clock, Dolores can spend some time with her husband in the living room, or more likely with her children in one of the bedrooms. At 9 o'clock the family retires.

After such a stimulating day, it is small wonder that Dolores does not communicate much of her inner feelings to the ethnographer, although this absence of personal information might be due to the fact that the ethnographer is a man. Although his wife worked with him, it is apparent from some of the later information that the direct approach in conversation is avoided even among close kin and compadres, regardless of sex.

A Conflict between Kin

In his study of a conflict over land between kin, Buitrago-Ortiz (1973: 131) demonstrates that the conflict is never brought out into the open. Resolution occurs through indirection. The conflict involved a couple who lived in Esperanza and enjoyed high status there. Their adversaries were the husband's sister and her husband who was a cousin. The sister and her husband had been living in the United States. Both claimed to own a plot of land on which the couple from Esperanza built a house. Eventually a surveyor was employed, but by the end of his field work, Buitrago-Ortiz still did not know the outcome. His analysis, however, indicated that the people most concerned, a brother and sister, tried in every way to avoid an overt clash. Each used his or her mate as spokesman to handle the dispute, and made every effort to enlist the support of other kin. Each disputant was careful to observe all the rules of respect traditionally associated with kinship. The sister even returned to the United States before the dispute was settled, after bidding her brother a warm farewell. But she left her husband behind in Esperanza to finish the matter which, among nonkin in urban society, might have been efficiently settled in a short time at the risk of creating enmity between the participants. Here it dragged on for many months, but there was no visible or consciously stated antagonism. The actions were patterned, almost choreographed. Significance was placed on the fact that Atanasia and her husband Miguel, the litigants from the United States, stayed with cousins when they arrived in Esperanza. They visited all their kin. Despite disagreements as to whose portion of the land Armando and Genoveva built their house on, Genoveva claimed that her sister-in-law, Atanasia, was an excellent housewife and a good cook. The entire real estate transaction was reduced to the dimensions of a woman's world, as it is measured in Esperanza. Never was the dispute permitted to violate the stated ideals of kinship — the respect of a sister for her brother, the duty of the brother to protect his sister.

Marriage in Esperanza

Here, as in much of Central America and the Caribbean, marriage can be contracted in several ways. Civil marriages, which are conducted by a judge, are numerically few. These ceremonies are followed by a reception at the bride's home.

A church marriage is by far the most common form, although such ceremonies must be held outside of Esperanza because there is no resident priest in the barrio. Again, a reception following the services is held at the bride's parents' home. These parties may be lavish or simple, depending on the relative wealth of the people involved. Both civil and church weddings are costly, especially to the bride's family. At every reception, friends, kin, and compadres (fictive kin) are present. Buitrago-Ortiz (1973:143) remarks:

> The occasion had a feminine air about it and the impression of the observer was that the women were enjoying the whole event more than the men who were more restrained in their behavior.

Many observers have noted that in peasant society, women show greater emotion at rites of passage, such as weddings and funerals, than do men. This may be due as much to the fact that these events provide women with the only legitimate opportunities for socializing as to the importance of the event or the emotional state of women in general.

The third form of marriage, the consensual union, was found to be least prevalent in Esperanza, although it is by far the most popular form of marriage in other areas in the Caribbean and Mexico, primarily because it is the least expensive. A household is set up just as is done in other marriages, and men and women perform the same functions toward each other and toward the children of such marriages. Consensual marriages, though neither legally nor religiously binding, are usually accepted by the community. The participants, especially the women, hope to regularize the union some time in the future. Buitrago-Ortiz has found that consensual marriages are usually the result of elopements caused by the failure of the groom to gain the support of the bride's father. Certainly this could not always have been the reason for consensual marriages. In writing of Armando and Atanasia's father, Buitrago-Ortiz states that he was simultaneously married to four wives; at least three of these marriages must have been consensual, a fact which Buitrago-Ortiz recognizes by putting the word "married" in quotes.

Compadrazgo

Once married, and particularly with the birth of children, a woman's social contacts are enlarged from only consanguinal and affinal kin to include comadres or the fictive kin. Although the compadrazgo relationship centers upon two men, the compadres, and is used to ease relationships and manipulate economic factors across class lines, it is still of major importance to women. Different compadres are chosen for each rite of passage for each child. Starting with baptism of the first child, another couple — usually husband and wife — must be asked to act as sponsors and godparents of the child. Given the large number of children in most peasant families and the frequency of rituals, a couple may acquire quite a large number of compadres and comadres. Although certainly some of them will be people with whom the husband desires to set up economic relationships, many others will be chosen from among neighbors in the barrio. These people will have little to offer in terms of economic value, but may perform invaluable services. Comadres address each other formally and treat each other with great respect. The relationship is a very serious one, usually accepted only after consideration. It carries a great deal of honor, but also great responsibility. In theory, at least, compadres are not supposed to refuse each other's request for help; in practice, however, compadres try not to make exorbitant demands. Compadres help in caring for each other's households in cases of illness and other emergencies. A woman can legitimately request her comadre to mind her children while she goes on an errand. She can entertain and gossip with her comadre. In areas other than Esperanza, where women are housebound, a woman may go to the stores or the doctor or visit public places in the company of her comadre, since they are responsible for each other. Compadrazgo serves to create durable bonds between strangers, often cutting across class lines and frequently cutting across the rural-urban dichotomy. For the woman, compadrazgo provides a socially acceptable companion with whom confidences can be shared and who can be counted on in need.

Summary

The bleak life of peasant women in Esperanza comes through clearly in Buitrago-Ortiz's writing, but nowhere do they articulate their discontent. Perhaps they are not at all dissatisfied. Perhaps this depressed attitude is a reflection on the ethnographer rather than the subjects of the ethnography. Esperanza does appear to be a rather extreme case in terms of segregation of women, division of labor, and status of women. It would be a good idea to examine other peasant societies before we attempt to draw any conclusion about this one.

2. ZAPOTEC WOMEN TRADERS

Women as Anthropologists

Modern interest in women's roles in society and the fact that women anthropologists have become interested in studying women of other cultures have led to valuable ethnographies written by women about women. Beverly Chiñas's (1973) work with the Zapotec women of lowland Mexico is one example. As has been noted throughout, a division of labor exists between men and women in all societies. It should also be noted that whenever anthropologists engage in field work, there is some natural suspicion on the part of the people under study, which is amplified when members of the opposite sex attempt to establish rapport within the culture. Women will talk more freely to other women, and thus female anthropologists have greater access to the private domain. This is demonstrated by Cançian (1964) in her work in Zinacanteco families.

Chiñas's work among the Mexican peasant women is notable both as a fine ethnography of San Juan Evangelista, a former barrio of El Centro, and as a study of peasant women.

The Isthmus of Tehuantepec

San Juan is located on the Pacific Coast of the Isthmus of Tehuantepec, in the state of Oaxaca, in Mexico. It is tropical in climate and semi-arid. During the dry season the area appears brown and dusty, but the wet season brings lush vegetation. The isthmus is a lowland, which is separated from the rest of Oaxaca by mountains and is a nearly self-contained area.

Chiñas did her field work with the Zapotecs, one of several language groups who inhabit the isthmus. The Zapotecs have been in this area for more than 1,000 years and have held to their distinctive languages and traditions despite the incursions of Aztecs, Spaniards, and Mexicans.

Subsistence

The people of this region are farmers, who grow subsistence as well as cash crops. Sugar cane used to be the principal crop, but today, due to the falling price of sugar on the world market, sesame, sorghum, bananas, mangoes, and coconuts have become the major cash crops. Maize, squash, and chili are the principal crops grown for subsistence. Irrigation is necessary to the production of crops. Protein is obtained from fish and shrimp, which abound in the area.

The Zapotecan area with which we are concerned contains two large population centers, El Centro and San Jacinto. The pueblo of San Juan

Evangelista trades with both of these areas. At one time, San Juan Evangelista was a barrio of El Centro, but now it is a separate political entity, which maintains strong trading ties.

San Juan Evangelista

San Juan Evangelista has a church just inside its physical boundaries. For a short time a resident priest and two nuns maintained the church and a parochial school. However, the people of San Juan do not feel committed to formal Catholic ritual, and prefer to practice a syncretism of Catholicism and Indian tradition. This manifests itself most strongly in the worship of particular saints and is practiced primarily in the homes and square of the pueblo. The central plaza, three blocks from the church, is bounded by streets and the small local market where there are always vendors. There is also a municipal building in which the jail and the upper grades of the elementary school are housed, and which contains a small, new library. Various artisans practice their crafts in the residential area: carpenters, sandal makers, seamstresses, and several small mills which grind corn for the women of San Juan, thus releasing them from this time-consuming activity. Like Esperanza, the lack of economic opportunity causes young men to migrate. These people, usually between the ages fifteen and thirty-five, may leave to attend school or to find jobs, and usually remain in the area to which they have migrated. This is a real problem for the young, marriageable women who remain in San Juan. However, as in Esperanza, the emigrants maintain close, affectionate ties with their home pueblo and actively work for its benefit through the larger political institutions. They are usually helpful to fellow Juanecos who migrate to their area, and often send money home to parents in the pueblo.

Land Ownership

There are two types of land tenure, private ownership and land which is owned by the community. The community-owned land has been the subject of much anxiety in the pueblo. Originally, upon its separation from El Centro, the community of San Juan was given several thousand hectares of land. This land has proven to be a point of contention between San Juan and El Centro and the larger Mexican government. Elsewhere, by various and often unfair practices, communal land has reverted to private or government ownership. Thus the people of San Juan are constantly suspicious of any attempts to survey or derive information about the size of the communal land and the uses to which it is put.

In terms of property inheritance, only privately owned land can be inherited. Those communal lands worked by families to whom they are allotted cannot be bequeathed.

Crafts and Skills

Most householders practice several skills in addition to their major occupation, which is farming. Men may be musicians, tailors, barbers, butchers, etc., as well as farmers. Women, although they refer to themselves as housewives, also practice other occupations, such as tortilla vendor, small *tienda* or shopkeepers, bakers, traders in the markets, and seamstresses. Chiñas (1973:30) notes that one woman, the school teacher, is employed for wages. Such employment is rare in San Juan and the competition for such jobs is heavy. Women are not normally trained for this type of employment.

Sale of Food

By and large, men produce goods and women process them. Any woman can make extra tortillas from the corn her husband grows, and sell them to neighbors or in the local market. Chiñas estimates that if a woman makes tortillas for sale, she can earn as much as eight to ten pesos. *Totopos*, another type of baked corn product, is even more profitable, although making them is more arduous and requires a particular type of oven. The sale of cooked food and sliced cucumbers, pineapple, or oranges to people on the street is also a common activity. Very few women are not regularly engaged in some form of trade involving prepared goods. Teen-age girls are often set to making totopos and are rewarded by being sent to El Centro to sell them. In fact, Chiñas says (1973:34): "The market places are overwhelmingly a woman's milieu."

The Market

The market at El Centro has more than 350 women who are regular vendors, and between 200 and 1,000 who have no regular stand, but sell their products in the markets, at bus stops, and in the street. In addition to selling in the market at El Centro and in the small, permanent market in San Juan, women regularly make the longer trip to San Jacinto, the regional center, where higher prices may be obtained. This involves a full day and 30-mile bus trip, and, consequently this can only be undertaken by women who do not have small children to care for. One phenomenon of women involved in trading is that these women, particularly in El Centro and San Jacinto, have little time to prepare food for their own family's consumption, and are therefore good customers of the prepared food vendors in the local market. San Juan Evangelista is a fully peasant society in that it is strongly integrated into the larger state economy. Soap, candles, jewelry, sewing machines, and radios are all highly valued and must be purchased for money. Women, as vendors, provide a more reliable source of money than their farmer husbands who are subject to the disasters of poor crops, bad growing seasons, and low world prices for their products. Moreover, men have fewer ways of earning money than women. For this reason, Chiñas (1973:40) notes: "The more women-hours a household can channel into processing and vending, the larger the household income."

Women as Marketers

In contrast to the house-bound peasant women of Esperanza, the women of San Juan are encouraged to use their skills outside the house and often have greater contacts in the towns and larger centers than their husbands. Young girls are always employed for food processing and selling. Shortly after they marry and start to have children, they must stop their outside activities until one or more of their children are old enough to take up the burden of caring for the younger children. As soon as this stage is reached, the women reactivate their former skills. In the interest of releasing time for this activity, household chores are simplified. The corn-grinding mill and the sewing machine are two technological innovations which save a good deal of time for the women. Laundry, which must be done by hand, is simplified by doing away with household linens, having people sleep in hammocks (which are far more comfortable than beds in the tropical climate) or on mats. Towels are not used; people dry their bodies with their hands, and their hair in the wind. Clothing is kept to a minimum; little boys go unclothed until they are five or six years old, and little girls wear only a small skirt or panty. Women prepare one large pot of stew for the day, which contains rice, vegetables, and as much meat as the family can afford. This is served at the main meal during the early afternoon, and the lighter breakfasts and suppers usually consist of coffee, sweet rolls, and cheese, all of which can be purchased in the market. Even the utensils used in cooking and eating are kept to a minimum. Tortillas are used as spoons to serve the stew. When plates are used, they are usually rinsed in cold water and left to dry.

Prestige of Women Marketers

It is significant that although the women's role in vending is very valuable, if not indispensable, to the economy of the household, few women claim to derive prestige from their work. Chiñas probably correctly attributes this to the model of the middle-class, Westernized woman who is often the customer, but never the vendor. San Juan is not cut off from the world, and the middle-class consumer can be observed both in the town, among the tourists, and in the movies. As a whole, the Zapotecs devalue any labor, no matter how remunerative, as opposed to "white collar" or office work. Women, particularly those who sell tortillas or other foods, feel that they must do this because they have no other skills.

At this point, it should be noted that although women of Esperanza and women of San Juan Evangelista live totally different lives in terms of contacts with the larger world, economic self-sufficiency, and their relationships with their families, both are inclined to devalue their own activities and their own status.

Perhaps the seeds of this devaluation are not to be found in the economic sphere, but rather in the life cycle through which each woman passes.

Childbirth

Babies, Chiñas tells us (1973:51), are born at home, aided by the local midwife, women relatives, and the father, whose role is very important. Not only does he encourage his wife during the period of her labor, but he places the afterbirth in a ceramic jar and buries it under the floor of the house. Baptism, under the sponsorship of a couple chosen as *compadres*, follows normally within the first month or two of the baby's life. Infant mortality is high, with critical periods being the first three months of life and again, after weaning, in the first year of life. If the death of a baby occurs, it is regarded as a responsibility of the mother who failed to protect it from supernatural evil forces.

Child-Rearing

Children are reared and socialized by women in the home. Chiñas (1973:53) notes that for the most part, children are raised gently, with mild scolding being the most frequent form of discipline. Although wife-beating and child-beating are known, they are not condoned. Boys are, as might be expected, allowed much more freedom than girls, and household quarrels often revolve about the unjust distribution of chores resented by the teen-age girls. Boys are more likely than girls to attend school until they are at least 12 years old. Girls, on the other hand, begin to help with household chores and care of younger siblings when they are as young as six. This care is, however, confined to the house and its immedeiate vicinity. By the age of seven, girls may go out to the market for their mothers, and learn to count and make change. After puberty, such trips may cease because, as in other Hispanic influenced cultures, much stress is laid on protecting the virginity of young women and rigorously confining and chaperoning their activities. After puberty, until she is about 16, the girl spends most of her time under the tutelage of her mother who teaches her the necessary preparative skills which she will use in adult life. Occasional opportunities to go to the market in El Centro have already been mentioned.

Courtship

Courtships may be generated at the occasional fiestas where the girl is under the scrutiny, not only of her own mother, but of every woman in the pueblo. "Every woman considers it her duty to report any misconduct to the girl's mother," writes Chiñas. Where errands must be run, the girl will be accompanied by younger siblings who tend to act as a distraction, if not as chaperones. However, one of the customs observed in San Juan is the *paseo*. On Sunday evenings the people of San Juan stroll around the plaza, two groups are formed, one walks around in one direction; the outer group walks in the opposite direction. Whole families participate and girls may walk out on Sunday evening accompanied by their small brothers and sisters. As people pass each other, boys and girls have a chance to "review the field." Often a young couple are attracted to each other and may even speak a few words to each other discreetly in view of the whole pueblo. In a successful courtship, the young man may eventually walk with the girl of his choice and her small chaperones, if she permits it. This is tantamount to an engagement announcement. Parents are well aware of these maneuvers, and if they object, they may forbid the girl to walk in the paseo or confine her to the house. If they make no objection, men of the boy's family will meet with the girl's parents to obtain their formal consent. In earlier years, a series of ritualized exchanges between the groom's family and the bride's family used to occur. Banns are posted and announced over a public address system a month before the marriage takes place.

Marriage

Marriages take place at the church at 8 AM on Sunday mornings. After the marriage, the couple and the wedding party return on foot to the home of the bridegroom. The ceremonials proceed throughout the day. In the morning the groom's friends and family are toasted and entertained. The bride's family arrives about noon and stays for two hours. The couple then remain alone with the groom's kin. Chiñas (1973:56) tells us that traditionally, the marriage was consummated in the presence of one of the groom's elderly female relatives. Today this is no longer done, but the groom's family waits outside the room until the groom delivers a handkerchief stained with blood to his mother as evidence of the bride's virginity. The groom's mother then leads a procession to the bride's house, carrying a basket filled with red flowers and the handkerchief. The procession to the bride's parents' home is marked by fireworks and music, and can scarcely be ignored. The young couple does not take part in the procession. The following day, the bride's mother leads her kinship group in a small fiesta in which the girls pass through the streets and the market, sprinkling red confetti on bystanders to mark the success of the venture. This ritual is so degrading and traumatic that many young couples elope in order to avoid it.

Residence after Marriage

After marriage, the couple resides patrilocally with the man's parents until several children make the building of a new house desirable. Sometimes the young wife finds it onerous to live with her mother-in-law, since she is generally held in low esteem until she has produced several children. More frequently they do get along and men continue to live with their parents and care for them in their old age. The status of a woman in her husband's household improves with the length of the marriage and the maturation of the children.

Women as Mourners

The final act in the life cycle, death and mourning, is more exacting of women than men. Women are the official mourners, spending long hours kneeling behind the corpse reciting prayers and chanting. Since burial usually occurs within 24 hours of death, such mourning usually involves only one day. However, prayers are said for the deceased on eight successive nights. Women of the household in which a death has occurred are expected to be secluded for 40 days. Men can resume their work immediately after the funeral. The length of time during which women are required to wear mourning varies with the closeness of the relationship to the deceased, but women's mourning clothes are always more elaborate than those of the men, who wear only an armband.

Women in Ritual

One of the most striking features of peasant life in San Juan Evangelista is the degree to which women take part in ritual. A very important aspect of village Mexican life is the fiesta, usually held to celebrate various saints' days, such as the patron saint of the village — in this case, San Juan. The patron saints of a particular church or barrio are honored by fiestas that last several days. There are elements universal to all fiestas. These are processions, fireworks, music, feasting, and dancing. Each fiesta must be sponsored by a Mayordomo who, acting alone or with several others, bears the expense of food, drink, hiring musicians, and buying the fireworks. This can be very expensive and, as Wolf (1966) notes, may be a means of redistributing wealth in a peasant community. In most areas, the men are mayordomos and the women work very hard to provide the food and drink, the decorations and costumes, but they do not receive formal recognition. In San Juan, however, the fiesta is regarded as a family contribution. Chiñas (1973:70) states:

> The role of each sex is so vital that if a man is unmarried, his mother, sister, or other close female relative will be chosen to act as mayordoma. Or if the household has no male head, the woman acts as mayordoma, and chooses a close male relative to fill the role of mayordomo.

Private Fiestas

In addition to the major public fiestas, private fiestas are also held. These are most often held to commemorate deaths or to celebrate marriages. Kin, compadres, and guests are invited. The guests usually include families who had previously invited the hosts to their fiestas. The more fiestas one gives, the more fiestas one is invited to and hence the greater one's status. Persons of greater status are invited more frequently than others. Invited guests are expected to make a monetary contribution to the hosts, but women pay less than men, and close kin pay more than friends. Men pay their contribution at a separate table from the one at which women pay theirs. A woman may pay her husband's share, his *cuota*, in his absence, but a man usually does not pay the woman's share called a *limosna*. When a woman pays her limosna, she is entitled to a portion of sweet wine and a cigarette. During the evening, the women may drink beer, as this is the only occasion when a respectable Zapotec woman will do so. Most fiestas are opportunities to socialize; often there is music and dancing.

Chiñas (1973:82) finds that jealousy is prevalent in San Juan, and the envy of others is strongly feared and guarded against. She noted that moving of goods from one residence to another or to market, or consummating a commercial transaction usually occurs after midnight. This is done to avoid the risk of having one's possessions seen and perhaps envied by others.

In terms of role behavior, or what Chiñas calls public and private images, she finds (1973:111):

> In San Juan Evangelista, one is first a human being, an individual, and only second and incidentally a man or woman. While the sexes are usually segregated, perform different tasks, wear distinct clothing, and behave differently, none of these differences is viewed as marking the essential inferiority of one sex in relation to the other. Women do not do agricultural work except to help or direct the picking of fruit on occasion, yet most of them know enough about agriculture to manage their land with hired labor, should it become necessary. Men usually do not do woman's work, but this seems to be more because there are women and girls to do it than because of any strict aversion to "doing woman's work." One father did the laundry by hand for a large family for a period of time when the mother was ill and no hired help was available. Nobody thought his actions unusual, and it was obvious doing the laundry posed no threat to his virility.

Women as Allies

Zapotecan women are also solidary in their relationships with other women. Sisterhood is extended to protect women from any threats to their safety or reputation. Drunken men are always feared as possible woman molesters, and a woman will warn others of the approach of a *borracho*, or drunkard. Women will find safety and protection in the tienda of another woman even though they may be scarcely acquainted. Secure as women, there is no evidence of jealousy between women over a man's affections. There is, however, jealousy between women when they feel that another woman threatens their close friendship. Women will band together to discourage a man whose behavior displeases one of them. *Machismo*, the Hispanic cult of violent masculinity, is disapproved in San Juan among Zapotecs in general.

However, despite these unusual values, there remains the fundamental distinction between public and private spheres or domains, as first expressed by Friedl (1967). Within the public sphere there are certain roles played by women. The women vendors of San Juan Evangelista perform functions in the public sphere. There are also positions in which a man and woman both have status, as in the mayordomo and mayordoma of a fiesta. However, in both public and private spheres there are differences in role which Chiñas designates as formal and nonformal. "Formalized roles are those which are given formal status and recognition by members of the society. That is to say, every adult member of the society recognizes the existence of the role and has a fairly clear concept of the rights and duties the role demands. . . ." (Chiñas 1973:93). Within the private sphere, a woman's formal role as mother and wife is clearly defined.

Women in the Public Sphere

A woman's role as vendor in the public sphere is distinctly lower than that of merchant or comerciante, the licenses for which are given to men or to husband and wife teams. However, there are no women vendors who are formally designated as comerciantes. A comerciante is publicly recognized as having higher status than a vendor. In the private sphere, in addition to their activities as mothers and housewives, women use, indeed exploit, social connections and kinship to maintain a network of communication. Many business arrangements are made through these channels of communication and men knowingly use them for such purposes. The networks are also valuable as mechanisms of social control and the women knowingly use them in this way. However, although men recognize and use these networks, they are not considered a formal role in the sense that being a housewife is a formal role.

Power and Authority

This seems to be an elaborate, if scientific, method of recognizing a fundamental fact of women's lives, one that has been mentioned earlier. Women have power, but they do not have authority. The women of San Juan regard the likelihood of a woman becoming a member of the local government as ridiculous as the idea of a woman becoming a priest. In actuality, due to their extensive social networks, their contacts with the larger urban areas of El Centro and San Jacinto, women may be better suited to become governmental officials on a local level. They do, indeed, wield power. Men recognize that having a wife is not only an economic advantage, but almost a social necessity. Without a wife or other adult woman relative, a man has no access to the network of communication between families in the pueblo. Without a wife a man is often at a disadvantage in dealing with another man whose wife has kept him informed. Chiñas (1973) cites several instances in which women, exploiting knowledge obtained from other women, have smoothed the paths of their husbands in both business and social matters.

Not only do women have power as parts of a network of communication, they also have power in terms of their mobility. Women can go to El Centro at any time and not arouse suspicion, whereas a man would be conspicuously breaking his routine. A woman, then, can often carry messages, or tend to business which her husband would prefer to keep secret.

Women and Social Control

Another informal role played by women is that of social control, particularly at fiestas and within the pueblo itself. When men become aggressive or abusive, it is their wives or mothers or sisters who act to keep them from harm. If a man drinks too much at a fiesta and starts to behave in a manner considered improper, his female kin, including fictive kin, will remonstrate with him, call his attention to his poor manners and his loss of esteem. They will, if necessary, maneuver him to the exit and evict him. Women regard sexual aggression as something they should take care of, and they will band together to do so. In fact, Chiñas (1973:104) says:

> It seems to be an unwritten law among Isthmus Zapotec women that women stand united in the face of any threat of any kind of unwanted or improper attention from a man, whether the man is stranger or brother.

Peasant Women in San Juan Evangelista and in Esperanza

In general, then, there is a strong contrast between the lives of peasant women in Esperanza and in San Juan Evangelista. In San Juan, although women have no authority, they do have power and mobility. In Esperanza, they seem to have neither of these. This should not be accepted at face value. It is entirely possible that the difference between two peasant societies may lie more in the sex of the investigator than in the society itself. Further investigation is warranted before any conclusions can be drawn. Of the status of women in San Juan Evangelista, Chiñas (1973:96) says:

Within the limitations just set forth — that women's roles are never dominant over men's roles in any society — there is, nonetheless, great variation from one society to another in the status of women as a group compared to men from equal at one pole (albeit different) to enormously unequal. Theoretically one might place all societies on a continuum designating the status of women as compared to men from equal on one pole to grossly unequal at the other pole. On such an imaginary continuum, I would perhaps place the Yanamamo of South America as reported by Napoleon Chagnon (1968) and the Tiwi of North Australia as reported by Hart and Pilling (1960) near the low status pole. The Isthmus Zapotecs, I believe, would be near the high status or equal pole. Where our own society would fall, I am not prepared to state at the present time, although it would certainly be lower than Isthmus Zapotecs.

3. SARAKATSANI WOMEN OF GREECE

The Shepherds of Greece

If we go by the strict definition of the term peasant, which means people who grow crops for subsistence and for the market, and are part of a modern state, the people we are to look at next would not be considered peasants because they are not an agricultural, but a herding, society. However, if we stick to the broader context of the term, which means people who live out in the country, and make their living by producing or processing a natural product for both local consumption and a national market, then we can include the Sarakatsani, or Greek shepherds. For many centuries these people led nomadic lives seeking pasturage for their sheep. Their travels took them across national boundaries in the Balkans, Turkey, and Greece. As nationalism rose in those countries, boundary lines became fixed and the nomadic shepherds found themselves restricted in their wanderings. J. K. Campbell (1974:6) who studied these people, claims that he finds no evidence to prove that the Sarakatsani were ever anything but Greek.

Transhumance

Whatever their origin, today they are confined to a limited area in which they practice transhumance; that is, they move from summer to winter pasturage each year. The Sarakatsani own their summer pastures, which are in Zagori, a mountain district in the province of Epirus; in the winter they move down to coastal plains and are dispersed over an area that stretches from the Albanian frontier to the southernmost tip of Greece. They must rent these pastures, which are increasingly scarce and costly. The particular group of Sarakatsani that were studied by Campbell numbered about 4,000 people, and had herds of about 85,000 sheep and 13,000 goats. The summer pastures are lush and receive plenty of water; however, snow comes early and they become bitterly cold. The people are thus forced to move to winter pasturage, where they feel alien, as indeed they are, and look forward to returning to their villages in the mountains for the summer.

Subsistence

The lives of the people are hard. The flocks of sheep are owned by families and constitute the wealth of the people. There is constant rivalry over both sheep and pasturage. Families vie against each other to increase the amount of either of these resources. Sheep-herding under these conditions is not an exercise in bucolic relaxation. Rather, the shepherd must stand guard day and night to prevent wolves or other shepherds from getting at his flock. He must move the sheep from areas with poor grazing to those with better grass and must help the sheep not only to bear lambs, but also to wean the lambs early so as to have a generous supply of milk from which to make cheese. This work taxes the physical strength of the shepherd, and also encourages the development of aggressive personalities, since man is constantly in contest with nature and with other men.

Social Organization

The basic unit of the society consists of a father and his sons living and working together. As the sons marry, their wives are brought into the father's household. Usually, after the death of the father, the household unit works together under the supervision of the oldest son; however, these units break up soon after the oldest grandson reaches his fifth birthday. When each brother begins to recognize that he will have to provide land and sheep for each of his sons, as well as dowries for each of his daughters, he stops working the family lands and flock and starts to concentrate on maximizing his own holdings. Although pasturage is reallotted each year, the flocks of sheep are the source of family wealth and every effort is bent toward increasing their numbers.

What is life like for women in this world of aggressive men, harsh, natural conditions, and constant struggle. Let us following Campbell through the life cycle of a typical Sarakatsani woman.

Childbirth and Childhood

As might be expected in a society where fortitude is necessary for survival, a woman is expected to bear her pains with dignity and in quiet. During labor, she is given a blanket to bite on to muffle her screams. Other women will talk or laugh or beat tin cans to drown out the noise of the mother. Usually, an older woman acts as midwife.

From the day the infant is born through his first four years of life, he is the recipient of the most tender care and attention from all members of the household. This permissiveness extends to both boys and girls. Between the ages of four and seven, when children of both sexes start school, they are kept close to their mothers. They are given appropriate toys to play with: girls pretend to spin wool or play "mother" to dolls made of rags and sticks; boys receive miniature shepherds' crooks, which they use in imitation of their fathers and uncles. From age seven on, the children attend school, which is compulsory. During this period, the father occasionally disciplines the children while the mother, although she never interferes, acts as comforter. When they are about 13 years old, both boys and girls leave school. It is at this time that sex differences become more marked. At 13, boys begin to work under their father's direction, and girls begin to do the myriad jobs of the mother. Usually the mother, knowing what is in store for her daughter, will not make her work too hard. Unmarried girls spend their time spinning, knitting, and doing lighter tasks, except during the lambing season, at which time they carry the lamb and the ewe to the pasture from the sheepfold early in the morning and early in the evening. The ewes and lambs are brought nightly from the pasture to sheepfolds which are cleaner and better protected and located nearer to the huts (Campbell 1974:32).

Growing Up

From the age of 17 until marriage, the nubile girl is supposed to exhibit an entirely different appearance, a sense of "shame" (Campbell 1974:45). During menstruation she is not allowed to approach the sheep directly, nor cross in front of the flock. Her relationship to her father becomes one of deep respect; she stands when he sits and she helps her mother serve him. Her clothing is designed to conceal her sexuality. Campbell (1974:287) states:

> The maiden's cultivation of her shame demands that her clothes hide her femininity. Her hair is hidden under a black, cotton scarf. A girl who, by artifice or accident, allows her scarf to become frequently undone, gains an evil reputation.

Her clothing consists of thick, black, homespun blouses and woolen sweaters buttoned to the neck. The blouses are deliberately shapeless to hide the developed bust. A long, black, woolen skirt is worn. Three or more underskirts are worn to enhance the shapeless effect. So great is the sense of shame at her own body that the girl never washes her body between the neck and ankles, and seldom changes her undergarments. Her hands, feet, face, and hair, however, are frequently washed. Her movements must be slow and deliberate. Running, or even falling, are regarded as shameless. A girl should walk with pride, upright, but her eyes must be ast downward. The entire object of this dress and behavior is to avoid the slightest hint of sexual attraction.

Woman's Honor

It is a young woman's greatest duty to remain a virgin until after she is married. Her fathers and brothers pledge their lives to this goal: if a girl is molested, raped, or shamed, the father is also dishonored and the duty of the brothers, usually those who are unmarried, is to find and kill the man responsible. In turn, the relatives of the rapist or molester are then under obligation to kill a relative of the avenger, and thus an endless blood feud, which threatens the delicate balance of relationship among the Sarakatsani, is promulgated. It is perceived that a woman is in some way responsible for provoking such assaults by improper behavior. Her sex is regarded as shameful in and of itself. If a woman so dishonors her family, she is killed.

According to his perception of the Sarakatsani, Campbell (1974:31) states:

Women and goats are conceptually opposed to men and sheep. Goats are unable to resist pain in silence; they are cunning and insatiate feeders. Greed and cunning are important characteristics of the Devil and Sarakatsani will often say that although Christ tamed these animals, the Devil still remains in them. Sarakatsani keep some goats to exploit that part of their grazing land which is unfit for sheep. But as animals they are despised and a stani with too high a proportion of goats to sheep loses prestige. Women are not, of course, simply creatures of the Devil, but the nature of their sexuality which continually threatens the honor of men, makes them, willingly or unwillingly, agents of his will. It is consistent, therefore, that in the practical division of labor, women rather than men care for the goats.

Marriage

Men regard sexual intimacies as a chore which must be completed in order to provide the desired goal, a son. Immediately after the marriage ceremony, the bride and groom usually have some privacy for about a week. After that they share common sleeping quarters with other members of the groom's family. A man out herding his sheep is not expected to return home more often than about once every 12 or 13 days. If he desires intercourse more frequently, he arranges to meet his wife clandestinely.

Rivalry among Shepherds

Since pasturage is redistributed annually, neighboring herders change annually. Moreover, good pasturage is in short supply. There is a great deal of tension between people whose grazing lands adjoin each other. The lack of fencing adds to the possibility that a neighbor's herds will "steal the grass" from one's own herds. Men do not leave their sheep alone at night for fear that some other group will trespass. This anxiety eventually spreads to all people except one's own kin. All other kin groups are potential "grass stealers," sheep rustlers, and, in general, enemies. George Foster (1965) has conceptualized the high level of hostility among peasant families on the basis of the idea of "limited good." According to him, in the peasant's world view, good things, pleasurable occurrences, and particularly wealth and resources are in finite supply, and therefore if one person or family has more than another, in terms of wealth or even good luck, it is at the expense of the rest of the population. Harris (1972) has more recently suggested that this concept is not unrealistic, in that the access to resources in peasant society is unequal. The risks to fields and herds are great and cannot cme under the peasant's control. Peasants do make conscious efforts to equalize wealth; for example, in Mexico the mechanism of fiesta-giving, where wealthy families act as mayordomos, redistributes the wealth. Among the Sarakatsani, even the annual redistribution of pasturage does not suffice to lessen hostility. The view of limited good, in this case, certainly, reflects reality because of the unequal quality of the pasture lands. If one group of kin gets better land, another group will get worse land. Even if it is recognized that next year a new distribution will be made, there is a drive to better the pasturage this year at the expense, if necessary, of the neighboring group. The attitude of constant hostility among different kin groups is based on real competition for land. The balance between sheep and land is precarious at best. A Sarakatsani must maximize his herds in order to provide dowries for his daughters and flocks for his sons to inherit. The drawing of finite national boundaries prohibits the shepherds from moving freely to other areas. The pasture land that they own is constantly in danger of being overgrazed. What land is had must be held on to at all costs, and an attempt to get a little more from a neighbor is deemed a fair practice.

Marriage as Alliance between Rivals

Marriage, which may not take place between kindred, involves "a contract between two hostile groups" (Campbell 1974:39, 124):

And since the prohibition on marriage within the kindred compels the Sarakataros to find a bride among families who are not related to him, that is among people who are hostile to himself and his interests, this marriage contract is in the nature of a peace treaty between two previously-opposed social groups.

Nearly all marriages are arranged. There are rare, sporadic bride abductions, but in most cases, the marriage negotiations are carried on between kindred of both the bride and the groom. In fact, the bride and groom may never have seen each other until the betrothal. The negotiations are undertaken by one of the groom's kinsmen, who must proceed indirectly in order to avoid a direct refusal, which would be considered an insult, which would have to be avenged in blood.

Dowry

The matters of most concern are the size of the dowry and the honor of the families. Both Friedl (1959) and Campbell note that the bride's dowry does not go to the groom's family, but is managed by the groom for the ultimate inheritance of the couple's children. The representatives of both families meet in a neutral place and talk about neutral things — the weather, the sheep. Eventually, the groom's representatives will state that he has a relative of marriageable age. Since these matters are common knowledge among the villagers, each negotiant always knows the purpose of the meeting and, indeed, the size of the dowry. The groom's representative then asks outright whether the bride's family will form an alliance with them, and he also states the terms of the dowry. The bride's representative asks for time to consider, and promises an answer in about a week. Since both negotiators were aware of the proposition prior to their meeting, such a meeting usually brings positive results. The betrothal itself is now formalized by a party given by the bride's family for the groom's family. At this function, which takes place on a Sunday, there is food, drink, and dancing. The bride and groom also exchange rings. Campbell (1974:126) says:

> There is something inappropriate about this act of commensality between future affines. At the moment of betrothal there are only feelings of suspicion and distrust between the two sides. This is reflected in the unhappy record of betrothal feasts since this village custom was adopted. Brawling between hosts and guests is not infrequent and generally the result of these celebrations is that relations between the two groups deteriorate yet further.

The actual marriage occurs within an agreed period of time after the betrothal. Seldom are such betrothals broken; to do so by either side would dishonor the other side and thus provoke a blood feud.

Claiming the Bride

The groom and his kinsmen go to the bride's home to claim her. A religious ceremony of betrothal occurs, and then the bride is escorted to the home of the groom, which will be her future home. The leave-taking from her family is very sad. The bride's family as well as the bride herself recognize that conditions will be hard for the young woman. It is taken for granted that after four or five years of marriage, the blooming young maiden will scarcely be recognizable.

Humility of the Bride

When the groom arrives at the bride's house, and before the ceremony of betrothal occurs, the groom's brother puts a pair of new shoes at her feet. Usually he places a coin in the right shoe. This is to mark her new pathway in life. The brother then takes the bride's right hand in his. She thanks him in a low voice and then bends forward, raises his hand to her lips, touches it to her forehead, and once more to her lips. The groom's sisters or sisters-in-law present the bride with jewelry and kiss her cheeks. She, in turn, kisses their hands. The bride then kisses her family and leaves. The girl, who has been through several days of ceremonials during which she spent most of her time standing, is tired, weak, and frightened.

The Journey and Arrival

During the journey to her husband's home, her horse is led by the groom's sister. Once arrived, she must respectfully greet her new father- and mother-in-law. She kisses their hands and, wearing bracelets of bread and carrying wine, she walks to the far side of the hut where she kisses the hands of all of the groom's family who did not form part of the procession. She even kisses the hands of the small children. In this way she indicates her submission. From Sunday until Tuesday night the bride remains in her husband's hut. She is surrounded by the women of his family. Whenever a person enters the hut, she must stand up to show respect and lower her eyes to the ground. She may have to do this for several hours at a time. On Monday, the following day, she must lead a dance, dancing with the man who arranged the marriage, her husband, her father-in-law, and brothers- and sisters-in-law. On Tuesday morning she makes sweetened coffee for her parents-in-law and serves them silently as they give her their blessing. At noon she prepares a special rice pie. Shortly thereafter, the guests, all relatives or friends of the groom, start to leave. Each one must have their hand kissed by the bride. They give her a small amount of money and she gives each a woven bag. The bag given the men contains bread, meat, and cheese. The women receive smaller, embroidered bags. The man who originally made the marriage arrangements gives the bride 100 drachmas and she, in turn, gives him the first blanket in her dowry. Now she gives shirts, socks, and embroidered bodices to her husband's immediate family and they give her clothing in return.

Consummation of Marriage

Tuesday night, for the first time, the marriage is consummated, and on Wednesday, the bride goes to the well with the women of her new family. A young man accompanies them carrying a standard which has flown from the roof of the groom's hut since Saturday. It is meant as a witness to the purity and virginity of the marital pair (Campbell 1974:63).

The Young Wife

The bride begins her new role of wife. Her first job is to carry a barrel of water back from the well. Since this is one of the hardest jobs, it will fall to the lot of the newest bride for quite some time. The following day, under the eyes of her mother- and sisters-in-law, she must do the whole family's laundry, including her own, which should show signs of blood, from the loss of her virginity. Campbell (1974:64) reports:

> The essential fact is that the new bride is subordinate to all other adults in the extended family. . . . In general, it can be said that any hard or unpleasant work will be delegated to her. . . . She addresses her husband's brother as "master" and his sisters as "mistress."

In all likelihood, except for the biannual visits to her own family, she will never hear her baptismal name again. She is now addressed as "bride." Early in the marriage, the bride will stand up and remain standing when any man of her husband's family comes into the hut. Her husband is careful to pay very little attention to her. He gives orders; she obeys. She never initiates conversation. She takes orders from all members of the household. After the first week of conjugal intimacy, the young couple share blankets on the floor with the rest of the family. Part of the bride's duty is to be the last to lie down. She covers each member of the family with another blanket, puts out the oil lamp, and then lies down.

The Visit Home

The second Sunday after the marriage, the bride and groom return to the bride's natal home. There is food, drink, and dancing. At first, Campbell (1974:136) states that behavior is formal and stilted. After a while, people relax and, although she is weary and worn, brides have been known to try to join in the singing.

There are two purposes to this visit. Primarily, it is an opportunity for the bride's parents to see how she is faring. Since one of the groom's female relatives is constantly near her, the bride cannot express her sentiments overtly, but in a covert fashion she is often able to communicate with her family.

The second purpose of the visit is to reconcile both sets of kin; their mutual interest in the offspring of the marriage is shown. In terms of conciliation, however, the "return" is often a dismal failure. Campbell (1974:127) tells us that after the bride and groom have left, there are lengthy discussions among the bride's kin: "Invariably the criticism is very unfriendly and reveals the hostility of the affinal relationship, a hostility, however, which must no longer be openly expressed."

Woman's Work

On her return to her husband's household, the woman's work will consist of preparing food and clothing, baking, cutting wood for the fire, carrying water and laundry. Women gather wild vegetables and in summer cultivate a small garden. They tend the goats, and card, wash, spin, and weave the wool. They care for sick sheep and lambs and they wean lambs from the ewes. Except for the initial help given by men in erecting posts and cross-beams, women build the huts in which they live. Campbell (1974:33) tells us that five or six women working together continuously can build such a hut in two or three days. All clothing is made of wool, and many hours of labor go into washing and preparing the newly sheared wool.

Naming the Bride

As time passes, and as new brides enter the houshold, the first bride may no longer be addressed as such. She is now called by her husband's name with the suffix "ina" added — for example, "Theodorina," "Periclina." With the birth of her first child, a woman gains some status in the eyes of her husband and his family. Her husband can now openly converse with her because she has joined in a common endeavor with him. They are both concerned with rearing this child and other children to come. A man's honor, his wealth, and his pride reside in his sheep and his children. His wife, who remains subservient in all respects to him, his father, and his brothers, is now responsible for rearing his children with honor. His sons must be brave, and his daughters pure.

The Breakup of a Joint Family

In a household containing several brothers and their wives and children, pressures begin to build up toward separating the common herd and breaking up the household into neolocal units. The men claim that this is necessary because the women quarrel. This may be true to some extent, but in reality each brother begins to feel the pressure to amass larger herds, and more property and money to endow his children. He has his wife's dowry which he may manipulate for this purpose. Jealousy arises when one sister-in-law feels that another sister-in-law drains the family wealth of more than her share. The young cousins who grow up in this environment inevitably feel the tensions and resent each other. On the other hand, they form close friendships with the cousins on their mother's side, whom they see once or twice a year, but with whom there is no rivalry.

Eventually, joint households break up, and each former bride becomes a potential mother-in-law. Only through her children can a woman hope to achieve status of any kind. Therefore, the mother is extremely agitated by any possibility of illness or defect in her child. Daughters, who will be suffering under the same conditions as their mothers did after marriage are usually treated kindly, and they return this affection to the mother. The bond with sons, however, is much stronger. The son is aware of his mother's suffering at his birth, at the harshness with which she has been treated, and the gentleness with which she has treated him. Campbell (1974:168) states: "The bond between mother and son is indestructible. She gave him life; in him she fulfills herself and transcends the moral inferiority of her sex."

As sons grow and marry and bring their brides into the household, the cycle repeats itself with the woman being regarded now as "mother." As such, the Sarakatsani offer her a measure of respect. There is a popular saying among them that the mother is the heart of the family. And yet, she cannot relax in her dress or behavior because her conduct reflects now, not only on the honor of her husband, but also on the honor of her children. This is particularly true of her daughters, whose marriages may be influenced by the mother's reputation. In transacting a marriage, the reputation of the father is important, but the reputation of the mother and the family from which she comes also play a large role.

Prevalence of Peasant Women's Roles

Many similar cases can be drawn from traditional China, Sicily, India, and from every continent and race where peasants struggle for existence. Whether anxiety, hostility, and jealously are perceived as irrational traditions or as realistic approaches to situations over which the peasant has no control, the fact remains that they are real, and are often displaced on to women. Women are cruelly repressed, physically assaulted, and deliberately degraded. Inevitably, women come to accept their society's assessment of their worth. One may wonder what conditions in the society would be like if the men turned their aggression from their women and their neighbors to those agencies responsible for their precarious economic condition.

Contrast among Peasant Societies

The contrast between the status of women in San Juan Evangelista, Esperanza, and here is probably due to many factors. San Juan Evangelista is not as isolated as the harsh Greek mountain habitat, nor is it as lacking in opportunity as in Esperanza.

The one common thread that runs through all three areas is the fact that men and women live separate and apart from each other, despite the fact that they share a common household. The Zapotec women upon whom Chiñas has reported are a refreshing contrast to the restricted lives of Puerto Rican and Sarakatsani women. There is, then, among peasant societies as among other types of societies, a broad range of conditions under which women live.

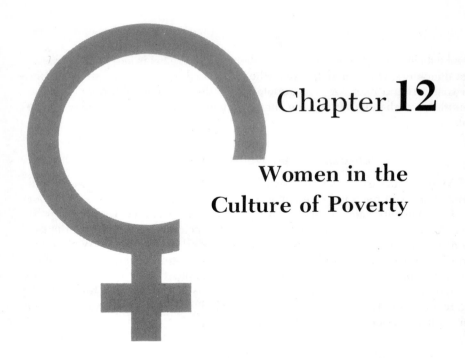

Chapter 12

Women in the
Culture of Poverty

1. NANGOLI AND ADUPA OF THE IK

Oscar Lewis (1961:xxiv) states his definition of the culture of poverty as follows:

> To those who think the poor have no culture, the concept of a culture of poverty may seem like a contradiction in terms. It would also seem to give poverty a certain dignity and status. This is not my intention. In anthropological usage, the term culture implies, essentially, a design for living which is passed down from generation to generation. In applying this concept of culture to the understanding of poverty, I want to draw attention to the fact that poverty in modern nations is not only a state of economic deprivation, of disorganization, or of the absence of something. It is also something positive in the sense that it has a structure, a rationale, and defense mechanism without which the poor could hardly carry on. In short, it is a way of life, remarkably stable and persistent, passed down from generation to generation along family lines. The culture of poverty has its own modalities and distinctive social and psychological consequences for its members. It is a dynamic factor which affects participation in the larger, national culture and becomes a subculture of its own.

The Ik

Nangoli, the Ik, tells the story of how modernization can destroy a society. As foragers, the Ik had lived reasonably well. The process of nationalization which followed World War II created boundaries that prevented the Ik from following their usual rounds. In addition, the story of Nangoli illustrates a conflict of values in modern society which may not easily be resolved. Conservationists are anxious to preserve the natural wild life of Africa. They are rightfully concerned about the extinction of species other than man everywhere in the world. But, they are often unaware of the fact that such preservation may take a human toll. The Ik, excluded from their usual hunting areas by the creation of a game preserve, are quite literally starving to death. Another reason for telling the story of Nangoli was to point out that, although extreme circumstances may erode those qualities we value as human, there are unusual people who can rise above such conditions. A real decision had to be made with respect to which category — Indigenous People or Culture of Poverty — the story of the Ik belonged. Since the condition of the Ik seemed to be due entirely to nationalization and its consequences, it was grouped with those of other people whose lives have been disrupted by the growth of modern society.

Strictly speaking, the Ik cannot be classified as members of a culture of poverty, since they have never been peasants and do not live in an urban situation. But in their own way, they meet all the criteria that Oscar Lewis originally set up for the culture of poverty. Their dire circumstances are due to nationalization, a product of modern society. They exhibit the violence, squalor, and physical and mental trauma of the culture of poverty. Colin Turnbull (1973) relates their story.

Prior to World War II, the Ik were a hunting and gathering population whose rounds included the areas of northern Uganda, southern Sudan, and western Kenya. Most of their time was spent in the high mountain valley of Kidepo. Turnbull (1973:21) makes the point that as hunters and gatherers, they depended as much upon vegetable food as on the animals they hunted. Sedentarism more quickly depletes the vegetation than the animal population. This makes seasonal migrations necessary and adaptive. Although they spent much of their time in Kidepo Valley, they left the valley during the rainy season and fanned out in small bands throughout the mountains into Sudan and Kenya. With the rise of nationalism, the Ik were encouraged to settle permanently in the Kidepo Valley. The borders to Kenya and Sudan were closed. Kidepo was declared a game preserve, and the Ik were expected to settle down and become good farmers. Whether this was possible or not remains a moot question because one of the worst draughts in history afflicted the area. Even seasoned farmers were unable to get along, and for the Ik, starvation became a way of life.

Of earlier conditions, when the Ik were still hunters and gatherers, Turnbull (1973:25) states:

> Although women and children are not used during the hunt which involves stalking rather than beating, their cooperation is still required. . . . The women are always close at hand, and occupy themselves by gathering while the men hunt. In this way they are even drawn into the evening debates when it has to be decided where to hunt the following day, since the vegetable food gathered by the women

is every bit as important in the diet as meat. This is another widespread characteristic of hunting and gathering societies, the cooperation and equality of importance between men and women.

Into an Ik Village

At the time of Turnbull's first visit, the conditions among the Ik were
neither known nor imagined to be as bad as they were. Turnbull's first contact
with the Ik occurred at the Assistant Administrator's post. Here, in the relatively comfortable village, he met two Ik who were studying at the mission
school, and with them he made the journey up to the mountains to find the
small Ik villages. Turnbull had to get the permission of the Mkungu, or chief,
before he could visit the villages themselves. The Ik villages are surrounded by
several nomadic herding societies who cross over and through Ik territory from
time to time, such as the Dodos and the Turkana, who are herders and rather
fierce cattle raiders. The Ik, particularly the young people, often accompany
the Dodos or the Turkana. There have been a small number of intermarriages,
but most often the relationships between the Ik and the herding tribes consist
of Ik attempts to steal some cattle. Similarly, the closest non-Ik settlement to
the villages is a police post, which is set up to administer the area for Uganda.
The police are often called upon, but not to mediate disputes; rather, they are
foils for some techniques the Ik have to use in order to obtain food. A typical
incident involved the third wife of one of the Ik who lured one of the police into
what might be described as "a compromising position." She thereupon began to
scream "rape, rape." Her husband just happened to be nearby; he set up a
tremendous fuss and had to be put in jail to quiet him down, but meanwhile,
the "guilty" policeman was so anxious to avoid having the details of the incident
become public that he paid off in large contributions of food, sugar, and tobacco.

Turnbull has been criticized for "moralizing," when he relates the fact that
when one of his guides from the mission school reached the village, he did not
inquire after his ailing mother, but rather was interested in food. Turnbull
(1973:49) said:

> Thomas came over then and said it was time we were going as there was no food
> here. I mentioned his mother and said she was sick, but he was not interested.
> . . . Then he moved on and at another spot called through the stockade to his
> sick mother a filial greeting, "Brinji ngag" to which he received the reply, "Vera
> ngag" (Give me food — There's no food") This exchange of formalities was ap-
> parently all that was required after a two-year absence, and without further ado,
> we set off, but not along the escarpment.

The criticism directed to Turnbull is not well founded. The shock apparent
in Turnbull's later encounters with the Ik are those of a sensitive and empathetic human being faced with the dehumanization of people who were

deprived of their basic needs. No anthropologist would logically deny this, and yet we may be too prone to the so-called scientific methods of strict neutrality and objectivity, even in the face of the horrors of Ik life. Turnbull's initial reaction was profound shock. He later tried in some small measure to help individuals in the society. When he found he was merely prolonging their agony, he desisted and lapsed into depression. He then reported as accurately as he could, not only the condition of the Ik, but also his personal reaction to them and even his pessimism about their survival as a culture. To do less would not have made him a better scientist. Turnbull shows how essentially fragile human values are, how people in dire need react. This is something we as scientists should value. Bronowski (1965:63–64) says:

> Science is not a mechanism but a human progress, and not a set of findings but the search for them. Those who think that science is ethically neutral confuse the findings of science, which are, with the activity of science which is not . . . . That is why the values of science turn out to be recognizably the human values; because scientists must be men, must be fallible, and yet as men must be willing, and as a society must be organized to correct their errors.

As scientists we need to know how hunger can destroy a people. And we need to feel strongly about it so as to "organize to correct our errors." Divorcing social science from values may be even a more gross distortion of what anthropology is all about.

The interaction between Thomas, the young boy from the missionary school and his mother was but a mild foreshadowing of things to come. In the village around the police post, most of the Ik were young and seemingly adequately fed. The real horrors lay up in the mountains where people who were too weak, too old, or too young to make it down to the police post starved to death in silence.

Starvation

Turnbull (1973:121) tells us that the villages are composed of individual compounds, each with a stockade. The compounds contain sleeping huts, granaries, and outside kitchens. Each wife, for the Ik practice polygamy, has her own hut. Every granary Turnbull saw was empty. Children are not allowed to sleep in the house after they are "put out" at the age of three or four at the latest. From this time on they must fend for themselves (Turnbull 1973:236). The children form into bands according to age because alone they have no chance of survival. These bands do not welcome newcomers because young children often are of little value in the constant quest for food. However, if the child stays with the band for several years, eventually he or she becomes adept at finding anything edible in the area. The food is often a matter of dispute because several bands roam the same area and often battles between bands who lay claim to the same food ensue. Figs were most sought after, but berries and tree bark were eaten most often. Turnbull states that when driven by hunger, children even swallowed earth and pebbles. After a period of time, the leaders of the band become too big and the other band members turn him out. If he survives, he must then become a junior member of an older band. Senior bands range further afield in their search for food. Children learn to steal, to lie, and to fend for and rely only upon themselves.

The two most touching examples of the Ik way of life are the stories of Adupa, a young child, and Nangoli, an older woman.

Adupa, the Child

Turnbull (1973:133) relates the story of Adupa simply:

Hunger was indeed more severe than I knew, and the children were the next to go. It was all quite impersonal — even to me in most cases, since I had been immunized by the Ik themselves against sorrow on their behalf. But Adupa was an exception. Her stomach grew more and more distended, and her legs and arms more spindly. Her madness was such that she did not know just how vicious humans could be, particularly her playmates. She was older than they, and more tolerant. That, too, was madness in an Ician world. Even worse, she thought that parents were for loving, for giving, as well as receiving. Her parents were not given to fantasies, and they had two other children, a boy and a girl who were perfectly normal, so they ignored Adupa except when she brought them food that she had scrounged from somewhere. They snatched that quickly enough, but when she came for shelter, they drove her out, and when she came because she was hungry, they laughed that Ician laugh, as if she had made them happy.

Partly through her madness, and partly because she was nearly dead anyway, her reactions became slower and slower. When she managed to find good fruit peels, skins, bits of bone, half-eaten berries, whatever, she held it in her hand and looked at it with wonder and delight, savoring its taste before she ate it. Her playmates caught on quickly, and used to watch her wandering around and even put tidbits in her way and watched her simple, drawn little face wrinkle in a smile as she looked at the food and savored it while it was yet in her hand. Then, as she raised her hand to her mouth, they set on her with cries of excitement, fun and laughter, beat her savagely over the head and left her. But that is not how she died.

Turnbull goes on to say that he started to feed her, which was probably cruel, because he had to physically protect her as he fed her. But the others beat her anyway, and Turnbull says Adupa cried, not because of the pain in her body, but "because of the pain she felt at the great, vast, empty wasteland where love should have been." Turnbull (1973:132) continues:

It was that that killed her. She demanded that her parents love her. She kept going back to their compound, almost next to Atum's and closest to my own.

Finally, they took her in and Adupa was happy and stopped crying. She stopped crying forever because her parents went away and closed the *asak* (door or gateway) tight behind them so tight that little Adupa could never have moved it had she tried. But I doubt that she even thought of trying. She waited for them to come back with the food which they promised her. When they came back, she was still waiting for them. It was a week or ten days later, and her body was already almost too far gone to bury.

The Realities of Hunger and Effects of Malnutrition

Hunger has caused the Ik to abandon all joy in having or rearing children, and it has made them lose all respect for the aged. Turnbull (1973:205) speaks of one old man who, emaciated and starving, nevertheless was a valuable informant. Turnbull made the mistake of giving him some food and tobacco. As a former ritual priest, Lolim's information was valuable. He had long lost any standing in the "community," since his intercession had not succeeded in getting the gods or ancestors to provide food. Nevertheless, Lolim took the packets of food and tobacco and headed for home. He was immediately set upon by two other Ik who beat him and nearly strangled him to get at the packets which hung around his neck. Turnbull stopped that attack, leaving Lolim on the ground rolled up in such a way as to protect his food. The children then set upon him, even his own grandson, beating him with sticks on the hand and everywhere that could be reached. They only ceased when the old man lay motionless and soundless on the ground. Turnbull tried to aid Lolim's widow who had been abandoned by her kin. However, this expenditure of medicine and food on a worthless old woman was fiercely resented by the Ik. As to famine relief, Turnbull tells us that the food was dispersed at a central village. Only the young were strong enough to make the trip to the village. Once there, they took the allocations for all the people in their village, and promised to distribute it. But they never did. The young people, if they did not prosper, at least survived. Children and the aged died.

All of life centered around two basics — getting food and defecating. Because of starvation, constipation was a major problem. The bloating of malnutrition made people uncomfortable and they tried very hard to eliminate. Sometimes they squatted for hours, just trying to relieve themselves. All ritual had been lost. The announcement of a pregnancy was greeted with deep hostility — another unwanted child to compete for food. Marriages and rites of passage were no longer celebrated. Even death came too often to be either feared or recognized. Turnbull (1973:22) states:

Villages were villages of the dead and dying, and there was little difference between the two. People crawled rather than walked — the very young and the very old, all crawled.

Nangoli, the Woman

Turnbull's attention was first drawn toward Nangoli by her neighbor, a potter, who had given her some water. The potter found Nangoli and her husband, Amaurkuar, to be very peculiar. They helped each other get food and water and they brought it back to their compound to cook and eat together. Turnbull says that both Nangoli and Amuarkuar were thin; Amuarkuar was merely skin and bones, but he was sprightly, and climbed and clambered up and down the mountains at that time when Turnbull first came to the area. After a while, Nangoli and her husband spent much of their time in the national park where they gathered what they could. Even if they had had the strength to hunt, it was forbidden. No doubt there was some poaching by some of the stronger young men, but they were equally good at stealing cattle from the Dodos and the Turkana. Nangoli's activities in the game preserve were probably illegal, which raises the question: Are people being destroyed while game is being preserved?

Traditions of the Long Ago

Old people like Nangoli and Amuarkuar remembered the traditions of earlier life. They recalled marriage celebrations and the frequent, but structured disputes between husbands and wives. For minor offenses, such as cooking food badly or not bringing water, a man had the right to beat his wife with a stick. She also had the right to fight back and, if she could get hold of the stick, beat him with it. In more serious offenses, a husband would, speaking loudly for the benefit of the neighbors, pronounce all the offenses which his wife had committed against him. He would then gather some thorny branches from a special plant with which to beat her. Usually a woman packed her possessions and left while the husband was haranguing the neighborhood.

There used to be a ritual which forbade the husband from entering his wife's hut for a week after the birth of a child. Now this has been discarded because the man has nowhere else to go. Women were expected to nurse their children for at least two years. Now women cannot even nurse for a short time. Certain foods were forbidden to pregnant women, but under present conditions, such food taboos are ignored. The woman in labor, angry at herself and her husband for having to bear this pain which only leads to another mouth to feed, ignores many of the earlier taboos against lying on her back, or looking at the peak of her roof. Formerly, when a child ailed, a ritual priest was called to perform ceremonies and prescribed herbs; now, no effort is made to save it. Upon her first menstrual period, a girl left home to seek another girl in the same condition. The two girls built a house together and stayed there until they married. There was no particular, elaborate initiation ritual, nor was there a sense of danger or uncleanness associated with menstruation. Girls are now "put out" long before their first menstruation.

The Death of Amuarkuar

During Turnbull's stay, old Amuarkuar died of thirst. He was too weak to accompany Nangoli on the food quest. Until the end, he was gathering grasses to make a little shelter in his compound, since the roof of the house had caved in and he had been unable to leave the house to relieve himself. He was too weak to go to get water, and Nangoli was off gathering food. He wanted her to have a shelter to return to. As Turnbull says, his last act was a social act, even though he died performing it. Turnbull (1973:210) says:

> When Nangoli returned, she did an odd thing, she grieved. She even expended energy to demonstrate her grief; she tore down what was left of their home, for it had been more than a mere house. She uprooted the stockade, she abandoned her little field running into the *oror* (ravine) . . . tearing up whatever was growing, and leaving it to wither still further in the baking sun. But if she cried, I did not see it. Then she fled, the skinny, old woman, with a few belongings rolled up and slung across her back, held by a tump-line against her forehead. She did not speak to anyone; she just left, heading for Kidepo.

Nangoli Leaves the Village

Nangoli then joined other people who were kin to her, and crossed over to Sudan where they built a new village. The new village had no resemblance to any of the other Ik villages Turnbull had seen. It was not barricaded and stockaded, but had only one fence of scrub along the outer perimeter. When he first saw it, Turnbull states that the village was empty. The Ik who accompanied Turnbull to the new village helped themselves to tobacco and water from unguarded stores. There were baskets of vegetables, and meat was drying on racks. The huts were clean, cool, and comfortable. There was a central hearth in the village center, about which people evidently gathered. All of this was in marked contrast to the villages Turnbull had seen, with their heavy fencing, the exclusion and mistrust of others, not only neighbors, but even close kin. After a short time, Nangoli, her three sons, her daughter and her husband returned from the hunt. They greeted their visitors with warmth, and did not appear concerned that the Ik had helped themselves to food, tobacco, and water. After dinner was cooked that night, people gathered around the fire and talked. They did not mention or compare their previous village to the present one. They spoke, rather, of the hunting that day — who had been adept, who had not. After a while, the women and children, Nangoli's daughter and daughters-in-law, and her grandchildren, went into the huts to sleep while the men remained around the fire. Turnbull remarks that it seemed like another world. One of the daughters-in-law even served her husband a dish of fruit, something that she had never done in the old village. The dramatic change in behavior could be due only to one simple fact: there was no hunger here. There was meat, there was fruit. Nangoli's family were hunting and gathering in the old way, and were behaving in the old way too. True, they were acting illegally; they had no "right" to be where they were. But they had food.

Return to the Village

Yet, Nangoli and her children were to exhibit even more remarkable characteristics, because shortly after Turnbull's visit, they returned to the village they had left. "They could not bear to be alone," Turnbull (1973:233) explains. Although Nangoli was joined by her daughter and son-in-law in the village in the Sudan, it was they who persuaded Nangoli to return to Pirre, the village they had left. Nangoli herself told Turnbull (1973:247) that she had been persuaded, not coerced, into making the return trip. The human side of Nangoli compelled her to prefer companionship, whatever its nature, to material sufficiency.

Indeed, Nangoli and her family remained unusual, in that they remained a family. Turnbull (1973:252) says:

> Never did I see a family member helping, even offering a word of encouragement. The only exception again, was Nangoli, for she was always with her family, and perhaps significantly she never was with anyone else.

Isolation of Starvation

Nangoli was unique in this miserable world in many ways. She managed to find pleasure and allowed her children to know pleasure. Her son, who was unmarried, was the only Ik who admitted to enjoying sex. Most Ik equated copulation with defecation. Their serious malnutrition undoubtedly affected their sex drive. But perhaps along with the problem of nutrition there was the problem of isolation. The Ik, isolated as they were from each other by starvation, greed, and jealousy, could not feel strong feelings of affection for each other. They had to learn to turn inward in order to survive. In fact, they did not even have the emotional capacity to feel their isolation; they were, with the exception of Nangoli, incapable of being lonely.

Nangoli did not feel lonely, since she lived with her family. She understood the harshness of the world in which she lived, but she met this harshness with a "bringing in" rather than a "putting out" of family, as did the others. Although too old and weak to work herself, she helped her children choose appropriate fields, showing them where to build terraces, and finally, well aware of the nature of her neighbors, she guarded the terraced field.

A "Good Year"

It would be pleasant to report that the drought ended, that the Ik returned to generosity, that they picked up once more the rituals and traditions which made them a distinctive group. Unfortunately, this is not the case. The drought did indeed end, and the rains brought a good crop, but:

The fields which at first promised to be so encouraging, were even more desolate. They were full enough, both those on the steep slopes and those on the lesser slopes.

Every field without exception had yielded in abundance and it was a new sensation to have vision cut off by thick crops that waved all around me, with maize reaching far above my head. The reason for the desolation in the midst of this abundance was that every crop in every field was rotting through sheer neglect.

People were stealing from other people's fields even though they had an abundance in their own. Nobody seemed to think of storing food; the granaries remained empty of grain to be used for seed in the following year. Turnbull said the Ik could not even reap the benefits of a good year. Their relationships with each other had fissioned beyond repair. Their sense of relationship with the environment had been dormant for so long that it no longer existed. According to Turnbull, the Ik as a people no longer exist. They continue as individuals in various places, but they have proved incapable of reviving that which made them distinctively Ik. There is a limit to any culture's capacity to adjust. The change from hunting and gathering to farming was traumatic enough. Setting up a game preserve and limiting mobility by creating national boundaries added stress to the situation. The drought which can be counted upon to return every four years was simply the final stress which fractured the society.

As for Nangoli, Turnbull (1973:271) says that he does not know what happened to her. He heard that she and her family made a futile effort to get the village to move. Failing in this attempt, they returned to Sudan. Wherever she is, if she still lives, she is proof of the possibility of remaining human even under extreme duress.

2. CAROLINA OF SÃO PAULO, CHILD OF DARKNESS

Favelas

In Latin America, some of the most stimulating cities, grand and new, or rich and old, are surrounded by a perimeter of shacks. Occasionally such shacks are situated in the heart of the cities. These shacks, built of scrap wood, with whatever materials came to hand, and roofed sometimes with tin or other scrap, form a *favela*, the haven of the culture of poverty in Brazil.

People who come to the favela are those who have been dispossessed from their land by a natural phenomenon, such as drought, or by human agency. Those who have never had land, but have merely worked for others also live there. The favela contains the urban poor, the unemployed, and the unemployable. The favelas are often equipped with a single spigot for water. Sometimes, one of the favela dwellers will run a single line of electricity into the favela and charge his neighbors for the use of the electricity for which he pays nothing. The cruelty and callousness, which we have seen among the Ik, are also found in the favela, for much the same reasons — hunger and desperation.

Carolina's Diary and Its Impact

Out of a favela in São Paulo, Brazil, in 1963, came one of the most articulate cries of horror. A woman, Carolina Maria de Jesus, a favela dweller, had miraculously written a diary. In 1958, a reporter, Audalio Dantas, covering the opening of a playground near one of the favelas, heard a woman shout at the grown men who were competing against the children for the swings. She shouted: "If you go on mistreating these children, I'm going to put all your names in my book." The reporter, curious, asked the woman what kind of a book she had. It took him quite some time to earn her confidence and to be permitted, finally, to see the notebooks which constituted the diary of Carolina Maria de Jesus. It was longer still until the reporter became chief of a São Paulo magazine, and was able to publish the diary. Finally, in 1961, the book became available in Portuguese. It became an immediate best seller. In 1963 it was published in English. It is a cry from the heart; it shows the indomitable courage some people have in insisting upon remaining human under the most dehumanizing conditions. The favelas are still in São Paulo and in other cities in Latin America. Carolina's diary was read, but had little impact on the internal and international conditions which make and keep favelas a way of life.

Hunger and Humaneness

The diary was so long in coming to light because Carolina herself had learned well the rule of the favela, which is the same as the rule of the Ik: do not trust anyone who seeks to do you a kindness; he may in some fashion be trying to take from you what little you have. The mutual distrust, the envy, the cruelty, the cunning which reside in desperate people can be brought forth wherever hunger undermines the basic humanity of people. To be penned up in an arid nonproductive territory, to be penned up in a ghetto or slum, to be deprived of the basic necessities of human life, to be deprived of the basic right to human dignity is a dehumanizing process. It should not be surprising that when such people find their way out of the ghetto, the slum, the favela, the barren hills, they are not sweet, pliable, understanding human beings. They have learned to be hard, cunning, and mistrustful or they would not have survived. As middle-class people sit down to their comfortable breakfasts to read the newspaper, deplore the crime rate and violence of slum areas, they have good reason to fear. No segment of society can be dehumanized and then be released and expected to become humanitarians. As the walls of the enclaves are breached, the hatred, the violence, will spill over. The only defense is to lower the barriers, to distribute resources more equally. Law and order are foolish slogans which are as unrealistic as most clichés. Law and order can only exist where there is justice. Carolina Maria de Jesus tells us of the justice she and her children experienced.

Carolina's Birth and Early Life

Carolina was born in 1913 in Minas Gerais, in the interior of Brazil. She was the illegitimate child of a farm worker. She completed two years of schooling, and learned how to read and write. At the end of those two years, her mother moved to a farming area where she got a better job, and Carolina's formal education ceased. Several years later, her mother moved to another town where Carolina, who was now 16 years old, got a job in a hospital. She held various jobs until she ran away to São Paulo, where she worked as a maid and was fired several times for insubordination. Eventually she became pregnant by a Portuguese sailor who deserted her upon learning of her pregnancy. She brought her infant son to the favela. She fed her child and herself by collecting rags, scrap metal, and papers and bringing them to a junkyard. She strapped her infant to her back and made the rounds of the city. She says that on good days she made 25 or 30 cents. Some days she made nothing. She had an affair with a white Spaniard who gave her some money during their relationship, but who eventually left her to return to Europe. Her second son was born. She continued the life of ransacking garbage cans and alleys for scrap. She next had a relationship with a white man, who gave her food and money for her children. She bore him a daughter.

Carolina Starts to Write

It was in order to escape the grinding poverty of her life, the cruelty of having to deny her hungry children more food because there wasn't any, that she started to write. She wrote on notebooks and papers salvaged from the trash bins. She lived as isolated as she could from her neighbors, fearing and despising them at the same time. When her book was published and Carolina was able to leave the favela, her neighbors surrounded the truck which contained her few possessions. She was moving to a small house in the suburbs. They shouted at her that she had made money writing about them and refused to share it. They shouted that she, Carolina, had done worse things than they, and she was profiting by it. Finally, they began to throw stones and debris at her and her children. It was with great urgency that she beat upon the hood of the truck to get the driver started.

Her diary for 1955 is relatively brief. She was only writing sporadically at that time. An entry for July begins:

> The birthday of my daughter Vera Eunice. I wanted to buy a pair of shoes for her, but the price of food keeps us from realizing our desires. I found a pair of shoes in the garbage, washed them and patched them for her to wear. I didn't have one cent to buy bread. So I washed three bottles and traded them to Arnaldo. He kept the bottles and gave me bread. Then I went to sell my papers. I received 65 cruzeiros, I spent 20 cruzeiros for meat. I got one kilo of ham and one kilo of sugar and spent six cruzeiros on cheese. And the money was gone.

Carolina states that she makes her living by picking the garbage cans of São Paulo. She sells whatever she can to rag and paper buyers. The amount of money she receives seldom covers the needs of her children.

Carolina's life in the favela is made more difficult by her neighbors who engage in drunken brawls, wife-beating, and malicious gossip. Carolina says: "I can't stand these favela women; they want to know everything. Their tongues are like chicken feet, scratching at everything."

Food Distribution

There are several groups and institutions which give food to the favelas sporadically. The Spiritist Church is one. Other churches also make food distributions from time to time. Carolina also states that occasionally merchants unload trucks of spoiled food in the favelas. She accounts for this by stating that the merchants hoard food, hoping to sell it at higher prices. When the food is old enough to be spoiled, it is given to the favelados.

Another form of food distribution occurs when election time draws near. Politicians invite people from several favelas to come to a central place where they will receive gifts of food. Carolina tells of the throngs who gather at the distribution point. The politician is there, as are the photographers. People are ordered to wave the bread they have received in the air for the benefit of the photographer. Carolina claims to have seen a pregnant woman faint during one of these distributions. Some people have come from as far as 50 miles away to receive a piece of bread, a little bag of candy, and a school ruler engraved with the name of the politician. Carolina states that the reason she cannot take regular employment is because she must care for her three children. This care involves carrying water from the community spigot, gathering firewood for warmth, laundering, cooking, and even safeguarding her children from the neighbors. On one occasion five sacks of paper which Carolina was storing near her house to take to the junk dealer were burned. Carolina is certain that one of her neighbors was responsible for this.

Carolina is extremely skeptical of the intentions and the actions taken by national or local government. On one occasion, the health department came to test the people for worms. Carolina did not even take the test. She did not believe that the government would distribute free medication, and she had no money to buy any.

Carolina has documented some of her interactions with the government. For her, the city is a paradise. She must trudge daily through the lovely streets, pass the fine houses and pretty gardens, pass the shop windows, pass the well-dressed and perfumed women, and return at night to the squalor of the favela, which stinks of human dirt and excrement, is muddy and filthy, and is filled with examples of human misery. Carolina is not naive, for if she were, she could not survive and pull her children through. She (1962:36) says:

> What our President Senhor Jusceline has in his favor is his voice. He sings like a bird and his voice is pleasant to all ears. And now the bird is living in a golden cage called Catete Palace. Be careful, little bird, that you don't leave this cage, because cats when they are hungry think of birds in cages. The favelados are cats, and they are hungry.

Carolina documents one of her efforts to get help from agencies of the government (1962:42, 43). In June 1957 she had injured herself carrying a heavy load of scrap iron. She went to the Social Service agency. She reports:

> How painful it is to see the dramas that are played out there. The coldness with which they treat the poor. The only things they want to know about them is their name and address.

She went to the Governor's Palace where she was sent to an office. There she was sent to the Social Service at the Santa Casa Charity Hospital. She spoke with a clerk who "said many things and yet said nothing." She then returned to the palace where, she says:

> I came here to ask for help because I am ill. You sent me to Brigardeiro Luis Antonio Avenue and I went. There they sent me to the Santa Casa. I spent all my money on transportation.
>
> "Take her," an official said to a soldier. They wouldn't let me leave. A soldier put his bayonet at my chest. I looked the soldier in the eyes and saw that he had pity on me. I told him: "I am poor. That's why I came here."

Eventually she is returned to the favela in a squad car and warned against making any further scenes in the welfare office. Her cynicism extends to all branches of the government. She speaks of the politicians who only show up at election time:

> This year we had a visit from a candidate for deputy, Dr. Paulo de Campo Moura, who gave us beans and some wonderful blankets. He came at an opportune moment, before it got cold.

Carolina's Relationship to Men

Carolina's cynicism colors her relationship to men. She has seen too many men mistreat their wives to want marriage for herself. She tells of one woman who gave birth to a boy, which for some reason so displeased her husband that he beat her up and threw her out of the house. She hears nightly the cries of her neighbors and despite her abject poverty, she claims to feel at peace.

Occasionally the father of Carolina's daughter comes to visit. He usually leaves a little money. When Carolina let it be known that her diary was to be published, he came to make sure that she would not mention him by name. On that occasion he gave her 100 cruzeiros. Her life on the streets of São Paulo has made her very tough. Once she passed a factory where she found a pile of kindling. She was about to pick it up when a black man who was piling the wood on a truck told her to stop or he would hit her. Carolina (1962:76) told him to go ahead and hit her because she was not afraid. He called her a "nut" and she answered:

> And it's just because I am crazy that you'd better not mess with me. I've got all the vices. I rob and fight and I drink. I spend 15 days at home and 15 days in jail. I am from the favela of Caninde. I know how to cut with a gilette and a razor and I'm learning how to handle a fish knife. A noresta (refugee from the Nord Este area of Brazil) is giving me lessons. If you want to hit me, go ahead.

She starts to search her pockets and then goes on:

> Where's my razor? Today you're going to walk around with only one ear. When I drink a few *pingas* I go half crazy. It's that way in the favela, anybody who shows up there, we beat them, steal their money, and everything else they have in their pockets.

Peace and Food

Carolina's two most important goals are peace and food. Peace is unobtainable in the favela. She tells of men beating women, young men beating their fathers. Of one teenager, she says that he beats his father "as if he were beating a drum." She is frightened for her children; she fears the impact of such violence upon them.

Food, too, is a constant problem. Often she and her children go hungry. Food that the boys find in the garbage is often covered with roach droppings.

The greed of the food merchants is uppermost in her mind. Brazil's high rate of inflation is a major factor in the inability of the poor to get food. Carolina says that lentils at one point were selling at 100 cruzeiros a pound, the same amount of money that the father of Carolina's daughter gave her to keep his name out of her diary.

When a warehouse was flooded and the rice stored in it was ruined, Carolina reacted in the same way as she had to the trucks which dumped spoiled canned sausage in the favela. She felt that the merchants were conspiring to hoard food in order to drive the prices up. She was happy when flooding caused their plan to backfire. Perhaps the best expression of Carolina's attitude toward hunger is in her diary (1962:108):

> October 7. A child died here in the favela. He was two months old. If he had lived, he would have gone hungry.

Success

Carolina's final words are recorded by David St. Clair, who translated the diary from Portuguese. He says (1962:150):

> Recently on a television program a well-dressed, well-fed Carolina said: "If I wasn't so happy, I would cry. When I first gave my manuscript to Brazilian editors they laughed at this poor Negro woman with calloused hands who wore rags and had only two years of schooling. They told me I should write on toilet papers. Now these same editors are asking for my works, actually fighting for them.

> Today I had lunch in a wonderful restaurant and a photographer took my picture. I told him: "Write under the photo that Carolina who used to eat trash from trash cans now eats in restaurants. That she has come back into the human race and out of the Garbage Dump."

3. CONSUELO OF MEXICO CITY

The Children of Sanchez

When Ocar Lewis defined and described the culture of poverty, he did so in connection with his work in a *vecinidad* in Mexico City. He established a long and strong relationship with a family whom he called Sanchez. His methodology was unique in its time. He had each member of the family record, on tape, the story of his or her life. They spoke in their own words, and each gave his own version of incidents which affected all of them. The family consisted of four children which Jesus Sanchez had by his first wife: two boys and two girls. The autobiography with which we are particularly concerned is that of Consuela, the elder of the two daughters. She was younger than the two boys, only four years old when her mother died.

The Vecinidad

At this time the family, who lived in the Casa Grande, was relatively well off. The Casa Grande is located in the heart of Mexico City, ten minutes from the Zocalo. It is spread out over a block, and surrounded by cement walls. Inside these walls are among the most poverty-stricken people in Mexico City. They inhabit rooms not unlike the huts they left in their peasant villages. Many of the inhabitants are related by consanguinal or affinal kinship. Of course, many are related through compadrazgo. There are shops on two sides of the Casa Grande. Most of the inhabitants seldom venture beyond these boundaries. For the most part, the men are unskilled and so their jobs are underpaid. Women and children work or beg. Young boys beg and steal and get into trouble with the police. The Casa Grande is, as Lewis (1961:xv) states, a world unto itself. The courtyard is where people gather; the women often do their work there, while the men and boys gamble and fight and also worship the two patron saints of the vecinidad.

Childhood

Of her early childhood, Consuelo remembers her great fear of her older brothers who used to beat her often. Her father, whose love she seems constantly to demand, was one of the few men in the vecinidad with regular employment. He was a waiter and food purchaser for a restaurant in the city. Shortly after her mother died, her father remarried. Her new stepmother, Elena, was kind to her and Consuelo remembers her with affection. Her brothers, however, tormented her and each other. She recalls one of them throwing a knife at her and nearly hitting her with it. Above all, she recalls the sternness with which her father treated the children. No one but Marta, the baby, could disturb him. Consuelo was in the unfortunate position of being a middle child and a girl. As such she was not protected by being the baby of the family, and she ranked lower than either of her two brothers. During her stepmother's life, the family acquired a substantial amount of furniture compared to others in the vecinidad. They had chairs, beds, a radio, a wardrobe, all of which were bought on time payments. Elena took the children to Chapultepec Park, and to Xochimilco, a favorite Sunday recreation for people in Mexico City. Often, but secretly, they went to visit their maternal grandmother. These visits were kept secret because Consuelo's father did not get along with his former mother-in-law.

Consuelo recounts that on her first day in school, a lady offered to hold her new cape and school supplies. Needless to say, the lady disappeared with them. Unfortunately, Elena soon contracted tuberculosis and had to be placed in a sanitarium. Shortly thereafter, she died. A series of bizarre living conditions now ensued. It seems that Jesus had another wife and daughter, and Consuelo was faced with a half-sister older than herself. This girl, Antonia, was brought into the house to take care of the children with the aid of a charwoman who did the heavy household tasks. Consuelo felt that Antonia usurped her place in her father's affections. She remembers being scolded for not obeying Antonia. Most of all, she remembers her father showing more respect and affection to Antonia than he did to Consuelo or her sisters and brothers. Antonia's mother, Lupita, worked at the restaurant with Jesus.

Consuelo, the Wage-Earner

Immediately after graduation from school, Consuelo went to work, first with a dressmaker and then in a shoe factory. During this year she started to attend the dances in the vecinidad. She accomplished this by sneaking out of the house after her father and brothers were asleep. Consuelo found, to her surprise, that some boys thought she was attractive. She claims never to have felt any particular affection for these boys with whom she danced. In truth, she may have been wary because the Mexican cult of *machismo* is based upon the number of successful conquests a man can make. Knowing this, fathers and brothers are especially protective of daughters and sisters because each is seen as a possible statistic in some man's machismo score. Finally, Antonia brought the Sanchez household to an end. She tricked Consuelo into accompanying her to the public bathhouse. She disappeared from there and was found later that night at the railroad station. She had been jilted by her boyfriend and was pregnant. Shortly thereafter she took some "strong herbs" to induce abortion, but which brought on a series of violent fits. She had to be taken to a sanitarium. When released, she and Jesus joined the household of Jesus's other wife and her two daughters. The other children were left at Casa Grande. Consuelo recalls it this way:

> One afternoon my father said, unexpectedly, "I'm moving to Rosario Street. That's where I'll be. I'll come to see you every day. Do you want to come or stay?" (Lewis 1961:132)

After Jesus left, Consuelo says he kept his word and did come every day to give them money for expenses, but she was disconsolate:

> My father's presence was everything. With him there, I felt my home complete. Now I began to have a feeling that was unbearable. "Am I not my father's daughter? Is it a sin to be an orphan, my Lord?" I kept asking. I cried for my mother and waited and waited for an answer (Lewis 1961:132).

The New Household

Now the household consisted of Consuelo's brother Manuel, his consensual wife, Paula, Roberto, Consuelo, and Marta, the youngest sister. Consuelo loved the children born to Paula. She especially favored the first baby, a girl, Mariquita. The entire family was disturbed by the lack of privacy. They all lived in one room. As Consuelo grew older, she took a more active part in the dances, games, and goings-on of the young people of the vecinidad. After a scolding from Jesus for her behavior on such occasions, she packed her meager baggage and moved to the home of Elena's mother. Her father came to get her and she moved with him into Lupita's house on Rosario Street. Consuelo admits that Lupita and her older daughters were kind to her. During this period, Consuelo was working in a shoe factory and giving her earnings to Jesus.

Working and Going to School

Later, Consuelo started to take a commercial course in secondary school. She was going to learn to do office work. But things began to go badly with the family in the Casa Grande. Marta, the youngest sister, became the consensual wife of Crispin, one of the neighborhood men. Their marriage was a stormy one, with Marta leaving and returning to the house in the Casa Grande periodically. Manuel, the married brother, beat his wife so unmercifully that she left him. But soon Jesus had to bring her back because she was dying. Now there were Consuelo, Jesus, Manuel, and his children, to be taken care of. Consuelo had a job in an office. She could not properly take care of her nieces and nephews. She persuaded her father to hire another girl, Claudia, newly arrived in the vecinidad from Zacatecas. Claudia took care of the children while Jesus and Consuelo worked. Soon the inevitable quarrels began. Consuelo saw her role as mistress of the house and Claudia as a servant. They quarreled and Claudia left. Consuelo sent for Delila, her sister-in-law's sister, to take Claudia's place.

Consuelo and the Middle-Class

During this time Consuelo first found employment as a typist. Her employer and his wife invited her to dinner and to the movies. She felt very uncomfortable at first because she was unfamiliar with the customs of middle-class people in her own country. She says:

> Seeing me disturbed, Senor Para said: "Would you like a drink?" "Caramba," I thought, "Are they going to drink? What will they say at home if I come back drunk?" I must confess that I didn't know it was the custom of the middle-class to drink aperitifs before dinner. In the vecinidad, to drink meant to get drunk. I was frightened, but I took the vermouth they offered. It was the first time in my life I had tasted it, and as I lifted the glass with my new friends, I felt very pleased and flattered (Lewis 1961:252).

About this time, however, Roberto, the younger of the brothers, was jailed for brawling and Jesus refused to bail him out. Consuelo borrowed the money to do so. In this way she put herself in debt to her employer who soon made it evident that he expected her to reciprocate by having an affair with him. However, since she was still unmarried and presumably a virgin, Señor Para told her that he would wait until she got married, when an affair would be easier and probably less risky for him. She then went to work for the licensiado who had helped her bail Roberto out. He, too, made sexual overtures. Consuelo left after two weeks, and went to work for an accountant.

Consuelo and Jaime

Her coworker, Jaime, was a young man who befriended her while she became familiar with the office routine. She began to see him socially and was soon "keeping company" with him. Unfortunately, Jaime soon showed his worst side. He was a heavy drinker, and Jesus refused them permission to marry. They had to wait three years, probably to see if Jaime could conquer his drinking problem. Jaime's mother encouraged the relationship. Although they were novios, Jaime flirted with other girls at the office, something Consuelo could not accept with the traditional stoicism of women in *machismo*-oriented cultures. When the three-year probabion period was almost up, Jaime confessed that he had spent the money he had been saving toward their marriage. He blamed this on the fact that Consuelo had quarreled with him and broken off relations at one point in their engagement.

Consuelo Leaves Home

At about this time, things became worse at home too. Delila and Consuelo fought as bitterly as Claudia and Consuelo had fought. Eventually, after one climactic battle, Jesus threw Consuelo out of the house. After this incident, Jesus says:

I did a bad thing when I chased out Consuelo. She went off with that fellow out of anger, pure anger, but it wasn't I whom she punished, it was herself who was hurt. I said: "My little daughter, you stained your life forever" (Lewis 1961:488).

It seems that while Jesus had a romantic attachment to Claudia, he managed to impregnate Delila, and felt honor-bound to marry her. He regretted, in his story, not having moved far away from the vecinidad after this marriage. In any case, Consuelo was homeless, and without prospect of marriage since Jaime was becoming more drunken all the time. She eventually found a home with her mother's sister and her husband. In Mexico, among traditional people, it is unthinkable for a young woman to have an apartment of her own; she must be under the protection of a male relative. At first, Consuelo enjoyed living with her aunt. She was permitted more freedom in attending dances in the vecinidad. Her father and brother found her at one such dance. Consuelo says:

> Face to face with my father, I stood up to him, ready for anything. He said: "What a spectacle you are making of yourself, you fool." He said it was a fine life I was leading, going to dances and from one house to another. "Do you want to end up on the streets?" When he said that, I exploded with rage. Before, I had always lowered my head at his words, but not since he had thrown me out of the house for that woman. I answered him, clenching my fists, "If I go out on the streets, it will be your fault. All I do is follow the example you have given me. First that Claudia and now this woman . . ." (Lewis 1961:270).

Although she was slapped by both her father and her brother Roberto, she refused to return home with them.

> I screamed at them, "Hit me, hit me all you want, but you'll never wipe out the hate I have. I am your daughter, but you'll get tired of *her* and afterwards no one will remember who she was. I warn you that if anything happens to me, it will be your fault and your fault alone . . ." (Lewis 1961:270).

Consuelo Loses her Job

At first, Consuelo found living with her aunt pleasant. The aunt even made an unsuccessful attempt to reconcile Jesus and his daughter. Toward the end of June of that year, Consuelo took sick, stayed home from work without reporting sick, and lost her job. Her uncle and aunt were unable to support her, and unwilling to have her live with them without making some contribution to the household. She soon found herself doing the laundry for the household, which she found difficult and demeaning. At the same time, Jaime arrived drunk. He felt that in her aunt's home Consuelo had lost status and he tried to attack her. After that, they had several confrontations, each more violent than the last. Jaime threatened her with a gun. He threatened to commit suicide. Consuelo tried to enter a convent to find the tranquility she needed. She was told that she had to be a legitimate child in order to enter the convent. Knowing her father and mother had never been legally married, Consuelo gave up the attempt. She subsequently met Mario, who lived near her aunt's home. She left her job and went back to live with her aunt.

Consuelo and Mario

At a particularly low point in her life, she agreed to go to live with Mario. Consuelo slept with Mario's mother, while Mario slept with his father, "Until the marriage ceremony could be performed," they said. His father got him a job in Monterrey, and he proposed to take Consuelo there. Consuelo says:

> Poor Mario. He took me to Monterrey, hoping to find true love. . . . But love is something both people must feel, a beautiful light that falls from above upon both man and woman. The light fell upon Mario but not upon me. I still loved Jaime and there was no room in my heart to love Mario. I was using him as a life rope to help me to get out of the deep well into which I had fallen. I planned that once he took me to Monterrey I would remake my life alone (Lewis 1961:286).

The Monterrey experience was a tragic one for Consuelo. Her relationship with Mario was stormy. She left him for a time and found a job. However, she soon became ill and had to go back to living with him. He tried his best to make her content, but she could not respond. Just as she was beginning to reconcile herself to living with Mario, a letter from his mother arrived. Consuelo learned that Mario had been married in church to another woman, by whom he had a son. Consuelo felt so helpless that she continued to live with him despite the knowledge that she could never marry him. In traditional thinking, she was "ruined," her life worthless. She had a miscarriage and sent a telegram to her father to come and get her. He did. Of that time, Jesus says:

> Imagine my heartache when Consuelo wired me from Monterrey a few years ago. I didn't have a centavo and had to borrow seven hundred pesos, a hundred here and a hundred there. I went and spent seven hundred pesos and there was no need to spend that money. Seven hundred pesos is a fortune. And then I left my work which I never do, even in vacation time (Lewis 1961:487).

Consuelo in Mexico City

Back in Mexico City, Consuelo again became embroiled in the family difficulties. She lived first with her aunt, then with her sister Marta, who had left her husband again. In each home, Consuelo quickly became dissatisfied. She took up with Jaime again, but this time on a different basis. He had been promoted and was earning a good salary, but his mother now objected to his courtship of Consuelo who was, in her terms, a fallen woman. Jaime offered to make Consuelo his mistress. Consuelo received several such offers. She found a room with a woman who lived alone with a servant. The woman, Juanita, told Consuelo that she was married to a doctor who only came home occasionally.

While he was away, she entertained male relatives. Consuelo says:

> I paid no attention to her goings-on, but she tried to influence me to take the same path. She wanted to introduce me to her visitors, saying, "Come on, Consuelo, don't be such a fool. You are so young. Who is there to stop you? I've had three husbands and I know that all men are the same cheats. You have to learn to take advantage of them. Life is for those who know how to live. Tell me what's stopping you?" (Lewis 1961:429).

Consuelo could not accept Juanita's advice although she confessed to an admiration and respect for her. A girl in her office urged her, also, to take what she could get. The girl, Carmela, offered to introduce her to a man who had lots of money.

Consuelo objected to the fact that the man was married.

> Married but not castrated, who tells his old woman not to know how to watch him? Listen, I'll introduce you to Leon. The old goat has lots of pesos (Lewis 1961:430).

It finally seemed that Consuelo was in reach of her goal. She got a job in a government office, making 540 pesos a month. She worked from 8:30 AM to 2:30 PM. In the evening she took lessons in English and applied for government housing.

At Christmas Consuelo found herself short of money. She had to furnish her apartment. She used candles, because she had no money for utilities. She commuted an hour to work; she had no time or money for food.

On Juanita's advice she tried out for the "Amateur Hour" on television. The judges decided that she would make a better dancer than a singer. They gave her a scholarship to take dancing lessons at the School of Fine Arts. After she had been trained, they assured her she would find ready employment in the theater, movies, or night clubs. She worked at her job during the day, and took dancing lessons at night. She had to take another loan to buy the necessary leotard, dance slippers, and pay the extra fare. Under such pressure she began to have headaches every morning and to lose weight.

One of her fellow students asked her if she would like to work as a movie-extra during the vacation. She accepted and earned 190 pesos for seven days of exciting and pleasurable work. That started her on a search for permanent work in the entertainment industry.

Consuelo's Gullibility

She was seduced by a minor actor, who, of course, offered to help her find work. She became pregnant and had to sell her clothing to finance an abortion.

This experience left Consuelo too "nervous" to work in an office anymore. She gave up her government job. She was in debt, three months behind in the rent, and Jesus refused to help her. She went back to the studio still looking for work. She was told she would have to join the union. At least this time,

Consuelo admits that she knew what was happening when the union official propositioned her, and promised to find her a job "on location." However, after that interlude, the man disappeared and no job materialized.

When making the final tape, Consuelo was living with an American student who had come to Mexico for a vacation.

Family Opinions of Consuelo

Her brother Manuel says of her:

The truth is, my sister was selfish. She was always looking out for herself. Ever since she got that bug about completing her studies, she felt set apart, as though she had nothing in common with us any more. Just because she had acquired a little learning, she became rebellious at home and no longer bowed down to paternal law. She claimed my father had no right to throw her out of the house because he was legally responsible for her. She was demanding a kind of legal justice from her own father, as though she were dealing with the government. But how could she do that? He was our father and had power over us (Lewis 1961:344).

Consuelo's brother Roberto sees Consuelo in another light:

My sister Consuelo had her own little apartment then, with a kitchen and bath. She had bought a wardrobe and sofa and with all that, it seemed to me she was high aristocracy. She kept telling me to come with Antonia to live with her. She thought we could start over again that way. Antonia was willing, but I didn't like the idea. "Look, sister," I said, "not with you. With your character I know that one day it will turn out bad for us. You better live in peace and let me set up a home of my own for Antonia so that I will feel like a man. . . ." (Lewis 1961:487).

Finally, Jesus Sanchez says of his daughter:

As much as I talk to Consuelo and give her advice, she doesn't listen. She doesn't give me a centavo. I don't want anything for myself. I want absolutely nothing from my children. Thank God, I am working for everybody What I build is for them. If she gives me anything, it would be put aside to pay for a lot to build a house for them. . . . Now my daughter must make her own way (Lewis 1961:488).

4. SOLEDAD OF NEW YORK AND PUERTO RICO

Comparisons

Oscar Lewis (1965) used his techniques of taping biographies, supplemented by questionnaires and participant observer methodology to study members of a Puerto Rican family, some of whom had migrated to New York. The relationships between the people in Puerto Rico and those in New York constituted what Carol Stack (1974:113) has called a network, or the matrifocal family.

The biography of Soledad is particularly interesting for the purposes of this volume because she spans the geographic distance between Puerto Rico and New York. Also, she represents a startlingly different personality from either Consuelo or any of the Esperanza women, and yet she is Puerto Rican and a member of the culture of poverty.

Soledad and Consuelo

Indeed, in the early years, the similarities between the lives of Consuelo and Soledad are striking. Both claim not to have been loved by their parents, both lived in households in which they were abused, both were children of a consensual marriage which was not the only marriage of either parent. Both women are young. We do not have Consuelo's age, but Soledad is 25. Both complain of many illnesses. This is where the similarity ends, because they have developed very different values and adaptive strategies.

Soledad and the Women of Esperanza

The contrast between Soledad and the women of Esperanza is even more striking. Esperanza is a rural area and Soledad lived her early life in a district of San Juan, the capital of Puerto Rico. The Esperanza women did not come through as emotional, sensitive people. They appeared to accept their lot with patience. There is no evidence that they tried to change the accepted order of their status or their lives. In contrast, Soledad is most vocal in her appraisal of her own and others' positions. She consciously works to change her position. She comes through as a very strong woman.

Early Years

Soledad tells us that the first six years of her life were uneventful. After that, her mother and father separated, and she went to live with her mother in a large household made up of aunts and cousins. After about two years, Soledad's mother sent her to live with her father and stepmother because she could not support her. This period is markedly similar to Consuelo's later years, when Jesus brought other women into the household. Soledad complained, not only of cruelty at the hands of her stepmother, but also of her father's indifference. Soledad returned to her mother, and her father paid child support. By this time, Soledad had a stepfather whom she neither liked nor trusted, and she found that her mother tended to side with her stepfather in most cases. She said that she grew up mostly in the street and was aware of the fact that her mother earned her living as a prostitute.

Soledad Goes to Work

At twelve, Soledad went to work as a housemaid for an Arab family. She went to school in the morning, to work in the afternoon, and was expected to do the housework for her mother and stepfather in the evening. In her case, as well as Consuelo's, she had not received any information prior to the onset of her menses, and felt frightened and guilty when she first became aware of the blood. She says: "I thought my stepfather must have dishonored me." She had several boyfriends, but in her words, "nothing serious." She felt kindly toward a boy from the country who treated her more courteously and romantically than the local boys. For some reason, her mother discouraged the romance. After a while, Soledad dropped out of school to work part-time in the laundry and part-time as a maid. Her mother had given up "the life" and also worked in the laundry.

Soledad and Arturo

Soon she met Arturo, her stepfather's foster brother. She was 13; he was 30 and already married. Soledad found him generous:

> I liked the smell of the lotion he used. He bought me clothes and he gave me money (Lewis 1965:158).

Soledad was aware of the fact that Arturo had a wife and child. However, she agreed to a consensual marriage with him. Arturo says:

> I got her easy, without any trouble. I told her mama about it right away. It has always been my custom to let a girl's parents know as soon as I get engaged to their daughter (Lewis 1965:167).

Soledad's life with Arturo was shadowed by the fact that they had no children for some time. They lived with Arturo's father and sister in the country, which also displeased Soledad. After three childless years of consensual marriage, Soledad moved with Arturo to San Juan. She adopted a little girl whose mother abandoned her. This child, Cataline, became the eldest daughter.

Almost immediately thereafter, Soledad became pregnant. By this time her relationship with Arturo had deteriorated to the point where he doubted the child was his. Soledad claimed that she never wanted marriage with Arturo. She says:

> I'm not marrying anybody. I don't like to be tied down. One can love without ever getting married. God only knows what would have happened if I had married Arturo. Maybe I wouldn't have been able to get a divorce. Some of my friends have married and been very unhappy. No, *hombre*, no. That's not for me. The day I get tired of a man, I walk out and leave him. That way I'm not obligated to him in any way (Lewis 1965:159).

Soledad accused Arturo of behaving badly toward her during her pregnancy. She claimed that she had to quarrel with him before buying any part of the layette. "It was my first child but it wasn't his first child, and you know what men are like." During the rest of that relationship, Soledad recalls moving into a government housing project which she did not like. Arturo became more violent, beating her and tearing her clothes. She claimed that he spent his money gambling, and then took money from her. Nevertheless, she became pregnant again, and had a little daughter.

Arturo, on his part, claimed that he could not stand the life in the district of San Juan, La Esmeralda, where Soledad had been raised and where she preferred to live. It was the wickedness of this area, Arturo claimed, which caused Soledad to neglect her children. Arturo came to visit them one night and found the door padlocked. He heard the youngest baby crying. He found Soledad and her mother at a bar, dancing. Soledad said that she had considered giving her youngest baby up for adoption. She was in desperate straits. She was weak after the birth of the baby; she owed eight months back rent. Her relatives, although they lived nearby, did nothing to help. At the last moment she decided not to give the child up. Soledad says:

> The only love I trust is the love between a mother and her children. Men come and go; only a child's love is sure, especially when he's small. But children grow up and marry and leave you, so the only real love is a mother's love which lasts forever (Lewis 1965:264).

Soledad in "The Life"

In order to support herself and her children, Soledad became a prostitute, working out of a local bar. She formed temporary relationships with an American sailor, Allen, and other local men. All this time, Arturo never completely severed relationships with her, and at one point offered to take care of the children if she paid him.

Octavio

It was at the bar that Soledad met her second consensual husband, Octavio, who was a professional thief. Soledad accompanied him on one mission, where he and his gang robbed a department store. Soledad describes him:

> Aside from the stealing, he gave me a good life. He loved me and he never beat me or mistreated me badly in any way. He was fond of my children. I never lacked anything as long as I lived with him. . . . He was good tempered, the kind of person who never gets angry. When we would have a quarrel, he would laugh about it afterward . . . I loved him very, very much, probably because he treated me so nicely. We're like animals, you know. Where we get good treatment, that's where we stay. . . . He gave me affection, he took care of me, he worried about me. If I got sick he watched over me (Lewis 1965:189).

Soledad had trouble with her teeth, and had most of them drawn early in her life. She had been self-conscious, and had the nickname "toothless." Octavio got her a set of false teeth. Of his stealing, Soledad remarks:

> When Tavio robbed a rich person I felt nothing but pleasure. The rich are sons of a great whore and they take plenty away from us. Robbing the poor is something else again. Tavio didn't steal from the poor (Lewis 1965:191).

Octavio was killed by a policeman during a robbery. Soledad found herself alone, pregnant, with three small children. She was, again, desperate. She tried to get a job a a nurse's aide but did not qualify. She went on welfare, but could not make do with the 18 dollars a month she received. Soledad expresses great bitterness at the political situation in Puerto Rico. The governor, she said, built fine streets and hotels for tourists, but did nothing for the poor. Every job she tried to get required experience. She claims:

> You can't get a job unless you already have one or unless you have experience. But the place to get experience is on the job. You aren't born knowing (Lewis 1965:195).

Soledad and Don Camacho

Finally, she went back to hustling at the bar. There she met an elderly gentleman, Don Camacho, who fell in love with her, and took care of her until her baby was born. The child was born syphilitic, because Octavio had been infected. Soledad says:

> I don't bear any grudge against Tavio because of my illness. If it had been incurable I would hold it against him. I had to go to the clinic for penicillin and streptomycin injections for almost 15 days. I felt weak, very weak, and I was thin,

thin, thin. The baby had to have treatments at the hospital for almost a year. Don Camacho kept helping me. He told me that if I didn't want to have any more children, he would give me the money for an operation (Lewis 1965:196).

Soledad decided to have the operation, and called Arturo in to sign the release required at that time. Although he was not her legal husband, she still considered herself in some way bound to him. After the operation, Soledad continued to live sporadically with Don Camacho who, she admits, was very kind to her. He was generous and gave her and her daughters jewelry. They quarreled from time to time, but Soledad's main complaint was that he could not satisfy her sexually. It was Don Camacho who paid Soledad's way to New York.

Soledad in the United States

She and her children went to New Jersey, where her sister lived. Almost immediately, she went to work picking vegetables. The living arrangements were not satisfactory. The small house could not hold both families and all the children, so Soledad went to live with a man, named Eddy, whom she met in her sister's house. Thirteen days after her arrival on the mainland, she had a job picking tomatoes, and a new "boy friend." She left her children in care of her sister. She discovered that Eddy had a wife in Puerto Rico and became upset at the idea. She resented this, although she readily admitted that she did not love Eddy. After about eight months she tired of her life in New Jersey, and Don Camacho sent her money to come back to Puerto Rico. She only stayed for a short visit and then asked Don Camacho for the money to go to Florida. This time she left the two older children, Catlin and Quique, with her mother in Puerto Rico. She rejoined Eddy in Florida, but his wife was there as well. She took up with another man, but soon quarreled with him.

Soledad now had the first of several episodes in which she lost consciousness, and evidently had to be restrained. She stayed in a sanitarium for a month, and then returned to San Juan. She paid half her fare, the other half was paid by the Welfare Department. Once in San Juan she resumed her network of relationships. Arturo took the children. Don Camacho sent a car for her. She refused his help, however, and went job hunting again, with no success. She began hustling at a bar once more and lived with her mother.

Soon she received word from one of her friends in New York, who sent her fare to come to the Bronx, a borough of New York which is now almost entirely Puerto Rican. This time Soledad left her son with Arturo, and her adopted daughter with her mother. She brought her two youngest daughters with her. She immediately found work in a purse factory at 43 dollars a week. She lived with the man who had sent for her, Jorge Luis. When she discovered that he had a mistress, she had another seizure of a sort and wound up at Bellevue, a city hospital with a large ward for the mentally ill. When she got out she was again behind in her rent, jobless, and getting no help from those of her relatives who were in New York. She applied for welfare, but was rejected because she had not established residency in New York. Finally, through her second cousins Virginia and Moncho, she got a job in a bar, working for 30 dollars from 6 PM until 2 AM on weekends. She also became a prostitute again.

Soledad and Benedicto

It was at this bar that Soledad met Benedicto, with whom she entered into her third consensual marriage. The relationship was entered into gradually.

Benedicto came to my house and stayed with me every other day. One day he brought over a few of his clothes. The next time he brought a few more, until finally he moved in with me. He paid the rent and he gave me money for the children's food. Then I stopped working at the bar (Lewis 1965:208).

Benedicto was a merchant seaman who was away for long periods of time. He could not give Soledad the dependent's allotment provided by the Merchant Marine because she was not his legal wife. He had another consensual wife, and several semipermanent relationships and six children. One of the bones of contention between Soledad and Benedicto was the fact that she would not permit him to bring his children to visit. Benedicto found Soledad difficult to live with because she was very jealous of him. He says:

There is a lack of understanding between Soledad and me. She wants to boss me. She is headstrong and so am I. At times I have no choice but to slap her good, because a man can't allow himself to be dominated by a woman. There should be proper respect and good mutual understanding in order to have a good marriage (Lewis 1965:221).

Soledad and Money

A major issue, on Soledad's side, is the money question. She accused Benedicto of coming home drunk and drinking up any money he had with him. Most of their quarrels concerned money; yet, Lewis has documented the possessions they had:

	Soledad		*Benedicto*
27	dresses	5	suits
3	suits	10	pairs of pants
11	skirts	23	shirts
11	blouses	25	undershorts
11	half-slips	25	undershirts
16	panties	4	pairs of shoes
7	pairs of shoes	40	pairs of socks
2	wrist watches	2	wrist watches
		1	gold chain
		3	gold rings

Their household was filled with cheap furniture, plastic ornaments, and a radio which was often in hock, as was the jewelry.

The Network of Relatives

Soledad resumed her work in another purse factory. One year Benedicto made arrangements to fly Soledad and her two girls to Puerto Rico, where his ship was to dock over the Christmas holidays. Soledad was anxious to see her children who remained in Puerto Rico, and intended to bring her oldest daughter, Catlin, home with her. She wrote Arturo who answered her, and also wrote the two little girls whom he addressed as daughters. Soledad's visit to San Juan was marred by several factors: Benedicto was drunk much of the time, and Soledad quarreled with her mother and her sisters. She had to pay Arturo to take care of her daughters because there was no room for them with either her mother or her sister. And that holiday was unhappy for yet another reason:

> Ay, the pain one feels after being in a nice hotel and walking by the Caribe Hilton, seeing so many pretty things and then having to go back to La Esmeralda! Such terrible poverty, so much dirt, garbage scattered everywhere! They live in a separate world, the poor and the rich. I'll never go back to La Esmeralda, may the dear God forgive me! I may go back for a visit, but not to live there with my children. Never again! (Lewis 1965:244)

Soledad returned to her home in New York. She brought her three daughters, Catlin, Toya, and Sarita with her. Her son, Quique, remained with Arturo.

Benedicto and Soledad set up housekeeping in an apartment on Fox Street in the Bronx. Soledad bought furniture on credit.

> I bought a living room set with three end tables, a bedroom set, and a breakfast set. The whole thing cost $800.00. I still owe $400.00. I'm paying $5.00 a week. My husband helped me, but not much. All he paid was $50.00. I was able to make the down payment because I belonged to an association and I got $110.00 from that. This is the way the association works. A number of people — twelve say — get together. Every week each of them puts $10.00 into the kitty. You make twelve slips of paper, one for each member. Each draws his slip in turn, one every week. The slip on top shows who gets the kitty that week. In that way, everyone gets the whole amount when his turn comes (Lewis 1965:214).

In addition to the Association, Soledad played the numbers daily. She invested 15 cents a day with the local numbers runner, Elfredo. She has not been very lucky, winning only small amounts occasionally. She feels that she is not a lucky gambler, although on a shelf above her kitchen door she has improvised an altar to Saint Expedito, who brings luck to gamblers. She keeps offerings such as a glass of rum, cigarettes, coins, dice, playing cards, and bread and butter to the saint on the altar. When she is short of money, she pawns her jewelry. Frequently, however, when these meager sources are exhausted, she turns back to "the life." She has a few steady customers, including the numbers runner and an older man whom she calls "the Polak."

Jealousy

Although Soledad has never been consistently faithful to Benedicto, she is very jealous of any relationships he has with other women. At one time, Soledad related, she found him in a house with an Ecuadorian woman:

> I fought with him right there, with as much courage as any man. Whenever I fight with Benedicto I use my fists. He has to bash me on the head to knock me down. I think I was born to be a man, no kidding. But if I'd been made with a cock instead of a cunt someone would have killed me by now because I have a terrible temper. I'm always ready to pick a quarrel and to stand up and fight.
> When I was through with Benedicto, I took on the Ecuadorian woman. I went at her with my teeth and bit her face. I had a small knife on me but someone snatched it out of my hand! (Lewis 1965:218)

Soledad and Her Children

Soledad's behavior toward her children is also highly charged, swinging from expressions of great affection and playfulness to moods of depression when she wants them to leave her alone. They have been in the care of several women related to Soledad by loose bonds of kinship. While she works, neighbors and various relatives of Benedicto's and hers take care of the children. Soledad's oldest daughter Catlin describes her relationship to Soledad and Benedicto:

> Benedicto never did anything to me. But it's that I hate all the husbands *mami* ever had. . . . When I am big, I am going to say to Benedicto, "How much money do you want to leave my *mami?*" Then I'll send for Arturo and Quique. If Arturo is around when Benedicto tries to take advantage of *mami* or if he grabs us and smashes us against the floor, he won't get away with it (Lewis 1965:254).

Attitudes toward Men

The contrast in attitudes toward men is well revealed in a dialogue between Soledad and Rosalia. Rosalia is an older woman who lives in the same apartment house and occasionally looks after Soledad's children.

Rosalia says:

> These days, women want to rule the men. In the old times when a man could leave his wife for a month and go do what he pleased. And when he returned she had to smile and take him back. I'll tell you something. A man who lived next door to us brought his mistress home to help his wife with the housework. Well, the two women lived under one roof as happy as could be (Lewis 1965:142).

Soledad replies:

That wouldn't work with me. If I don't satisfy a man, let him leave me and get himself another woman. I won't stand for my man having a mistress. That's the reason why I'll never get mixed up with a married man. In the first place, I wouldn't do anything I wouldn't like to have done to me. And, in the second place, I don't want to be some man's toy, to play second fiddle (Lewis 1965:142).

Soledad's attitude toward Benedicto is further aggravated by the problem of money. Benedicto asserts that he gives Soledad as much money as he has whenever he comes ashore. He says:

I have always liked to dress well and to have some nice jewelry. In my good times, I've had as many as fifteen suits, many of them made to measure, about ten pairs of shoes. . . . Soledad has a wrist watch of her own in hock, a chain I gave her, a ring, her sewing machine and a radio-victrola. I left some money with her and she spent it all and pawned the TV set. We owe the pawnshop about $400.00 counting the interest (Lewis 1965:222).

A typical dialogue between Soledad and Benedicto concerning money goes as follows:

"Soledad, give me five dollars to buy beer,"
Benedicto said, "The whiskey is all gone." "What, are you crazy." Don't you dare ask me."
"Yes, I will. Give me three at least."
"Not even one, you drunken bastard. We have so much money, don't we? You give me such a lot."
"Didn't I just give you 150 dollars? What do you expect anyway?"
"That you shouldn't take them away again. With that money I have to pay the insurance, the furniture stores, two months I owe for milk, buy food, get the TV set out of the pawnshop, and I don't know what else."
"There must be about $200.00 under the pillow," Benedicto said. "I put the money some place but I can't remember where."
"I've already looked all over the house for it. That money isn't here. Two hundred turds is what you must have left. God knows where you lost that money, you idiot" (Lewis 1965:144).

Soledad's attitude toward men is summarized in her own statement:

Can you imagine what it's like to fall in love and think the man loves you for yourself only to realize that all he's interested in is having his pleasure with you and then send you packing? And then to humiliate you by refusing to give you a dollar when you ask for it. Most men want women to support them. That's why I'd just as soon there be no men in my life. . . . What I feel toward men now is a desire for revenge. If Benedicto and I break up I'll never marry again. I'm 25 and I'd marry again if I could find a man to spend all the rest of my life with. But I've never yet come across a perfect man, and that's what I want. A man who doesn't drink or smoke, who has no vices of any kind, who's attached to his wife, his children, and his home. A man who won't cheat on me because he knows that if he's unfaithful to me I'll be unfaithful to him. But the man who will have no woman except his wife hasn't been born yet. I've never known a man who doesn't have a mistress on the side (Lewis 1965:148).

Contradictions

Realism appears and disappears as Soledad rationalizes her situation. She wants a man who will accept her children but she will not accept Benedicto's children. She wants a man who will be faithful to her, but she earns extra needed money through prostitution. She lacks money for necessities, yet owns an extensive wardrobe.

Soledad does not have much interest in Spiritism, a cult involving medicine and guidance from departed spirits, but she does complain of "bad luck." At her most realistic, Soledad says:

> I know I won't last with Benedicto much longer. He stayed in Brazil two months and a half without sending me a penny. Yet he expected me to be faithful to him. Who the hell would be faithful to a man like him? I didn't take such behavior from Arturo who is the father of two of my children, and I won't take it from him. It isn't that he was so terribly good looking or a representative of the government of Puerto Rico or something. He's just a shitting sailor, a Negro with nostrils big enough to let a transport through.
>
> I haven't left Benedicto yet because I have to get even with him first for everything he's done to me and because I don't want him to have the apartment and the furniture. I'm defending my rights. As long as I live with him he has to support me (Lewis 1965:216).

Soledad has been a very plucky woman. She has fended for herself and her children as best she could, with whatever assets she had. She has not been a pawn, as Consuelo seemed to be so often. Soledad has manipulated her life and her men.

What lies in the future as Soledad sees it?

> Look, I give the impression of being tough, but really, I'm not. I have my feelings and I can suffer for another person. I pity the weak, the poor. I would like to help the needy. . . . Look at me. Right now I'm thinking about myself, about how I'm 25 and already a sick woman. By the time I'm 30 years old I won't be good for anything. I've lost my teeth, I already have high blood pressure, my nerves are shot, any little thing startles me. Last night while I was mopping the floor I blacked out and had to sit down. And I tire easily. After I walk a while my back and my chest hurt. . . . I have borne many troubles and I can bear many more.
>
> I wrote to my mama but she didn't answer. I wrote to Arturo and a letter from him arrived a few days later. As always he offered to help me. . . . He offered me a home but it is not the home I want. I will never go back to Arturo again. If I were alone, I would go to far-off places. I would go all over the world far, far, anywhere I wouldn't have relatives or know anybody (Lewis 1965:265).

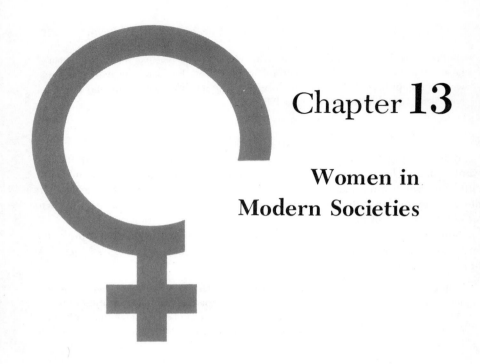

Chapter 13

Women in Modern Societies

1. THE WOMEN OF LIU LING IN THE PEOPLE'S REPUBLIC OF CHINA

How These Biographies Came To Be

In 1962, when relationships between China and the United States were still cut off, Jan Myrdal, the Swedish anthropologist and his wife applied for and received a visa to enter the country and study the peasants. Myrdal states that he was given a free choice of villages to study, althouth certain military areas were off limits, of course. Otherwise, his choice was based primarily on his needs. He wanted a peasant village that had been part of the "old liberated area," one which brought the revolution to the rest of the People's Republic, rather than one which had been passive in the revolutionary movement. Myrdal also wanted to interview old communist revolutionaries. For that reason, he chose the village of Liu Ling.

Myrdal's book, "Report from a Chinese Village," gives much basic data about the economy, the price of goods, the yield of crops, the organization of labor brigades, but more than all this, Myrdal has given the peasant in China a voice. Myrdal (1965:xxxviii) states that in his very first assignment as a journalist, he was sent to interview a 100-year-old lady with the advice "Just get her to talk about her life, what she experienced, what she remembered." He has done that in his book and, through an interpreter, has brought us the words of the people of Liu Ling.

The Village of Liu Ling

Liu Ling is located among the hills in northern Shensi province. This is fertile agricultural area in which the people live in houses constructed inside caves. Both the valley and the hills are under cultivation; the soil is quite fertile if properly watered. In 1962, there were 50 households made up of 212 people. The caves can be built of earth or stone. Stone caves are longer lasting, but they also take more effort to make. Both types of caves have outdoor kitchens for use during the summer, and are warm and comfortable in the winter. Liu Ling farms communally. There are both collective and private plots in the valley and on the hillside, and each family has some private land. People grow most of their own food. They are organized into labor brigades who work together, not only to farm, but to terrace the hills and build dams where needed. Some of the goods that must be bought are rationed and some are not. Rationing is called "planned supply of goods." Books, paper, earthenware, bicycles, handcarts, electric light bulbs, and washing powder were among the items that were not rationed in 1962. Cotton for clothing as well as many other consumer items is rationed. Labor brigades keep records of their man-hours, and are entitled to goods and services according to the number of man-hours they have worked. People receive coupons for their labor and products, and there are, in addition, regular distributions of goods.

Myrdal's book gives Americans the rare opportunity to hear directly from people who lived through the revolution into the present. Nowhere is the change in their lives more outstanding than among the women of Liu Ling.

An Older Woman Speaks

Chia Ying-Lan was 53 in 1962. She had been born into a very poor family. At 16, she married a man who was a tinker and peddler; they had a daughter. She also worked for a farmer who owned his own land. At the age of 22, her husband sold her and their daughter for 220 silver dollars to a slave dealer. A farmer bought them. She lived with him until his death and bore him a son and a daughter. After the death of her second husband:

> I was, of course, a widow and a burden on the village. The landlord wanted to marry me off. My husband's relatives, that is Mr. He's relatives, wanted to marry me off in order to get the house and my children. There was a man in the village who was willing to buy me. I don't know how they arranged it, and I don't know who he was. But I didn't want to any longer. I just wanted to be with my children. In order to get out of this new marriage, I lied and said I was already 41. Then he thought I would not be fertile any more and wouldn't have me. That was what I had reckoned on. After that I was left in peace (Myrdal 1965:235).

Ying-lan uses the phrase "a man in the village who was willing to buy me," and since the conversation passed through an interpreter, we are not sure whether the actual purchase of a woman as a chattel or the more common custom of paying "bride wealth" was involved.

Some time after that, the revolution came along, and Ying-lan was free to go where she chose. She came to Liu Ling because her sister lived there. Her son works with the brigade, and her one problem is that he has not married. She very much wants to have grandchildren.

Another Older Woman

Tu Fang-lan was 56 in 1962. She, too, came from a poor family. Her father gambled, drank, and beat her mother when he lost. She recalls:

> He said, "I'm utterly useless. I can't support them." Then he took out a rope and was going to hang me. Then we all cried out: "Don't hang us, Father. We can work and help to support the family" (Myrdal 1965:237).

Tu Fang-lan was one of six children. Her feet were bound as a child, and thus they are crippled and deformed. At 16, her mother arranged for her to marry a farmer, who was even more poverty stricken than her own family. She recalls that in her day, daughters-in-law were entirely at the mercy of their mothers-in-law. She only ate after the rest of the family had finished and thus had little food. She was pregnant eight times during her marriage, but only four sons survived. After her parents-in-law died, she went with her husband and family to work on another landlord's farm. Her husband died within days after their arrival. The hardest times that she recalls came thereafter. Her two older boys worked as herdsmen. She worked in the fields, despite her mutilated feet. In 1939 she took her family to Yenan where the boys again worked as herdsmen and she worked the land. She lived through the bombing of Yenan and moved to Liu in 1955. Her boys fought with the guerillas. In Liu Ling she worked as a shoemaker. The labor brigade did not want her to work in the field, but she insisted and eventually was awarded a certificate for her excellent work. She married Ching Chung-wan. People in the village comment:

> She was obliged to marry Ching Chung-wan. It's the custom for people to marry. Women marry, even if they are over forty. They can even be fifty when they marry. After all, a woman can't live alone. If a middle-aged woman wants to marry, people will have no objection. Tu Fang-lan was known to be wanting to marry. She needed a man. She married Ching Chung-wan. He is eight years younger than she is. He is the younger brother of Ching Chung-ying, leader of the labour group for vegetable cultivation. As I say, people remarry a lot here in Liu Ling. As soon as the husband or wife has died, the survivor tries to remarry. People should not live alone, and if a woman can remarry, she should do so. Who is going to carry the water otherwise? (Myrdal 1965:241).

Unfortunately, the marriage did not go well. Her husband had been rejected by all the available younger women, and married because he needed someone to cook for him. He now nags her because she cannot give him children. People in the village feel sorry for her on this account.

A Young Girl

Li Shang-wa was 16 in 1962. Her mother was dead. She finished school and would have liked to go on for higher education, but her father needed her at home to run the household. People in the village say that they tried to persuade her father to let Li Shang-wa continue to go to school, but he was adamant. Unfortunately, Li Shang-wa's remarks sound like a recorded message. There is no way of knowing whether she actually made the following statement, or whether the tone was that of the interpreter. In any case, she says:

> I am proud of being able to work on the land. Agriculture is the foundation of society. No society could exist without it. Of course, I would be happy with whatever work the party gave me to do. We who are young now have a bright future ahead of us. I hope to be able to make my contribution on the agricultural front and be a good "swallow" as the teachers in school taught me. I'm not contemplating marriage. I shall marry late. I'm altogether too young to be able to think of love. I'm running the house for my father. Later, I am going to work on the land (Myrdal 1965:246).

A Pioneer Woman

The person who comes through most articulately is Li Kuei-ying, a woman pioneer and member of the communist party. She was 32 in 1962 and can recall the fighting during the Chinese revolution, when areas were ravaged by war lords of various political persuasions. She moved with her family to Yenan in 1950. The family — mother, father, and four children — walked to Yenan, and Li Kuei-ying recalls being so tired that she cried. In Yenan they were very poor and went to work as tenant farmers. The area was ravaged by a war lord called Hu Tsung-nan. Li Kuei-ying was sent with her brothers and sisters to their mother's brother in Ansai. She says:

> One day when the troops came to the village, my little brother and I were ill. We had high temperatures with bleeding at the nose and mouth, and diarrhea. One of Uncle's female relations was staying with us in the cave to look after us and Uncle. The woman's husband was a stretcher-bearer for the guerillas. She was living with Uncle, as she had been left alone in the village. Now she was able to look after us children. That is why she was not hidden when the solidiers came. They stood outside the cave and told us to come out. We replied: "All those who are well are away, it is only we ill ones left." Then they asked us what illness we had. "It's catching." At that they took two paces back. Then they said: "Those who are not ill must come out, otherwise we shall shoot." After that Uncle and the woman stepped outside. They did not bother Uncle, but they took the woman away with them. Two hours later she came back. Her face was gray then and she was silent. That night her husband came. They sat side by side for a while, then they stood up and walked out, in the middle of the night. No one has heard of them since. No one knows where they went. They just walked out into the dark (Myrdal 1965:248).

In July of that year, the family reassembled in Liu Ling. The fields were desolate and there were no seeds for planting. During that first summer Li Kuei-ying and her mother did the laundry for the troops of Hu Tsung-nan. In the spring of 1948 Hu Tsung-nan withdrew his troops, and Li Kuei-ying's father brought seed corn from Lochuan. He kept bringing corn until their own corn was ready for harvesting. It was her father who organized the first communal labor group for mutual help. The people, we are told, were very poor. In 1951, the communist party school in Yenan started a school for female *ganbus*. Myrdal explains that the term *ganbu* originally meant communist party functionary, but now is applied to any civil servant. Li Kuei-ying says: "It was said that as half the population consisted of women, trained women were needed as well."

Li Kuei-ying at School

The labor group which Li Kuei-ying's father founded nominated her for training at the school. Although she had always wanted to become literate, she was fearful both about her ability to learn and about the neglected chores at home. The curriculum at the school consisted of fundamentals such as learning to do arithmetic and to read and write Chinese. The classes were held consecutively, with 15 minute intervals in between. The girls were fed better than they had been at home. They formed friendships, and spent the evenings discussing the villages they had come from and how conditions in these villages could be improved.

Li Kuei-ying reports:

That time at the party school was the decisive time of my life. It was then I realized what I must do with my life. I came back to Liu Ling in July, 1951. I could then read and write, and I took part in the autumn harvest, and in the winter I began organizing women to study. When I got back, the women said: "We didn't think grown-ups could learn to read and write, but you have." Because of that, the younger women now wanted to learn to read too, and I told them all how good it was to be able to read and write, that she who could read could see; and she who couldn't, was blind (Myrdal 1965: 250).

Li Kuei-ying as a Teacher

Li Kuei-ying taught ten women that winter, but admits that she has not had great success with them. She married in 1952, a man of her own choice, who had been studying a different course. Her parents posed no objection.

In 1953 she was elected to head a woman's labor brigade. She states as one of her objectives the desire to get the women moving:

I wanted them to break away from the past. I was thinking of the time when Hu Tsung-nan had occupied the area. There was a cavalry regiment quartered here in Liu Ling then. Its duties were to track down and capture deserters. They shot the deserters in our potato plot. Every day I used to stand by my cooking stove in the cave and see them shoot deserters down there. I thought then that that must never be allowed to happen again. That we women must all get together to see that it never happened again (Myrdal 1965:251).

In the following winter, she opened a winter school where lessons were given in poultry feeding and spinning, as well as help in making shoes and clothes, and fixing agricultural tools. She also tried to get the women to tell how life had been for them in the past, how it was now, and what they would like to see in the future.

Woman's Traditional Status

One of the problems she encountered was the traditional thinking of both men and women. Some women said that they considered themselves equal to men, since both worked in the fields, but felt the men should help them at home. However, the older women stated that men and women were born different, that women were not able to work in the fields, and consequently should have the whole responsibility of the home.

During this period, although women were working in the fields and earning money, older men still said: "What does a woman know? Women know nothing. What is a woman worth? A woman is worth nothing."

The first time the women took part in an open discussion on changing the name of the cooperative, and means of maximizing production, some of the older women felt they were unqualified to take any positions. The younger women, on the other hand, discussed the question of whether to pay dividends on land or on labor. When they had finished speaking, one of the older men said:

We should not listen to women when it is a question of serious business. They understand nothing. After all, they are only women and ought not to disturb our discussions. We do not need to concern ourselves with what they have said (Myrdal 1965:252).

A younger man disagreed with the older gentleman, and eventually the women's proposal was accepted. Li Kuei-ying was elected a member of the larger cooperative. From 1953 to 1958, she had three children, two boys and a girl.

Li Kuei-ying joined the communist party in 1966. Although her husband had urged her to join earlier, it was the persuasion of other comrades which finally motivated her to do so. Through her study of party literature she learned how cooperatives were working in other parts of China. Some ideas seemed workable and others seemed impractical for her part of the country.

In 1958 the Liu Ling people's commune was formed. This commune incorporated larger areas of land and greater numbers of people than did the earlier cooperative. By this time, things were going so well that most of the people, except for some of the older ones, were committed to the idea of enlargement, since it would provide capital and labor for a large scale enterprise.

As a result of the new commune, during the winter of 1958 to 1959 great irrigation works were built and fields were terraced. In 1959 there was a drought, but the harvest was adequate; this strengthened the people's belief that they could help themselves.

Activities of the Women's Committee

In 1959 to 1960, a discussion was held about working among women. A special women's committee was set up to deal with the particular problems of women. This committee had five tasks: (1) to organize women to take an active part in production; (2) to spread literacy and get women involved in decision-making; (3) to help them do domestic tasks efficiently and give economic help where needed; (4) to teach personal and public hygiene; and (5) to help and advise in matters concerning marriage and domestic life.

An example of the last was a case in which one of the young girls in the village fell in love with a lad from a neighboring village. Her family opposed the match because they felt they could arrange a marriage with a more prosperous person. Li Kuei-ying spoke to the parents and told them that they no longer had the legal right to "sell" their daughter. The father remonstrated, saying that he had paid for his wife and had invested a great deal of food and clothing in raising his daughter and wanted to be repaid. Li Kuei-ying finally persuaded them to accept the marriage, using as a point of persuasion the fact that the parents were secure in their income due to the functioning of the People's Commune, and that both daughter and son-in-law would help them should the need arise. The girl's mother was silent throughout, and then said that her parents had sold her to her husband at such a high price that he and his family went into debt. As a result, they had been particularly cruel to her as a bride, and she did not want her daughter to have to go through the same sort of thing.

The women's committee is active in changing childbirth procedures. Tradition demanded that a woman sit up straight upon her couch for three days after having the baby. Li Kuei-ying has had to persuade women that they will not harm themselves or the baby if they lie down to rest or nurse their babies. She has had difficulty with older women who find the young women too outspoken, too forward, and disapprove their informality toward men. The older women have been told that women work as hard as men, and that they are equal to men, and for that reason they do not have to modify their behavior toward men.

Birth control is one of the major problems encountered among village women. Condoms are sold at a very inexpensive price — 33 for one yuan.

However, many people still believe that they will not become pregnant while they are lactating. Men often disapprove the idea of birth control, while their wives would like to limit the number of children they have. In such a case, members of the women's committee will point out to the man how much extra work each child is to his wife. Contraception is introduced as a temporary measure, merely to space the children more conveniently. They persist in talking to the man until he concedes.

In 1958 a children's day nursery was established, as well as a collective dining hall. These are used primarily at times in the agricultural cycle when people are too busy in the fields to tend to private household chores. People pay work points for the care of children and the use of the dining hall.

Li Kuei-ying explains:

> In 1960, the women elected me their delegate to a conference of merit workers that was being held down in Sian. They did that because I taught them to read and write. I was very touched by it; I could not help thinking how they were commending me, though really I had not done all that I ought to have done. I determined to work even better, seeing that the women believed in me. I want to solve all our women's problems here. You see, not all women by any means are aware that they are their husband's equals. Some still look up to their husbands as in the old days before women became free. They suffer from that, and they must be freed from it (Myrdal 1965:259).

The people of the village admire Li Kuei-ying because she is soft-spoken, decisive, and hard-working. One woman admires her most because she has succeeded in planning her family.

A Chinese Housewife

The final biography Myrdal gives is that of a 29-year-old housewife, Li Yang-ching, who is married and has three children. Li Yang-ching was betrothed to her husband at the age of 13. She married at 18 and went to live with her husband's parents. She says that life then was much harder for her than it is now. She gives an account of her time as follows: January and February are spent making clothes and shoes for the family; in March and April she works in the fields, turning the earth the plow has missed and spreading manure; she weeds the fields in May and June, and in July and August, in addition to weeding a second time, she begins to cut wheat; in September and October, the fields are harvested, and wheat is threshed; women do not work in the field in November and December. While working in the fields, Li Yang-ching is still responsible for preparing the family meals and taking care of the domestic animals — a pig and some chicks. The winter season is easier for her, since she does not have to go to the fields. In these months, she prefers to do her sewing and shoemaking in the company of other women. Groups of three to five women gather together to do this work and chat. About once a month she goes to Yenan. She is fond of Chinese opera, and attends, in the daytime, whenever a special troup is in Yenan; her husband attends in the evening so that the children are not left alone. Every two weeks she goes to the nearest village to buy salt, soya, vinegar, cooking oil, biscuits, and sugar. Her shopping costs four or five yuan. She observes the traditional Chinese festivals.

The pig and goat are slaughtered for the New Year's festival, and special dishes such as millet cakes and Chinese bean pudding are prepared. She also observes the spring festival when food is brought to the graves of her ancestors. Everyone in the village observes this custom. There are several summer festivals marked by eating foods prepared from plants which have just ripened, as on September 9th, the new buckwheat is made into noodles.

Li Yang-ching makes her own wine, ketchup and special dishes. Clothing is made without a sewing machine, although there is electricity in the village. The quilted cotton clothing must be picked apart, washed, and then sewn together again. Once a year, she makes a new coat for every member of the family. In between, she mends the old ones. She does many things by hand. She makes her own paste and jute thread in order to make the family shoes. She pastes the layers of cloth together to make the soles of the shoes, using two layers of new cloth and filling between them as many layers of old unusable cloth as she can get. She makes the jute thread with which the shoes are sewn by first cutting the jute, removing the leaves, and soaking the jute in the stream for a week. Then she removes it from the water and peels it, revealing the fibers.

Her husband knits the stockings for the family. He does this in the winter, when there is less agricultural work.

In evaluating these biographies, we must be aware of the prerevolutionary conditions of women, before judging their present position. It is probably true that women work harder in the People's Republic of China than they do in the United States, but they work less now than they did before the revolution. Although it is true that some of the statements appear to be propagandist rhetoric, we must bear in mind that previously women were not expected to speak out at all. Although their marriages seem rather unromantic to Western eyes, they apparently satisfy the Chinese. It will probably be some time before people in the United States become sufficiently familiar with conditions in the People's Republic of China to make any judgments at all.

2. BEING A SENIOR CITIZEN IN THE UNITED STATES

Older Women

In looking at contemporary American life, one expects to find many roles, many classes, many different lifestyles led by many different types of women. Much scientific and historical literature, exists concerning vocal and conscious women, that is, conscious of their femaleness, and how it has patterned their lives. With women like Simone de Beavoir, Betty Friedan, and Germaine Greer writing about the meaning of womanhood, any words by the anthropologist would be both redundant and superfluous. There are, however, in this society, groups of women whose consciousness has not been raised, and to whom womanhood is a fact of life; such women have not deeply explored their potentials. One such group is composed of women who are now in their 60s and 70s. The idea of liberation, although certainly known since the time of the suffrage movement, has not penetrated the core of their lives. They are more concerned about their membership in the community of the aged. How does growing old affect women? Do all women react in the same way to aging? Does being an old woman mean more problems than being an old man? For answers to some of these questions, this chapter will be devoted to an examination of the lives of ordinary women growing old in America.

The Retirement Community as a Form of Age-Grading

Jerry Jacobs (1974) has written about people in a retirement community, which he calls Fun City. Jacobs has not focused in particular on women in such a community; however, since they are there they have been interviewed in his work. Women penetrate any study of the aged, because women live longer than men.

The idea of a retirement community is unique to the United States. Many societies around the world have age-grades, whereby individuals of a certain age are grouped together in ritual for practical purposes. East African societies are best known for this, but only the men are age-graded. Among the Masai, for example, boys at every age have precise functions assigned to them; they act as a group and maintain lasting ties with their age-grade companions. In most societies, certain tasks are assigned to young people and other tasks to old people. In traditional societies, Mead (1970) points out that older people are respected for their wisdom, since the problems young people have to cope with have already been experienced by their elders. In our society, however, the exponential growth of technology has created problems for which there is no precedent, and with which people have never before been confronted. Pollution, overpopulation, energy shortages, and food shortages are all felt to be new phenomena that older people lack the resources and wisdom to solve. But, in fact, few people are called upon to help solve the problems of the world. The ordinary person does pretty much what his or her father or mother did. People hold jobs, they marry, they have children, and they grow old. Despite the fact that the wisdom of the elders may still be relevant in our daily lives, in the United States the elders are treated most unkindly. They are often neglected, relegated to impersonal institutions, ignored, and dehumanized. It is a sad commentary, but the disdain for the old is so great that many of them prefer the segregation of separate communities to participation on the fringes of the larger society.

Reasons People Come to Fun City

People said they came to the Fun City retirement community for various reasons. Perhaps they felt the streets were safer, that the community was good for their health, that it was less crowded than cities, or that it offered many activities, or was well situated. Jacobs (1974) points out that the people in Fun City came from middle-class communities in which the streets were just as safe as in Fun City. He also points out that the health facilities in Fun City are really quite inadequate: there is no hospital, no clinic facilities, and the only ambulance service is run by volunteers. Although it is true that Fun City is not congested, that is because few people take part in the activities for which they ostensibly came. As far as being well situated, Jacobs (1974:57) points out that the community is very poorly situated for older people who do not have cars or cannot drive. There are no shopping areas within walking distance, and other communities can only be reached by car, over freeways which are neither safe nor convenient for older people. Jacobs suggests that perhaps financial reasons play a part in their decision, because Fun City offers homes at low prices, or maybe people want to live fairly close to their children and grandchildren, and yet be apart from them. The most cogent reasons are stated by Jacobs (1974:66) himself:

> Second was the theme of the "common enemy." This referred to citizens in the neighboring towns to whom Fun City residents pay substantial school taxes and for which they receive no benefits; the younger generation who neither understood nor cared for the aged, and who had "peculiar" or "immoral" ways; the greater outside political process that had long ignored the economic and social needs of older persons; those responsible for the country's current economic plight; and that amorphous mass responsible for the lack of "law and order" in the streets — "colored," "communists," "hippies," and "welfare types," who are now found everywhere.

The Exclusion of the Aged

In actuality, then, the people living in Fun City do so because they do not feel welcome, or cannot cope with society as it is presently constituted. They cling to each other and hope they can ignore the world outside. This theme is stated most articulately by one women:

And I'll be honest with you. Sometimes when I go to a large meeting down here at [Fun City] Town Hall, I look around and at first I used to get a feeling of repulsion because there is something about older people; they are ugly. They don't look nice. . . . But now that I've been here longer, I've overlooked that and I just see my friends. I recognize faces now, and people I know are glad to see me. And suddenly I come tight with that old feeling, well, sister, who do you think you are? Perhaps you're not so hot either. After all, your figure is going, your hair is getting grey, you're getting brown spots on your hands and I think, oh, brother, this business of getting old, the aging process. But where on earth would they [the residents of Fun City] go. This is a retreat. It's sort of a false paradise in a way. We're not of the world and yet do we want to be? (Jacobs 1974:66).

Fun City

Demographically, Fun City seems to be located in southern California. The total population is 5519 (Jacobs 1974:45), and nearly all white. Residents must be over 50. The majority come from other areas in California, but there are sizable representations from Illinois, Michigan, Ohio, and Wisconsin, with some people from nearly every other state except Mississippi and South Carolina. There are 2,238 households composed of husband and wife. Five hundred and four women live alone; 166 men live alone, 19 households are shared by two women, and 10 are shared by two men. Although most of the retirees list their former occupations as professionals, owners of independent businesses, skilled laborers, salesmen, civil servants, ex-military men, unskilled laborers, farmers, and ranchers as well as a category "managers" (which Jacobs puts in quotes), are all represented. This list is not complete for the purposes of this study because in the case of married couples, Jacobs gave only the husband's occupation; however, where women headed the household, or lived alone, their occupations were listed.

As can be seen from those figures, the residents of Fun City represent a broad spectrum of white middle-class Americans, whose values represent their backgrounds. They are overwhelmingly politically conservative, their interests do not lie in intellectual directions. In summing up the books Fun City residents read, the librarian notes: "mostly mysteries, escape literature, you know — things to go to sleep by" (Jacobs 1974:13).

Activities in Fun City

What can a woman do in Fun City? For one thing, she can go to the shopping center if she has transportation. The places which provide informal sociability are the beauty parlor, the laundromat, and the supermarket. Here women tend to meet and form superficial acquaintances. The formal activities provided by Fun City are held in several rooms of different sizes. One is designated as the women's club room, another as the men's club room. Actually, members of both sexes use either room, depending on the activity.

Classes in arts and crafts are very popular. Here there is evidence of the enculturation of sexual differentiation. The women do artwork, sewing, and ceramics; the men attend carpentry sessions and make jewelry. The camera club has both male and female members.

By far the most popular activity is playing cards. There are both formal and informal card groups. In addition to the combined bridge club membership of 760, there are a canasta club with 100 members, two pinochle groups with a combined membership of 94, and an infinite number of informal card playing groups which meet in various people's homes. Some are exclusively male, some exclusively female, and some mixed.

The largest number of participants in active sports play golf, and here also, there are women's and men's golf clubs. There are also people who play shuffle-board, bowl, and cycle, although the last has a relatively small number of enthusiasts. There are chapters of service clubs and church groups; for instance there are a large number of Masons in Fun City. Their duty here is perhaps more onerous than elsewhere. Masons are pledged to attend each other's funerals. In Fun City it is not unusual for Masons to attend one or two funerals weekly.

Retirees and Work

Some people, mostly men, try to work. Jacobs (1974:26) says:

Retired admirals paint houses, retired colonels pump gas, or transcribe math problems into Braille for the blind, while housewives act as realtors. Other well-to-do residents work as handymen or gardeners.

Jacobs correctly ascribes this to the work ethic by which people in this age group have guided their lives, rather than to the need of money. The average fixed income of the residents was revealed to be about 8,000 dollars per year. Jacobs (1974:28) says:

Work, among those holding a work ethic, is the source of one's identity and self-esteem. This is especially true of those ascribing to "the Protestant ethic and the spirit of capitalism" and a rugged individualism and a strong anti-welfare state ideology. "Work makes life sweet" is no idle expression to those whose biographies read like Horatio Alger stories. Such persons find the abrupt transition from a work to a leisure ethic especially difficult.

This applies particularly to men. For women, even those who had been employed, there is no transition to leisure because running a household, cooking, cleaning, and myriad tasks which fall in the category of housework must still be done. These women have simply been relieved of one job. Women who have been housewives find their daily routine similar to the ones they had before coming to Fun City.

Retirement and Marriage

Some may find that the constant presence of the men creates extra work, in that lunches, which the men probably ate out at restaurants, now have to be prepared. Women in similar retirement communities have also complained that they cannot get their regular chores done with the men always "hanging around." For some marriages, retirement is particularly stressful. Women who are accustomed to setting their own schedules to suit themselves, to work at their own pace, and to spend part of the day in privacy now have to cope with the more or less constant presence of their husbands. Other marriages, however, have prospered in that with age, a mutual dependence comes into being. Where one of the partners in a marriage becomes infirm, the dependence upon the other partner is greater. For the most part, these couples have lived together for many years, have adjusted to each other's idiosyncracies, and share beliefs and values. This is evident in some of the conversations Jacobs (1974:63) held with couples who seemed to be able to complete each other's sentences. A conversation with Mr. and Mrs. B. starts as follows:

Mrs. B.   But here it's (the forms of interaction) mostly
Mr. B.   social.
Mrs. B.   social, recreational, that's what it is. And as they say, when you reach that age . . . a lot of people miss the other kind (intellectual and political forms of integration. . . .

Dr. Jacobs and Mrs. B. discuss the local Democratic Club.

Mrs. B.   That's what it is. It's not a Democratic Club that has taken an interest in worldly affairs.
Mr. B.   Well, local and county politics, oh, yeah.

Etiquette

Putting aside discontent with facilities and rootlessness, there is an attitude which Jacobs (1974:66) characterizes as a "kind of bourgeois gentility." This is marked by a conscious effort to avoid boasting of former positions held. Jacobs remarks:

Allowing that some formerly influential persons may find a ready audience among other formerly influential persons (for example in the stock exchange room of the bank during morning "bull sessions" or at the Ladies Club) the general attitude of Fun City residents toward boasting or name-dropping ranges from boredom to resentment. This stems, not only from the resident's recognition that others are not what they once were, but also from the tacit understanding that one should neither give nor take offense (Jacobs 1974:66).

The Founder of the Ladies Club

The Ladies Club is one of the formal associations in Fun City which Jacobs (1974:26) accurately describes as a passive membership club. There are 596 members, but meetings are poorly attended and only a small group participates with any regularity. Mrs. R., who was one of the first residents in Fun City, describes the founding of the club as follows:

Well, then, one of the next things we had to have was a Woman's Club. You can't live in a town without a Woman's Club. And we said, well, we will call for a meeting and if we don't get fifty people there, why we will know Fun City is not ready for a Woman's Club. Well, we had 300 and some. The biggest woman's club that was ever organized at the start. And this last year we had 607 members. And it is one of the liveliest organizations in town. We have beautiful programs. We have a wonderful tea at the beginning of each meeting. That girl (Mrs. K.) was my stage (designer and stage decor), I was president this past year and she did the stage decorations. And they were fabulous. That girl is something. It is just simply a work of art. And we do a lot of philanthropic work. We give scholarships to — you know —, little old (Jonesville) over here. It is a very poor town. And last year we gave $1,800 in scholarships. This year we gave $1,000. Our students have gone on, really, they have done exceptionally well. Now one of our students three years ago was a boy named Jackson. Now his grades were not good, but he had talent, but not scholarship. And last night I saw a whole bunch of his pictures. They are simply fabulous. That boy has just done wonders. And then that little Paul Jones, you know, that we gave a scholarship to, he took dress designing, and I attended a wedding over in Jonesville in the Baptist Church — he decorated the church, he made the girl's wedding dress, he made all the bridesmaids' dresses, and it was the most gratifying thing you have ever seen. He is a little colored boy and he never world have gone on if we hadn't of helped him. . . . (Jacobs 1974:29).

The women in Fun City have not had to change their lives to any great extent. They were preadapted. They continue their household activities, they found chapters of clubs they belonged to in their original home towns, they play cards, and attend their various philanthropic functions. They are, perhaps, more isolated physically from the demands of younger people and the needs of others.

Isolation from the Outside World

These women were probably always mentally isolated from political and social change. They have achieved an adaptation to life which depends, in part, on misperception of reality. Jacobs (1974:27) gives an account of one of the philanthropic gestures of the Fun City Players, a volunteer drama group. They put on a 20-minute, one-act situation comedy for patients at a nearby nursing home. During the performance, dinner was served. Jacobs (1974:27) says:

Many patients were eating their meal, frequently with the assistance of nursing home aides and paying no attention whatever to the play. Others nodded, half asleep with their backs to the performers, while the rest stared blankly out of the windows. In fact, of the 20 or so persons comprising the audience, only three seemed to be paying any attention whatever to the performance.

Nevertheless, the players were pleased. Jacobs continues :

> What did the players make of this audience response? They were gratified. They told each other how well it had gone and how well it had been received. They were pleased that they were able to help those less fortunate by entertaining them and felt they really should stage performances there more often in the light of so appreciative a response.

Jacobs ascribes this "misperception" to the need of the players to be needed. This is, of course, partly true, but not completely true. In fact, it is doubtful whether the players' perception of their performance was faulty. In emic terms, they had set out to stage a play and had done so. Whatever the personal frictions, lapses of memory, or absenteeism which plague volunteer organizations, they had, indeed, succeeded in their goal. The audience's reaction was peripheral to the basic fact that a group of volunteers accomplished a project successfully. This is a central value in volunteer organizations, both male and female, whether one of aged or young people. People are highly gratified, despite an etic doubt as to the value of the accomplishment, because they have entered into and carried through an activity for which they receive no compensation. Success is, in our society, often measured in terms of money, and money is gained through work. People who work and are not paid in money are enormously altruistic, and subject to failure since one cannot command cooperation without payment. Therefore, any project carried through to fruition by a group of volunteers is, by definition, successful.

Aging and Death

However, there is one reality which cannot be ignored. That is the fact of death. Jacobs (1974:42) recounts a conversation:

Mrs. B.   When we first moved out here (six years ago) we were the first on this block. And at that time there was only one widow in this whole block and now there are seven of us in a row. I don't know, I think this is a bad side of the street. They're all on this side of the street. The other side of the street seems to be all right.

Mrs. F.   No.

Mrs. B.   Well, there's one widow over there.

Mrs. F.   No, they lost three over there.

Further study of this group, or another similar retirement community, would be of value to determine whether widowhood is easier to bear in a leisure community made up of people of all age groups, both sexes, with people involved in normal living processes. Since the widows of Fun City continue to live there, it may be assumed that their financial status had not been affected by the loss of their husbands.

Information from retirement communities in Florida indicates that widows in such communities fare better than they would elsewhere. They have formed informal self-help groups, which use a system of checking on each other every day to be sure each individual is alright. In one such community, each resident goes to the office and turns over a disc near his or her name. One side of the disc is a bright red. If a resident has not turned over his disc by noon, management or neighbors investigate. One of the real terrors of the aged living alone has been the possibility of the occurrence of a disabling stroke or other catastrophe, which would prohibit the person from actively seeking aid.

Another problem for Fun City residents is the lack of transportation to shopping and medical facilities. Women who are now in their 60s and 70s often have not learned to drive or are troubled by such factors as poor sight and hearing and are thus unable to drive. Mobility, then, becomes a problem. Many such women had formerly relied upon their husbands for transportation. As widows, they find themselves more isolated. Often the one or two widows who do drive feel inconvenienced by the demands of the nondriving widows for transportation.

Widowhood and the Division of Labor

The division of labor has been so strongly encultured in people of this generation that few women can handle simple household repairs or large gardening projects. As a result, in Florida, at least, many women with living husbands resent the fact that widowed neighbors often call upon their husbands for help.

Fun City as Middle America

To the observer, Fun City may not live up to its name. Jacobs states that most of the people spend much of their time in activities that can be performed in any setting, such as watching television or sleeping.

Would they do other things if they were in other settings? Probably not. In Fun City, the aged are a majority rather than a minority. They have brought with them all the cultural baggage of a lifetime of Middle American living. They have transplanted their life styles. There is the possibility that they may be more comfortable because they live in a community of people who share their problems as well as their values.

3. LINDA, SUBURBAN WIFE AND MOTHER

Children of the 1940s

To be born in the 1940s was to be born in the eye of the hurricane. Parents of these children had lived through the great depression and World War II. Such experiences had left indelible impressions on them, which affected their values as well as their views on childrearing. The forties and fifties provided a period of relative calm, conformity, and togetherness; the tumultuous 60s were in the future.

Suburbia and the Child

Linda is a child of the 1940s. She grew up in a family where material security was very important. After years of deprivation first due to the depression, and then due to the war, her parents finally realized their dream of a little house in the suburbs of New York. There they tried to simulate the lives of the family in the Dick and Jane readers of the time. The suburb, so close to the heart of the city, was nevertheless a world of its own. There was a high degree of homogeneity. The only blacks present were the occasional cleaning women; the only elderly people were the grandparents who came to visit. Linda was constantly reminded that she had everything a child could want, but she could not believe this since she never saw children who had less than she did.

Schooling

Her schooling was consistent with the relatively bland existence she lived. She was ten years old before she visited Harlem, and then she merely passed through. She remembers asking her father what all the "colored people" were doing there. She also learned that America was the most powerful and richest country in the world, and that communists were enemies, that "everyone" wore "Villager" shirtdresses and bobby socks, that Frank Sinatra was the greatest, that boys were people you dated, and that her ultimate goal in life was to find a nice boy and settle down to replicate the life her parents had at last achieved. Although she was exposed to literature, science, and government, these subjects did not motivate her to further development.

Activities

Her "leisure" was as structured as her studies. There were Girl Scouts on Tuesday, dancing lessons on Thursday, Sunday school on Sunday. As she grew, her activities grew in number. She became a cheerleader, which required hours of after-school practice. She also became active in the youth group of her church. Voice lessons were added to the dancing lessons. Endless hours were spent with the dentist to have braces applied and removed. She acquired girl friends of varying degrees of intimacy: there was the best friend to whom Linda revealed all; there were good friends with whom one shared pajama parties, secrets about boys, and plans for the future; and there were those girls Linda did not associate with. Some of them were unpleasant and some were excluded merely because an "in" group, by definition, implies an "out" group.

Retrospection

Linda fondly recalls the memories of those years of growing up. Discipline was never harsh. Mother was, perhaps, a bit too fussy about the neatness of her house, and father was perhaps overly concerned about things left on the driveway or the lawn being trampled. But life, on the whole, presented no challenges. Linda says that until recently she never realized that her life was so one-dimensional. Her parents, too, recall Linda's childhood with warmth. She was always a good girl, never gave them a moment's trouble, but after all, "why not, didn't she have everything?" Linda was totally unaware of the fact that only a few miles from her neat home there were enormous slums, where children literally fought over a nickle or a dime, and where mothers were not always at home whenever they were needed, and fathers, when they were home at all, were often drunk or violent. World affairs played no real role in the conversations of suburbia. Of course everyone knew about communists and Joe McCarthy, and good, dear President Eisenhower, but the important thing was getting a date for the prom, being taken to football games, getting a real cashmere sweater set. Suburbia encouraged early dating. Children in the first grade escorted each other solemnly to "mixed" parties. Of course, both children were actually escorted by a parent.

College

Linda attended a college within commuting distance of her home. It was here that she had her first contact with the varieties of experience offered by the large city. Linda's parents sent her to college because they wanted their children to have the best education. Linda's brother was sent to a college in Boston. The family could not afford to send two children away to school.

"After all," said her mother, "she's going to get married anyway." At college Linda at first suffered a kind of culture shock. There were whole groups of people she never realized existed. There were people who were serious about politics, art, or reading. There were libraries full of books she had never heard of. There were professors who talked about far away countries and spoke the languages of those countries. She learned for the first time that the world had problems, and that she was expected to contribute to the solution of those problems. She heard about the devastating destruction of Hiroshima and Nagasaki. She began to question the validity of that nuclear strike.

Activism

During Linda's second year at college, she terrified her family by joining a group of students who were marching about the White House, demonstrating against nuclear warfare. President Kennedy, less terrified than the parents, sent out word that he, too, deplored nuclear war, and had the kitchen send out coffee and doughnuts for the demonstrators. Thus began a series of political activities. Out of deference to her parents, Linda refrained from marching in Selma, Alabama, but she did buy Christmas cards sold by CORE and even attended meetings of student activist groups. She began to think of doing something with her life in addition to being a wife and mother.

Courtship

It was at one of the activist meetings that Linda met David. He was studying law, and hoped to join his uncle's firm. Their courtship was agreeable in every way. Linda's parents and siblings all approved of David, and his family liked Linda. They shared many common interests. They were both political liberals, more or less lapsed Christians. Both began an exploration of the cultural heritage of New York. David acted as guide and teacher. His family had been more interested in intellectual and cultural events than Linda's, and so he had more experience. Together they explored the Cloisters, the ballet, the foreign films, the Guggenheim Museum, and the Modern Museum of Art. Linda began to think of taking a job after graduation. David, who still had another year of law school ahead of him, thought it might be a fine thing, especially if Linda could get a job doing something significant. In 1964, Linda graduated from Hunter College. During the last months of the semester, she became somewhat insecure because so many of her classmates were going to get married immediately upon graduation. But David still had that year of law school to complete, and there was the possibility of a job as a social worker.

Engagement

In June, a compromise decision was reached. David and Linda became formally engaged. A large reception was held to make this announcement. Linda's family home was too small for the 100 invited guests, so the family rented the reception hall at a local club. Linda looks back on the time of her engagement with mixed feelings. She and David were, as she says, "right for each other." There were the candlelit dinners at small and obscure ethnic restaurants, because they were saving money toward their future home. They took the subway rather than cabs, and took advantage of the many free events available in New York, such as Shakespeare in the Park, and the outdoor concerts in local parks, zoos, and museums. But as David began to prepare for the bar exams they had less time for such activities. Linda, too, found herself more and more depressed by her case load. There were simply too many problems, and too few people to deal with them. More and more Linda came to doubt the effectiveness of her welfare work. Increasingly, she came to lose respect for her clients. She came to see them, not as people who needed her to help them over the rough spots, but as leeches who drained her physically and emotionally without any possibility of standing on their own feet. In March 1965, Linda missed her period. This proved to be a false alarm, but nevertheless, David and Linda decided to get married that June. They came to this desperate decision for several reasons. Linda says:

> I felt that we were growing apart. Dave was always studying for his exams. I was so tired and depressed by my work that we weren't even having any fun together. I thought if we didn't marry soon, we'd lose each other. We were already losing so much.

The Wedding

Linda remembers the next few months as a kaleidoscope of "happenings." Actually, it was Linda's mother who arranged the formal wedding — the church and the reception which followed. Linda's old friends planned showers for her. David, still seriously studying, became lost in a welter of bridal veils, bridesmaids' dresses, gift lists, thank you notes, altar decorations, and all the minutia which accompanies the traditional middle-class American wedding. Linda found her time and her thoughts concentrated on the wedding as though it were to be the last day of her life. The wedding became more important than getting married. Endless decisions had to be made — whom to invite, what to serve, should some people be invited to church only, or to the reception only. How to word the invitations. Should they be engraved or printed? Should little cousin Ellen be asked to be a flower girl? Who were to be maid of honor and best man? And should there be a single or double-ring ceremony? And the bridal gown. And even the wedding cake, and the small boxes provided for the guests to carry a piece of it home with them. The caterer had to be chosen, as well as the band. David? Oh, David was busy, he'd be there when the time came.

Early Married Life

And so he was. In June 1965, David and Linda were married amid an extravagant ritual display. They took a short honeymoon at a cottage which David's uncle lent them. And then they moved into a small apartment in the city, so that both could get to work easily. Besides, as yet, they could not afford a house. Their first few months of married life, though not idyllic, were good. Linda says:

> It was a tiny apartment, really, but we loved it. There were many other young couples like ourselves in the neighborhood and we had small dinners together. We went out as much as David's work would permit. It was good. We didn't have to say goodnight at the door. Of course, I was tired a lot of the time. My work was really getting me down. So, when I became pregnant, I was kind of relieved. At least I wouldn't have to work any more.

Children

Little David was born in 1966. By this time David had passed the bar exam, and was working in his uncle's firm. He was not earning very much, but by cutting a few corners, they were able to live reasonably well in the small apartment they had. Linda found herself living a life programmed by the needs of her son. She breast-fed him, but after six months decided he would do better on baby food supplemented by bottles. In nice weather, Linda took little David to the park. She was soon one of a group of young mothers who flocked together on the park benches, watching their children in perambulators or in the playground. She became conversant with Dr. Spock and Dr. Gesell. She kept a little diary of firsts — David walked at ten months, David got his first tooth at eight months, and so on. She was completely absorbed in the development of her child. She bought only recommended, educational toys. She read Dr. Ginott on how to speak to your child. She and David seldom went out together. To save the expense of a baby sitter, they alternated nights out. David did not mind this because he often brought work home from the office. Linda went to the movies with other young mothers. But soon both David and Linda found the little apartment in the city too cramped for their needs. Linda wanted her child to grow up in a "safe" neighborhood and to attend a good school. These were only to be found either in the extremely high-rent districts of the city or out in the suburbs. David began to feel the need to meet his clients in less formal, more social situations. Country clubs with golf courses were ideal for this.

The Move to Suburbia and Isolation

With encouragement from both sets of parents, as well as substantial loans, Linda and David bought a house in the suburbs, but not the suburbs of Linda's youth. These homes were not regarded as permanent abodes. Rather, the young couples who went rather heavily into debt to live there, saw the first home as only one of a series of homes of increasing luxury, as their affluence increased. It was important to have a "good" address. The country club was a must, even though the dues were high, because one could meet clients and entertain there as well. Little David, at three, began to attend a Montessori kindergarten. Linda drove her husband to the station every morning, and then used the car all day to drive little David to and from kindergarten. She needed the car to get to the market. She lived bounded by the telephone and the automobile. Without them, she was isolated. But it was an enchanted isolation. Little David was growing up and she was molding him. Some neighbors were also parents of small children. They formed informal groups who met at each others' houses to drink coffee and talk. They lived in a relatively manless world. Husbands were picked up at the commuter train, usually after the smallest children were in bed. During the weekends, husbands often had strategic golf games, or more recently, tennis games, to be played with potential clients. Saturday nights were reserved for the club, or entertaining or being entertained by potentially useful people.

Woman's Work in Suburbia

In 1970 Linda's second son, Seth, was born. Now, Linda's life was truly bounded by her children. With a four-year-old and an infant to care for, she was inundated by work. The values of her culture were demanding. Each of her children had to be as close to spotless at all times as they could be. Her house had to look like a "House Beautiful" illustration. Her kitchen must look as though no one had ever prepared a meal in it. David must be brought to and from the station. The car must be kept in good repair; the food brought from the supermarket; tasteful dinners prepared for the adults and nutritionally sound diets provided for the children. The lawn required attention; to neglect it even slightly would mean ostracism in the neighborhood. The house was large and needed a good deal of care, and there was no help. Indeed household help, where it existed, was the one thing women fought over possessively. If anyone found a minimally reliable maid, she could be sure that her neighbors and her best friends would try to entice the woman away. Linda found the work more demanding and physically exhausting than anything she had ever done. She attempted to live up to impossible standards. When David came home, he had to find a beautifully groomed wife, a spotless home, two well-scrubbed boys, and a good dinner. Anything less might tempt him to forego the long train ride home and find a more amenable woman closer to the office.

A Typical Day

In 1974, Linda was 30 years old. Her day begins at seven. She wakes her husband, prepares breakfast for him, gets the boys up and sees that they dress with a minimum of fuss. After breakfast, they all pile into the car; Linda drops her husband off at the train station and little David at school. Then she takes Seth to the nursery school. Her return home begins the endless round of washing, drying clothes and dishes, cleaning the house, much of which is done by mechanical appliances, which have a way of breaking down. Then it is essential to wait for the repairman, who never comes at a definite time. After a small pickup lunch, it is time to retrieve Seth. Occasionally the morning is taken up by a meeting of one of the many volunteer organizations to which Linda belongs. There is the book club, which meets monthly to hear a member report on a classic or new book, and the garden club. Actually, the garden club ladies are a bit older, and usually meet in the afternoon, but they sometimes schedule a morning meeting. The church also has a women's group to which Linda belongs. In the city, Linda and David never felt the need for formal religious organizations. But out here, in Maplewood, where it was difficult to meet people unless you made an effort, it seemed necessary to become church members and to affiliate with the men's and women's organizations connected with it. The meetings themselves took little time, but stimulated a lot of activity. There were committees for fund-raising, committees for education, committees for getting new members. All of these enlisted the energies of the young women of the community. Linda says:

> Sometimes it seems much harder to get things done by asking people to do certain things. I could probably get it done better by myself. But then, serving on these committees, helps me to get to know other people. Out here nobody sits outside, or walks anywhere. You can't meet people casually. You have to belong to a group. And then you get to meet some of the really prominent people and that helps Dave, I guess.

Whatever the activity of the morning, after Seth comes home and is put to bed for a short nap, Linda spends at least an hour a day on the telephone. She calls various people in regard to committee work which has been delegated to her. She calls her mother and David's mother. She makes arrangements for a baby sitter for an evening during the weekend. About these calls, Linda comments:

> Well, most of the time I'm cooped up with the children. I don't often get to talk to other adults, not as much as I'd like to. And I don't have the time to drive into the city to see my mother or my mother-in-law. I only have about two hours between picking up Seth, and little David's coming home. I am always so busy.

The school bus deposits David about the time Seth wakes up. Linda gives both boys milk and cookies. David changes to his play clothes. Some afternoons Linda has to drive David to a Scout meeting or a Little League practice session. She takes Seth with them. Often, while David is occupied, she stops at the local shopping center and picks up clothes left at the cleaners or does some marketing. On the afternoon when David has no organized activities, she may drive him to a friend's house, returning to pick him up at five. At other times, friends may come to play with David; Linda tries to use such relatively free time for special tasks like ironing, mending, or polishing silver. On rare occasions she may bake something special for the boys. While carrying out such projects, however, she is always alert for the sounds of quarrels or injury which may come from outdoors, if the weather is nice, or the playroom, which the boys use in inclement weather. Little Seth is often a problem. He wants to join the older children in play, and they have little patience with him. Linda encourages Seth to make friends his own age. Maplewood is as conscious of age differences as Fun City.

At five, the children are picked up by their mothers. Linda picks up David, wherever he may be, and Seth on the rare occasions he is away from home. Both children are then bathed. David manages his bath alone very well. Seth still requires a little help. Dinner is served to the boys at six. David is then relegated to his room to do his homework, and Seth is allowed to watch TV. Linda goes to the station to pick up David. She says:

> That is the worst part of the day for me. I'm tired, sometimes it is icy out, or raining, and I hate to drive to pick Dave up. I hate leaving the boys for even a few minutes. By the time Dave and I get back, they are often quarreling, or little David isn't doing his homework, or something.

Once at home, Dave fixes the predinner cocktail and talks to the children, while Linda prepares the adults' dinner. Seth is put to bed before his parents have dinner, while little David is allowed to watch TV until nine o'clock.

A Marriage Matures

Conversation between Linda and Dave is limited. He asks whether she has gotten the car or the washer fixed. She tells him that they have been invited to a party Saturday night. Rarely do they discuss matters unrelated to the immediate needs of the family. Dinners are sometimes rushed; P.T.A. meetings are held in the evening, as well as church fellowship meetings. Often either David or Linda will go alone to such meetings, while the other stays at home with the boys. Sometimes it is possible to get a babysitter and they can go to the P.T.A. meeting together. The church fellowship meetings are restricted to men. By 11, the evening is over. Linda and Dave, with their two children, are home and in bed.

Both Dave and Linda are intelligent people who are aware of the changes that suburban living has brought to their marriage.

On several occasions they have left both boys with grandparents and have gone to Puerto Rico or Florida for a weekend. They both feel it is important not to disrupt the boys' schooling by keeping them out for a week. They also feel that a longer stay would be an imposition on the grandparents, and besides, David can seldom spare more time from work. These weekends have been conscious and futile efforts to resurrect their marriage. Linda says:

I always think that if Dave and I could only get away by ourselves, things would be all right. I love my sons, but I know I spend most of my time talking about them, worrying about them. Even when we go away and I leave them with mother, I worry about them. And I'm always so tired. Maybe I do too much. My mother always says I join too many committees, but how else am I going to see other adults? If it weren't for Dave and the kids, I'd move back to the city. Maybe then I would be able to do something, to be a part of something important. But, even when I was working, I didn't like it. It's funny, you grow up thinking you'll marry a nice guy and have a couple of kids and a house in a nice area, and then when you've got it, you wonder why you wanted it. When Dave and I lived in the city, before the children came, we talked politics, went to concerts, saw the latest movies. But most important, we always had so much to tell each other. He knew so much, and I wanted to learn so much. Now our conversations sound like a laundry list. Even our sex life isn't that good any more. We are both so tired at the end of the day. And sometimes when Dave wants sex in the morning, I'm afraid the boys will walk in or something. Then when we go away for a weekend, it just can't happen, you know, it's like we both know why we went away, and we've got to feel sexy and it is hard to feel sexy when you have to.

David says:

I don't know what gets into Linda sometimes. She's got everything a woman could want. We live in a really fine place with some pretty darn important people. I don't know why she's tired. I'm the one who does the commuting. I'll say this for her — she's a very good mother. A little too good, maybe. All she can talk about are the kids. And she hates to leave them, even with her own mother, or mine. I sometimes wish she had a little more sense about choosing these committees she works on. I know she does a lot of this work to help me socially and professionally, and I appreciate that, but sometimes I'd like to come home, just once, and not hear about the newest fund-raising gimmick, or David's crooked front tooth. Still, I like Maplewood, and it's a wonderful place for the kids.

Asked about her future plans, Linda says:

Well, maybe it will be better when both kids are in school all day. Then maybe I can go into town once in a while and see plays and museums, and shop, and meet friends. But I don't know. A lot of my friends here have children in school all day and they don't go anywhere. I guess what I'd like most is to have it the way it used to be between Dave and me. Maybe if I could come to town for lunch once in a while. Right now, it is as if we live in different worlds, and we can't share our experiences or interests. I have no time to read the newspaper, most days. And Dave is always talking about people in his office, and clients, and so on. He thinks I don't listen to him, but I do. It's just that I don't feel a part of it. I'm stuck in Maplewood, but it is a wonderful place for the children.

4. CAROL, PROFESSIONAL WOMAN

Early Life

Where Linda opted for the conventional life of a young wife and mother, things did not work out that way for Carol. She, too, is a product of the 1940s baby boom. She, too, lived much of her life in the sterile, raw, new suburbs which blossomed in and around the cities, suburbs built for the newly released soldier and his bride, where the down-payment was paid for by the G.I. Bill. But Carol's family was less houseproud than most. They read more, and were more concerned about Carol's education than Linda's parents had been. In lieu of siblings that her parents could not give her, Carol's house was often filled with pets. Patches, an unhousebroken rabbit who wore rubber panties indoors, shared the house with a large and rather stupid Irish setter, a guinea pig, a female canary, which persisted in laying eggs instead of singing, and Priscilla, a garter snake brought home from camp.

Prep School

Carol went to a prep school instead of a community high school. She quickly became a member of a rather select set of young people who were being carefully and thoroughly primed for college entrance. There was never a moment's doubt about the fact that she would attend college. However, in those days, the baby boom had just reached college age, and the colleges found themselves unprepared in that they lacked facilities, particularly dormitory space for the many students who applied. Carol's parents both felt it was important to her development that she go away to college.

College

Eventually she found herself at a less well-known university in Washington, D.C. In the summer, between prep school graduation and college entrance, Carol joined a group of young people on an organized tour of Europe. Once at college, her freshman year was relatively easy for her because of her prep-aration. She found time to join a sorority, she dated freely, and in fact, had a very good time. Carol started out as a political science major, but lost interest. She then decided to major in English, but soon realized that this led to a dead-end professionally. During her sophomore year, she suffered a minor episode of depression, something that academics called "sophomore slump." This malady, which afflicts our most sensitive youth, was probably caused by a multiplicity of factors. For one thing, though she liked her sorority sisters as individuals, she disliked being restricted to friendship with members of the sorority. She resented the time sorority affairs took from other activities, and finally decided to disengage herself from the sorority.

She was intrigued by the possibilities offered by an anthropology major. She also was most comfortable and at home in an academic atmosphere. During the summer of her freshman year, she had worked at a bank in New York, and had gone with friends to some of the activities at Columbia University. Academia, she decided, was her thing.

Seeing Europe

During the summer of her sophomore year, she and several of her friends from Washington went to Europe. This time, on their own, they explored places only briefly visited during her guided tour. She also went to places she had not previously seen. They traveled as students do — without much money — foregoing the luxury hotels and restaurants. The trip was marred by the death of Carol's father.

Fears of Possessiveness

She returned home, unsure of what the future held. As an only child, there was a good deal of pressure on her to transfer to a local college and to live with her mother. Eventually she, together with her mother, decided to return to Washington where her career was already charted and where most of her friends lived. Both women felt it was necessary to rebuild their lives as individuals, rather than become too dependent upon each other. Given the time and place, it was a typical modern American decision. Visions of "momism" and fear of possessiveness and overprotection prevented mother and daughter from giving way freely to their need for each other, and to the grief and insecurity they both felt. It was to be a long time before either regained sufficient emotional balance to accept each other fully. During Carol's junior and senior years at college, she became more totally absorbed in anthropology. Her grades, always good, became superb. She learned to use the resources of the capital city. She worked in the storerooms of the Smithsonian Museum, and learned to repair and preserve anthropological collections. Carol began to date young men, usually fellow anthropology students.

The Open Country

Of all the subdisciplines of anthropology, archaeology interested her most. During the summer she attended a field school in the Southwest. Here she fell in love with the country. The Southwest, with its incomparable scenery, its open spaces, its fascinating population of Indians, Chicanos, and Anglos, its deep roots in archaeology — all of these appealed to her. On her short visits to

New York, she found herself stifled now by the crowds, the city itself, but even more by the burdensome etiquette of dress and manner so necessary to a densely populated East Coast. The casualness, the openness, and the relaxed relationships of the west held greater appeal. During her senior year, 1965, Carol made Phi Beta Kappa, and was offered a scholarship to complete her graduate studies at the University of Oregon. Young women did not yet freely accept the idea of casual heterosexual residence. Many if not most of Carols' classmates were engaged or going to be married right after graduation. For herself, she was torn by several personal problems. For one thing, she was anxious to continue professionally but was not quite ready to go clear cross country on her own. For another, she had not yet come to grips with her ambivalent feelings toward her mother and the loss of her father. Reason dictated acceptance of the scholarship, emotion dictated that she not go it alone. Among the young men Carol knew, one was particularly persistent in his pursuit of her. He was a bright young man, another anthropology student who came from a small, western community. Bill was a year younger than Carol and had another year to complete his B.A. He had a charming manner and what appeared to be a deep devotion to Carol. Bill transferred to Oregon.

Marriage

These two young people demanded and got a very traditional wedding after having lived together more or less openly for months. As in Linda's case, there were invitations to have engraved, caterers and hotels to be selected, a menu and a guest list to decide on. But whereas Linda had been pleased to receive the usual sterling silver bowl, platter, or dish, these gifts were singularly inappropriate for a graduate student marriage. After a week at Cape Cod, the pair set out for Oregon in a well-used Volkswagon.

Graduate School

Oregon proved a disaster for Carol. The grey, fog-shrouded climate was depressing. After an initial period of mutual discovery, Carol and Bill found themselves in active competition. Each had structured stereotypes about the role of husbands and wives, but neither was conscious of the fact. Although both were students and each received scholarship money, this money was not enough to keep them in even the modest style they chose to live.

Role Expectations

Carol thought Bill should be the one to get outside employment. Bill was particularly anxious to complete his B.A. so that he could be a graduate student on a par with his wife. He also expected Carol to run the household in the same way his mother had. He expected her to make her own clothes and to bake and cook.

Depression

In addition to these problems, a real physical problem developed. The birth-control pills that Carol had been taking caused her to develop an edema and a severe depression. Her weight fell drastically and she was very ill. In 1966, small town doctors were not aware of the problems that could be caused by "the pill." They treated her depression through that particular school of psychoanalysis Phyllis Chesler (1972) describes so well. She was told that her problem was psychological and that she had to adjust to being a good wife. She was also told that she must put her infantile dependence upon her parents behind her and accept her new role as wife and potential mother. The problem was actually that she had accepted the role of mother too well, for she had been acting as a mother to her husband. He demanded her constant presence, her care, her nurturing. She exhausted herself in her efforts to be a student and a wife. After a year at Oregon, Carol received her M.A. and Bill his B.A. and some credits toward graduate school. The couple decided to move to California. Here, while Bill enrolled in graduate school, Carol's depression was so bad that she lost all professional ambition. They took a tiny bungalow, the only thing available in their price range.

Carol as a Social Worker

Carol got a job in social work; Bill went to school. Carol left for work early in the morning and returned late in the day to find the sink littered with the dishes used by Bill and his friends. Bill was now the intellectual in the family. He was the student; Carol was the working wife whose privilege it was to put him through school. His comings and goings were irregular at best. It was not Carol's business where he went or with whom. She was to provide and that was all. The gap between the two widened to the point of no return. Still Carol clung to her marriage. She felt that divorce was an admission of failure. During this period, Carol finally located a fine, young physician who recognized that her symptoms were produced chemically. He took her off the pill and her recovery was spectacular. Unlike Linda, she found her work with the welfare department satisfying in many ways. She felt pride in being able to support herself financially, and felt deep responsibility toward the people she served. She felt a sense of accomplishment when, through her efforts, they achieved some small triumph — finding a job or getting proper medical attention. As her depression lifted, she realized that her marriage was simply an impossible situation. She and Bill decided to try a camping trip to Baja, California, as a remedy. As in Linda's case, this did not work.

Divorce and Return to Graduate School

Shortly thereafter, Carol and Bill separated. Within a few months, Carol learned that she was pregnant. There was still time, at this point, to return to living with her husband and bearing his child. But Carol had the intelligence and the experience to recognize that a child or several children would do no more than to imprison her in a bad marriage. Unsure of her mother's response, and unwilling to involve her husband, she had an abortion alone. She was testing the limits of her strength and her independence. She found herself adequate and capable. Shortly thereafter, she enrolled at another California University to get her Ph.D.

Life in California in the Late 1960s

While the storms of student protests raged, Carol remained staunchly apolitical and unattached. During the days of study at the library she learned to dive quickly beneath the table at the sound of students' running feet. These were usually followed by running police's feet, and then it was safe to emerge from under the table and resume studying.

An unpleasant side effect of the police vigilance against student activists was the fact that the police left many residential areas unguarded. Most universities are ringed with low-cost housing for which students compete with local poor people. During the late 1960s, these became hotbeds of "crime in the street." It was while living alone in such housing that Carol was attacked and raped. Shortly thereafter, she moved to share a house with two other girls. Despite this sordid experience, proving to herself that she could cope with personal problems and support herself, all served to give her a new kind of inner strength, a sense of security and independence which would serve her well in the years ahead.

Entering the Job Market

In anthropology, as in other disciplines, it is customary for a student who has completed all required course work and passed comprehensive exams to take a teaching position at a college or university while completing the last phase of doctoral studies and writing a dissertation. Carol came into the job market in 1970, a most opportune time, for if she had come years earlier, she might have faced more difficulty as a woman. But in 1970, anthropology was looking for young women. In another two years, few academic jobs would be available for men or women. Carol entered the job market just in time to take advantage of a self-critical movement within anthropology, which attempted to right the balance in the hiring of women and minority groups.

Anthropologists, just as any subculture, have their own tribal rituals. One of these is the annual Meeting of the American Anthropological Association, where anthropologists meet annually to exchange information through symposia and reading of learned papers. They also come to see old friends. Here, new, young anthropologists seek out possible employers, and vice-versa. It is doubtful that any contracts are signed at this time, but the employers form opinions regarding people they would like to interview further. And employees learn a bit about the competition and general state of the market. For reserved and sensitive people hunting jobs, the annual meetings are a kind of slave market. Carol attended a meeting in San Diego. She did not receive any commitments at that time, but several potential positions were available. During the following months she traveled to several universities for interviews.

Choosing a Job

Choosing a place to work is quite different for a woman as opposed to a man. A woman must consider such factors as the safety of the community. Carol knew that a university campus in the great cities is usually surrounded by pockets of poverty and slums. Living close to the university is not physically safe. Living far away from the university is both expensive and uncomfortable for a single woman. There is little room for the lone woman among the pair-bonded families of suburbia. Moreover, the universities with the greatest prestige often pay the smallest salaries, making it financially impossible for a woman who has to make her own living to attain a standard of living commensurate with her status.

Carol was fortunate in that she found a welcome at a university in the Southwest. Not only was she back in the area she loved, but she also found employment at a university which enjoyed an excellent reputation.

Carol at Present

By 1974, Carol had completed her doctorate and had been teaching for several years. She is in charge of the field school at which she got her initial training. Professionally, she is respected and liked. She has published several articles and is looking forward to further publications. She serves on several administrative committees, both department-wide and university-wide. To a greater extent than ever before, she is content. But she recognizes that there are areas in her life which, if not barren, are not altogether satisfying. Socially, her closest friends have been the relatively few women in her department, and some of the neighbors in her apartment complex. The Southwest has never conformed as strictly to the couple-pairing tradition of the East. Carol recognizes that she could not enjoy as free a social life back east as she can here. She is decidedly uncomfortable in any dating situation. She would far rather attend a concert or a play with a young couple she knows well than go out with an unknown or less well-known man.

Carol and Marriage

Carol says: "I've had it with marriage. I am contented with things the way they are." Things as they are include a relationship with a man which approaches a living-in arrangement. Both remain financially independent of each other, but they are emotionally dependent upon each other. Carol regards this arrangement ideal for the present. She and her lover share much, and yet do not feel bound. They are intellectually stimulating to each other, as well as physically attracted. Marriage would present a number of problems. Neither really needs or wants the formal responsibilities of marriage. They both prefer to have a less structured relationship. Not the least important reason for this is academic mobility. University jobs do not come in pairs, and if either Carol or her lover were to move to another university, the relationship would have to be ended. Carol is quite outspoken about this possibility, although she gave up the opportunity to move to a prestigious Eastern university in 1973. Marriage would simply formalize the bond, but would not necessarily strengthen it. Carol explains:

> Marriage is important if you want children, but I don't want children. I can't see myself giving up at least eight years of my life to care for a baby now. And I know if I had a baby, I would want to stay home and take care of it. Eight years out of my career at this time would be impossible. I worked too long and too hard to get where I am, and I still have a lot of work ahead of me if I am to become established. I love John and he loves me. We are together most of the time. If either one of us were ill, the other would take care of things. We need our privacy, and this way we get it. The only time that things become difficult is when there are family functions. It would be nice to go to some of these things as a couple, but that is relatively less important than the satisfaction I derive from the freedom of our relationship.

Carol had never been a baby-watcher. When other little girls played with dolls, Carol roller-skated. As an adult, she likes "small people," but feels no great sense of loss at not having any of her own. She does have a small terrier, who is a less demanding surrogate child.

At this point in their lives, both Linda and Carol are busy people. Linda is raising a family; Carol is building a career. It cannot be known at this time which one will ultimately derive the greater satisfaction. They are both in progress; neither is a finished product. Biologically, it is more likely that Linda can raise her boys and then go on to a new career, than that Carol can build her career and then decide to have a family. Chronologically thirty is quite young, but as the mother's age increases, the likelihood of Down's Syndrome or mongolism in the child increases. Carol knows this, but at present refuses to be too concerned about it. If she ever does marry, she can adopt a child. And to what extent do children constitute a fulfillment for their mothers? While they are young, children absorb the creative energies of their mothers, but when they grow older, mothers in our culture are constantly constrained lest they overprotect, be too possessive, or in some way cause psychological damage to their children. We rear children to be independent. We want our privacy, and we want our children to have their privacy. And we become, finally, a rigidly age-graded society. Young professional women like Carol must make very difficult choices, choices which do not have to be made by men. Men can procreate at any age; women cannot. Men are expected to work hard at their careers when they are young but women who do so are often suspect. They find it difficult to form friendships with other women. If other women are in the same profession, there is a degree of competition between them. If other women are wives of colleagues, they are often jealous of the relationships between their husbands and women colleagues. Most of all, women who have no careers of their own are often awed and a bit frightened by the capacity of the professional woman. They may admire her, they may envy her, but they will seldom befriend her.

Women and Mobility

In our society, men have much more mobility than women. Though they may be robbed if they live in a high-crime area, they are not likely to be raped. They can afford to live almost anywhere — a woman cannot. Men can pick up wives and children and move to new locations, but a woman must remain alone if she desires such mobility. The rare men who would willingly chuck their jobs to follow their wives probably lack ambition more than they value woman's liberation. A woman who places a high value on her own career could not respect a man who placed little or no value on his own career.

These are the realities that the Carols of the world face, but the final word has yet to be said. The courage, spirit, and independence shown by these women may lead them to discover new solutions to old problems. We have yet to see the finished products of the generations of the 1940s.

5. ANNIE ROBINSON

In Annie Robinson we have an unusual woman who we would expect to fall in the category of "Women in the Cultures of Poverty." However, through innate intelligence and successful application of adaptive strategies, she has placed her foot on the rung of the ladder leading to middle-class America. She has a long way to go, and she may never make it, but she is trying. This is her story.

Childhood

Born in a cabin in Mississippi, Annie's early life parallels that of most poor black sharecropper families. She was the youngest in a family of five, the only girl. Her childhood memories are bittersweet. There are memories of grinding poverty, and the drunken brawling of her father and her older brother. Illness, and the lack of proper medical attention, remain in her mind. She once broke her collarbone and the nearest doctor would not treat blacks. It healed badly and still troubles her today. There is also the bitter memory of her older brother, who was shot and killed by the local sheriff. Sweet memories consist of her mother's tenderness, the fun of fishing in the local creek, her closeness to the earth and growing things, and above all, Sunday church, when people sang and clapped and rejoiced in the Lord.

Segregation

In Mississippi in the 1930s, segregation was so complete that Annie imagined that the white people were, somehow, another species. She could not imagine that they worked, sweated, drank, or quarreled. Children only knew that they must cast their eyes down when addressing the white person, that they must speak only when spoken to, and then only in the most polite and short phrases. For the sake of safety, it was better to steer clear of whites, to be faceless in the crowd, to keep one's own secrets within the community. To this day Annie is badly shaken by the overt anger of a white person. Speaking of a nurse who unjustly shouted at her, Annie says: "She reminded me of those white bitches in Mississippi. I could feel it, like living with that hate all over again."

Annie went to school long enough to learn to read and write, not fluently, but passibly. At home she spoke a dialect which is not easily understood by people speaking Standard American English. At school she learned the latter, and although she has an adequate vocabulary, at times of great emotional stress, she lapses into the local dialect of her childhood, which is unintelligible to the white people around her.

At 12 she was working in a local laundry, ironing shirts. Some 30 years later, she still hates to iron a shirt. At 16 she married a local man and set up housekeeping in a cabin like the one in which she was born. At this point, her life might have taken the path her mother's took. She might have given birth to several babies, worked to raise crops, and remained isolated in rural Mississippi. But, for several reasons, things did not work out that way. For one thing, she developed severe complications in her first pregnancy, which not only cost the life of her baby, but also left her reproductive organs severely damaged. Her husband soon took to staying out drinking, and became abusive at home. Her beloved mother became terminally ill. Annie is particularly bitter about the lack of care that her mother suffered.

> The doctor wouldn't come to the house, he wouldn't treat her. I used to go to him and he gave me some medicine for my mother. I don't think he even knew what was wrong with her, he certainly didn't care. Maybe if she had gotten the proper care in time, she'd have lived. Anyway, she died. I did my best for her, I nursed her, but she died. And my baby died. And my brother went off to Florida to pick fruit. I was the kind of a girl who had always done things with my brothers. I fished with them, I climbed trees with them, I learned how to fix engines. I guess I was a tom-boy. Anyhow, when my brother Tom decided to go to Florida to pick fruit, I went with him.

Life in Florida

At first Annie enjoyed life in a migrant workers' camp. It wasn't any harder than chopping cotton and the weather was warm and pleasant. But very soon she learned her physical limitations. She could not work fast or hard enough to earn any money. What little she made, she already owed to the commissary. Her shoulders hurt, and her internal infection gave her constant misery. When Tom and the others left for camps in the North, Annie stayed behind.

Growing Up

Annie soon found herself living in the black slums of St. Petersburg. She started out as a domestic, doing day work. This meant she had a whole house and laundry to clean for a different family every day. She worked from 8:00 AM to 5 PM or 6 PM, getting two to two and a half dollars, plus carfare for her work. She had a small room in a run-down house to which she returned exhausted every night. Too tired to prepare her own dinner, she lived on soft drinks, snacks, and when the loneliness became too much to bear, liquor. But she was learning. She learned that the white people for whom she worked were as human as she was. Some were certainly not as smart, some were mean, and some were well intentioned. But she quickly realized that the life she was living was not going to lead to anything but trouble. And she had enough of that in Mississippi. She applied for and got a job working for a family with several small children. In this new position, the chores did not have to be repeated each day; laundry came only twice a week and windows were washed monthly. Raising the children was difficult, but at that time she could cope with it. Now she made 10 dollars a week. She found herself doing the things that many poor black people did in St. Petersburg. She went to the dog track, hoping to win enough to buy some extra clothing. She played the numbers, and even ran them for a while. She took up with Joe, who was "a drinking man." They began to live together in a consensual marriage. Annie learned some of the adaptive strategies of poverty. For example, her utilities were billed under her own name, Annie Gainer. But she bought a second-hand car under her "married" name, Annie Scott. Hence, if she missed payments on one, the other would not be jeopardized. She was still drinking and still ailing. Eventually, her illness became too severe to permit her to go on working.

There were black doctors in St. Petersburg, and Annie could and did have an operation. Her health was restored, but at the cost of all her savings. Moreover, she went deeply into debt and lost her car. Her life was at a very low ebb. Her husband was of little help. He worked in construction, and made good money when he worked, but construction jobs were vulnerable to weather, financial conditions, and many other vagaries, including the availability of needed lumber or pipes. Even when he worked, he drank heavily, and Annie saw little of his pay. In a short time the relationship ended. Annie was now close to 30, and still not very strong. She had major surgery, and her ill-nourished, exhausted body needed time to recuperate. She had no job, and no money. Her brother Tom had come back to Florida, but he had a wife and small children now and could do very little for Annie.

Return to Church

It was in the depths of her despair that Annie turned again to the church, which had sustained her in her childhood. In so doing, she lost none of the values she had absorbed during her years of work. Annie knew that somehow, some day, she was going to live, if not as well, then nearly as well, as the people she had worked for. She knew now that whites and blacks were both humans. She was very conscious of the prejudice which kept blacks from white jobs, white money, white status, white power. She had seen enough of life in the black slum to know that "the man" was out to get you. She had dealt with slum landlords who accepted sexual favors in lieu of rent, and then turned the tenant out anyhow. She had learned to deal with the landlord who collected money from the tenant for the water bills, but failed to pay the city, so the tenant has his water turned off. Like Carolina in the *favela*, she learned to distrust politicians, white or black, who promised jobs and then forgot.

Annie now knew that she would never have any children of her own, but she desperately wanted the respectable domesticity of the middle class, and she set about getting it. Through her church she met Bill Robinson. He, too, had physical problems which kept him from holding a full-time job, and aspirations, which he had no ready means of fulfilling. But above all, he had a gentleness which Annie badly needed. He saw her through her bad days, when she was in physical discomfort. He helped her through with prayer, rather than drink. When Annie lost her temper, and flew into a rage at some obvious act of discrimination or injustice, Bill could calm her down. They were good for each other. Annie was sophisticated, cynical, ambitious, and hot-tempered; Bill was impractical, a dreamer but kind and soft-spoken.

Marriage and a Family

Bill and Annie bought an old house in a black neighborhood in Tampa. Annie took a part-time job as a domestic. Bill worked at odd jobs, and studied to become a pastor in his church. Founding a new church in the black community involved not only the ability to lead a congregation, but also the ability to help in the actual construction of the church building. Bill was paid by the contributions of the members. This seldom amounted to more than 25 or 30 dollars a week. Annie's part-time job paid about the same. In order to help with the house payments, Bill and Annie reached out into the kinship network which surrounds the matrifocal family. Bill had been raised by an aunt who was now very old and ill, and was receiving old age benefits. Annie and Bill made a home for the old lady. In return, they used her monthly welfare check for household expenses when they needed it. In this way they struggled along, barely keeping up with their expenses. But they had a house, and each had a car, old and rebuilt though it was. Bill's congregation was in a small town outside of Tampa. He needed transportation to get to and from church. Annie's job required transportation as well.

Soon they added to the family. Bill's niece, a girl of about fifteen, came to live with them. Unfortunately, this did not turn out too well. Bill and Annie had hoped that Carrie might finish school, get a job, and contribute to the support of the household. Instead, she became pregnant, married a very young man, and proceeded to have a series of babies.

Annie says:

> I told Carrie, I told her and told her. I said, "you'll come to the point where no man will have you." Why would a man take on a woman with four babies? Wouldn't a man rather have a wife like me; pulling him up instead of dragging him down?

In her midthirties now, Annie's goal was only partially achieved. She had the honor of being a pastor's wife, and a Mother in the church. It was a beautiful and memorable day when the new church was dedicated. Notables from other Primitive Progressive Baptist churches attended. Annie and the women prepared food. Annie led the women ushers in song, and Bill, the reverend, spoke from the pulpit. People smiled and clapped hands and sang. It was a beautiful occasion. Respectability had been achieved, but security had not.

Changing Jobs

It was at this point that Annie realized that the extended family network was not adaptive for Bill and herself. She found that, after the old aunt died, the other efforts to use the family network did not work well. Carrie had turned out to be more of a hindrance than a help. Bill's young son by a previous marriage had come to live with them, but the situation was impossible. With both parents working, the boy could not be adequately supervised. He required more care and money than either could expend. He has sent on to another relative. Annie felt the network was draining her rather than helping her rise in the world.

By this time Annie was much stronger than she had been. She knew full well that the key to security, like the key to respectability, lay in employment. Annie took a job as a nurse's aide in a local nursing home. She worked the night shift so that she could hold on to her part-time domestic work.

Life as an Employee

This new job was probably the most important single factor in orienting Annie's world view. At first she found it very difficult to work as one member of a group of black and white women because she was accustomed to the very personal relationships between the domestic and her employer. She took offense at the impersonal way in which orders were issued. She was hurt by the obvious prejudice of many of the senile patients who called her "nigger," even as she tended their most basic needs. She suspected her coworkers of plotting against her, and felt that her supervisor made her work much harder than the white nurses' aides. She was distressed by the inevitable institutional politics, but she persevered. Always a capable person, Annie soon came to be valued as a coworker. She began to understand that the patients were helpless victims of their time, and that the white aides had problems similar to hers. They began to socialize. They shared coffee breaks and dinners. After a while, they went to occasional luncheons in local restaurants. Always astute, she learned much from the other women. She learned to eat regular meals instead of snacking. She went to the beauty parlor to have her hair done. She began to feel some sense of purpose and security, which she had never known before. She was part of a large institution. She was no longer subject to the whims of an individual employer. She had social security. She had regular paid vacations. Annie and Bill used one of those vacations to drive cross country to visit one of Annie's brothers who had moved to the West Coast. They were impressed by the size and variety of their country. They learned that white people were not uniformly hostile. Bill took sick in a small town in Wisconsin, and was admitted and treated in a Catholic hospital. The sisters found a room for Annie, and she had her meals in the hospital. In deference to Bill's position, they were not charged for any of the medical care. Annie and Bill marveled at this, particularly because of her early years in Mississippi.

The New Home

About this time Annie and Bill became eligible for an experimental government project. Their old house was condemned as unfit for habitation. The government, through its Project Pride, provided money for the Robinsons to buy a house in a middle-class, predominantly white neighborhood. Part of the money provided went for a down payment on the house. Annie used the rest to furnish the house. She converted one room into a den for Bill. She furnished the rest of the house in excellent taste. For the first time Annie and Bill had a home they could be proud of, a home to which they could invite their friends, black and white. Annie proudly presided at a dinner party for Bill's deacons and their wives. They got along quite well with most of their neighbors. Certainly, overt prejudice has not been shown. Most of the other families in the area are white working-class people. Many are civil service employees. Many have working wives. They contradict the oft-stated claim that working class people are most prejudiced against blacks. They also contradict the theory that the cycle of poverty cannot be broken. Annie and Bill are examples of the fact that one way to overcome poverty is by providing employment opportunities, and judicious amounts of money for capital expenditures.

The Future

Annie and Bill have their feet on one of the low rungs of the ladder. Their grip is still not very firm. They need time to consolidate their position. The rate of inflation in 1974 and 1975 is doing them great harm. Utility bills are mounting. The high prices of heating oil and gasoline threaten their precarious economic balance. As the economy worsens, they may lose their jobs to other people. Already Bill has felt the pinch. There has been a halt in the building of new congregations and churches. He found some short-term employment, but he has been his own man too long. He seems incapable of making the kind of adjustment to regular employment that Annie has made. For the present, their marriage seems solid. He provides the coveted status of Reverend; she supplies the income to pay the bills and meet the house payments. As long as they balance their needs against each other in that way, things will go smoothly. But, given economic pressures, their relationship may become stormy. Always tempestuous, Annie may feel that her own position gives her sufficient status, or Bill may regard their home as a constant and unnecessary drain on his strength. Annie's middle-class values may include the need for a working husband. This seems a remote possibility, however, in the face of their mutual devotion. Always strong and self-reliant, Annie will not lose her home. At all costs she will seek to preserve that hard-won symbol of middle-class status.

The saddest event has already occurred. In the cyclical belt-tightening efforts of the federal government, the program which provided a home for Annie and Bill has been discontinued. There will be no more Robinsons setting their feet on the first rung of the ladder for a while. And this is, indeed, a tragedy, because it closes the door upon people who should be free to enter what is supposedly an open society. We will again hear that the culture of poverty is so embedded that it cannot be eradicated. We will again be told that welfare families are self-perpetuating. Perhaps we will even be told that poverty is a mark of racial inferiority. Or that racism is endemic to low income, white neighborhoods. None of these statements is true, as Annie Robinson has shown.

> I think where I started, and I know no one helped me, and I see where I am. I work hard, true enough, but Bill helps me make breakfast, he rubs my back when I ache. Sometimes I get disgusted; work, work, work, and what for? Then I look at my house and my yard, and I remember the cabin in Mississippi.

Annie says that if she were to live her life again, she would become a registered nurse.

Epilogue

Summary

Friedl (1975:2–3) sums up the attitudes of anthropologists towards sex roles. She states that there are two antagonistic schools, one which stresses the biological differences between men and women and one which stresses the social and economic differences. Friedl (1975:2) states:

> The particularly genetically ascribed constraint which the biologically oriented contestants believe underlies such a universal division of labor between men and women is sexual dimorphism in *Homo sapiens*.

Friedl points out that the opposing group, the "environmentalists," recognize biological evidence but point to the fact that in some populations, such as Southeast Asia, there is considerably less difference in muscular development between men and women than in other populations, and that cross-cultural studies show that women fill many different roles in various societies.

The mass of evidence assembled tends to show that the "environmentalists" have the better of the argument. Not only is there an enormous range in the status of women as among foragers, agriculturalists, and industrial society, but even within each of these rubrics there are great differences in women's roles and the status they achieve.

Among foragers, Friedl distinguishes four patterns of sexual division of labor. In the first, each sex provides for itself; both men and women gather food

239

and men only occasionally hunt. The second type involves both men and women in subsistence activities, such as communal hunting and fishing. The third is the one in which men hunt, and women gather, and then pool the results. Finally, there is the form prevalent among the Eskimo, in which all food is provided by the men through hunting and fishing, while women are processors of food and clothing. Friedl correlates the status of women with their contribution to subsistence, noting that the lowest status is found among those women who contribute the least, that is, primarily among the Eskimo. The assignment of low status to Eskimo women is based upon the fact that:

> After puberty, a girl is considered fair game as a sexual object for any man who desires her. He grabs her by the belt as a sign of his intentions. If she is reluctant, he may cut off her trousers with a knife and proceed to force her into intercourse (Friedl 1975:42).

Friedl also points out the fact that a man can share his wife's sexuality with trade friends or any other male at the husband's will; the woman is thereby deprived of control over her own sexuality.

Hart and Pilling also referred to the fact that women among the Tiwi were pawns to be traded at the will of the mother's husband. But the material gathered by Goodale among the same Tiwi tends to show that the women themselves did not resent being passed to other men; they regarded this as an opportunity for variety.

In Eskimo society, Friedl (1975:42) says:

> Whether a girl consents or not, these transitory sexual encounters are regarded as matters of no particular importance among the Eskimo. They are not occasions for vengeful action on the part of her kin, nor do they lessen her desirability as a sex partner or a wife, unless she comes to be known as especially promiscuous.

How do we know that the Eskimo woman emically sees herself as sexually abused? Perhaps she too sees the sexual customs of her people as providing her with variety, especially since there are no public sanctions against this activity. Certainly, Pitseolak did not recall her life as a young wife in terms of deprivation. Though memory might have dimmed through time, it seems impossible that had wife exchange been extremely distasteful to her, she would have mentioned it, as she mentioned shamans, who were distasteful to her. Even were we to regard Pitseolak as a singular exception among Eskimo women, the greater our ground for stating that a variety of life experiences exists even among foragers who are dependent solely upon the man for subsistence. Among the Mbuti who would fall into Friedl's second category of foragers, we found that there is relatively equal status between men and women. Here, as among the Mundurucu, it seems to be only in ritual that women are excluded. Sanday (1973) would apparently be correct in stating that it is in the area of ritual that most of the denigration of women resides. However, for those anthropologists who see ritual as a reinforcement of existing attitudes, this status of women vis-à-vis ritual would merely be a dramatization of a condition which exists in other subsystems of the culture.

Friedl (1975:8) makes the point that it is not child-bearing and rearing that determines women's role in subsistence, but rather women's role in subsistence which determines the frequency with which children are born, and the amount of time spent rearing them. There are methods of population control in all societies. Infanticide is much more widely practiced than a cursory survey of the literature would indicate. Moreover, Friedl rightly points out that in foraging societies, child care is often delegated to older siblings, older women, and occasionally even to fathers. This situation parallels that found in the modern, matrifocal family in which child care needs are subordinated to women's place in the subsistence economy, and surrogates are used to rear the children.

Among horticulturalists, Friedl (1975:52) suggests that the higher status accorded males is due to the fact that they clear new plots for cultivation, often in areas where other groups dispute their right to the land. Thus men, who are traditionally the warriors of society, are used to expand the community boundaries through clearing plots of new land. Friedl offers a logical explanation for the fact that even in those societies where sexual dimorphism is minimal, men most commonly carry on warfare. Friedl (1975:59) states:

> The number of children that a woman can bear is severely limited, particularly where the average spacing is frequently one child in every three years. Under these circumstances a woman can scarcely have more than a dozen children between menarche and menopause. One man, on the contrary, is capable during his sexual maturity of impregnating an extremely large number of women. Therefore, for the maintenance of a population, men's lives are decidedly more expendable than women's.

Although in Dahomey women serve as warriors, and some other societies take their women into the field with them, in most societies, men are unquestionably the warriors and earn prestige and esteem in this role as they do in hunting. No similar esteem is earned by women.

Friedl (1975:54) classifies four distinctive types of horticultural societies: (1) men raise crops for exchange and women raise staples; (2) men and women cultivate both exchange crops and staples; (3) men and women raise the same crops; and (4) women raise the prestige crop for exchange and men raise the staple. This last type of society is not, at this time, known. One reason might be that men are more likely to be in contact with other groups and, as we have seen among the Mundurucu, act as the representatives of the women in trading with outsiders. The transition from trading representative to initiation of cultivation of crops used for trading is a small one.

Even among horticulturalists the status of women varies. The Mundurucu woman has far less power in traditional Mundurucu society than she does in the

tapper villages where she resides neolocally. The Bemba women have relatively high status. This difference may be explained in terms of the fact that it is
the Mundurucu men who, even in traditional Mundurucu society, deal with
the traders who come to buy manioc flour, even though the flour is produced by
women. Among the Bemba, men and women cultivate together; however,
women make beer which may be correlated with the Tibetan woman making
butter.

Certainly, in peasant societies there are extreme differences, from society to
society, in their treatment of women. One need only contrast the Zapotec
women of Mexico with the Greek Sarakatsani women. Again, one of the factors
influencing such diversity may be the importance of the women's role in subsistence. Zapotec women, through trade, have more ready access to money
than their farmer husbands. Sarakatsani women raise goats, which are not
valued in their society. Yet, this explanation does not suffice. Sarakatsani
women help with the lambing. They are assigned to rear goats simply because
goats are considered inferior to sheep. Even the women who do work in
Esmeralda are granted no greater status than those who do not.

In modern society, there is an even greater variety in roles and status. The
women of Fun City seem to enjoy a degree of self-esteem that neither Consuelo
nor Soledad have. Yet both Consuelo and Soledad work, whereas women of
Fun City are not evaluated in terms of earlier careers, if they had any. Is it
poverty alone that separates middle-class women from the Consuelos and the
Soledads? Annie Robinson is poor by the standards of Fun City women, and by
the standards of Carol and Linda, yet she does not lack self-esteem.

Probability theory has long replaced simple cause and effect explanation in
scientific analysis. We should be naive to suppose that women's status can be
deduced from her role in subsistence alone. We should be equally naive to
expect societies with similar subsistence patterns to grant their women identi-
cal status. Earlier it was stressed that culture is a system made up of subsystems, each of which interacts with the other. Any attempt to explain a condition
in any society must do so within these constraints.

Woman's status in a society may be said to be higher when she contributes
to the subsistence of the society and does so in such a form as to retain control of
the wealth and/or products she produces.

She can usually do this best in a society in which the social organization is
such that she finds herself part of a group of related women, as in a matrilocal
society, or where she is free to choose the associates with whom she will share
her responsibilities. This can occur in a polygamous society, as among the Tiv
(Bohannan 1965), where the first wife, through her training activities can pay
bride price for successive wives and/or daughters-in-law. It can also occur in the
matrifocal family where a woman can manipulate networks of kin to her advantage or in monogamous societies such as our own, who have the right to
choose their own mates and thereby select their affines. Friedl (1975:21) states:

"Probably the development of the cultural concept of the 'in-law' is as important a human invention as is the incest rule." If women have the right to choose their in-laws, and their colleagues, they are in a more advantageous position to maximize their freedom and productivity than if they live in a society which gives the right to dispose of a woman's sexuality to fathers, husbands, brothers, or any other group or individual.

Finally, a woman's control over her own sexuality and her own life is strongly influenced by the ritual and religious customs of her society. Where women are denigrated by the belief system, the other subsystems will be so articulated as to prohibit women's full participation.

However, it is equally true that where women are perceived as hostile aliens in the family, or where their work effort is regarded as insignificant, this will be reflected in the belief system.

Women who contribute to and participate in the production of wealth, or who select and are selected by mates who respect them as persons, or where customs and beliefs of the society measure individuals in terms of their contribution rather than as stereotypes, will receive elevated status.

In the light of women's need for economic independence, it is a poignant truth that Friedl (1975:136) notes:

> High school counselors report that they have difficulty convincing girls of the hazardousness of relying on marriage and wifehood as a permanent way of earning a living. The statistical probabilities of losing husbands or their earning power through divorce, widowhood, illness, or unemployment are very real but hard to demonstrate to adolescent girls.

The role of crypto-servant not only has respectability, but the pseudo-romance of Hollywood and dime novels working in its behalf. More than that, the entire industrial and advertising world seems bent on perpetuating the myth of the wife-mother-concubine-consumer.

With growing numbers of women entering the work force and retraining in colleges and universities, women may develop different goals in the future.

The Future of Women

Modern industrial society is the proving ground for entirely new conditions for women. For one thing, the division of labor need not be as rigidly defined as in other societies. This is due to several factors, among them the more efficient technology which places a premium on dexterity and intelligence rather than on brute strength.

Another factor which has made the boundaries between men's work and women's work more flexible is the fact that for the last 50 to 100 years, it has been possible for girls to get the same education as boys; in fact, in many places, the young people are not segregated by sex within the educational system.

Granting the argument that schools often still teach sexual stereotypes, one must also take into consideration that the fact that only 200 years ago it was not considered necessary for women to have any education and, until quite recently, it was still separate and apart from men.

Still another factor contributing to the breakdown between men's work and women's work has been the nearly constant state of warfare our civilization has been undergoing during this century. In some nations which experienced heavy losses in manpower due to warfare, such as France after World War I, and the Soviet Union after World War II, women had to take over many jobs which were heretofore regarded as men's work.

Women in the Public Sphere

All the factors mentioned have contributed to bring the modern woman into the public sphere. They have also contributed to a new evaluation of womanhood by both men and women. The economic and social climate of our time has contributed to this growing movement of women into the public sphere. Economic inflation and the proliferation of consumer goods has made it necessary for many women to work in order to live well. There is also a burgeoning public sentiment, not as yet clearly defined, against the complexity, waste, inhumanity and general confusion of our culture. This is reflected in the "anti-establishment" sentiments voiced most clearly by the young, but also to be found in every age group. The "establishment" is undeniably male. Women, though not necessarily leaders of the "antiestablishment" factions, are in a position to contribute alternatives to establishment policy and to get a hearing. A generation ago, this would have been most unlikely. It would be tragic if the opportunity to make such contributions were lost in a morass of trivia. It would be tragic if women confused equality of opportunity with equalness or sameness. Women are not the same as men, and therein lies their strength.

The Need for Feminine Gentleness and Empathy

There is a real possibility that through the ages, cultural selection has operated in favor of the adaptable, pliable woman, as opposed to the aggressive, combative one. Shakespeare illustrated this in his "Taming of the Shrew." Behavior which would be tolerated or even admired in men has usually been unacceptable in women. Such aggressiveness would be detrimental, not only to the male-female relationship, but also to the mother-child relationship. Rearing children requires a great deal of tolerance, patience, and human warmth, qualities which are perceived by our culture to be feminine rather than masculine. It is precisely such characteristics which are desperately needed now in the public sphere.

Women and Child-Bearing

Until very recently, conditions for women had not changed at all. They were still primarily child-bearers and rearers, and as such had limited freedom of action. The truly revolutionary change in the status of women will probably not be felt for another generation, because evolution occurs in terms of cumulative modification. Thus, the results of the great scientific and technological discoveries of the 1960s may not bear fruit until 1980 or later. These breakthroughs are the contraceptive devices which now, for the first time in millions of years, make it possible for a woman to control her fertility. For the first time, women have a choice. There need no longer be unwanted babies. Women need no longer be confined to the domestic or private sphere all their lives. The full impact of these facts has yet to be absorbed. Institutions have not yet begun to move in the directions necessary to deal with these conditions.

Models of the Future

It would not be true to say there are no models to point the direction. In every generation there have been women who have chosen to enter the public sphere. Sometimes they did this at the sacrifice of a family, but quite often they managed to have both. Again, in our own time, we have women who, of necessity, combine the role of mother and breadwinner.

The matrifocal family is such an example. Also, nations such as Israel, the Soviet Union, and the Republic of China, which need the labor input of women, have experimented with communal methods of child-rearing.

Women in modern Western society stand on the threshold of an entirely new era. Women can now assume responsibility for their biology. They can choose where there has never before been a choice. They can marry or stay single; they can have children or have none. They can plan their families to best meet the parents' needs.

It is not entirely certain that most women, let alone all, will want to assume the responsibility involved in these choices. It may be bewildering for many to have so many options. This could lead to frustration, but it does not have to. As never before, women can now divide their lives into periods. There can be a time for preparation; a time for child-rearing; and still a time for a career. In order to do these things, women may have to acquire a maturity for which they have never before striven.

Careers as Opposed to Families

The mature modern women will not think of careers and families as opposing choices. She will seek to combine them so as to live life as fully as possible. She will spend her early years in preparation for a career, based not upon stereotypes, but upon her own abilities and capacity. Her preparation should make it possible for her to compete successfully and to act effectively in the public sphere. Legislation is now making it possible for women to enter industries which heretofore have been closed to them, and is closing the gap between men's and women's salaries. The mature, modern woman, having prepared for a career, will want to use her training, but if she does so, she must recognize that she will face specific problems which men do not. In a society in which employment opportunities are limited and population pressures continue, there will be many men who will feel competition for jobs from women is unfair and unnatural. And there will always be the men who, perhaps justifiably insecure in their own abilities, will use femaleness as an excuse for bigotry. However, there are growing numbers of mature men who resent bigotry in any form, and who can and do work with women in an efficient manner.

Mate Choice and Rearing a Family

The problem of rearing a family will prove more difficult than entering a career. Mate choice will be critical. It is very possible that in the future selective criteria will favor men who are empathetic and mature over aggressive and immature men who, in myth, have dominated the scene. Such changes can only occur in the long run. In the immediate future, a woman will have to be careful in her mate selection for two reasons. First, of course, she will need a mate who is strong enough to avoid feeling threatened by a strong woman. Secondly, as Stack (1974:121–122) has shown there is the danger that a woman may be economically exploited by a man, just as some men have been economically exploited by women.

Having and rearing children presents a grave problem at present, because neither institution nor custom is prepared to deal with the problem. In certain professions, such as teaching, maternity leaves are possible. In time, this custom may find its way into other institutions. Other women may find themselves so situated that they can afford to devote a portion of their lives to the task of child-rearing and then return to their careers. Still others may find this impossible, or undesirable, and will have to search for alternatives.

One alternative is the surrogate mother, such as existed in the days of the "Nanny." In order to provide this service, the image of domestic service will have to be improved. Wages will have to rise considerably, as will conditions of employment. These are all feasible. Working hours, paid leaves, arrangements for illness, can all be worked out. The stigma, however, of being household employees is more difficult to erase. Concerted efforts, both through the media and through vocational advisors, will have to be made to induce young people to enter child-rearing professions. It has been done before. The career of nursing, for example, had a severe problem in recruitment at one time. The hours were unorthodox, the routine work was not glamorous; yet with the addition of uniforms, professional status, and a little help from Florence Nightingale, nursing has become a career of choice for many women. The actual work of an airline stewardess is less glamorous than the popularity of the vocation would lead one to believe. The return to respectability of the housekeeper, the professional nanny, is long overdue.

There will be other women again who will find their solution in institutionalized child care centers. Here, again, corporations have not provided this type of care because heretofore they dealt primarily with male employees. Unless women can demonstrate unique abilities, it is not likely that the business community will, in the face of consistent five percent or higher unemployment rates, incur additional expense for child care. The private child-care centers may have to fill this need; however, more rigid standards of licensing and periodic inspection should be demanded of the state.

Finally, another alternative would be for a woman to establish wider networks of relationships which include facilities for child-care. The matrifocal family, it has been shown, has succeeded in doing this. Precisely who would be included in the network would have to be a matter of personal decision. Some people might seek this type of network in a peer group, community residence pattern. Others might prefer a network of kin who span two or three generations, and include affines and consanguinal kin, grandparents, and aunts and uncles on either side of the family.

Realistic Approaches to the Future

Above all, women will have to be realists. Except for very unusual and individual professions, it is not realistic to expect husband and wife to alternate roles as homemaker and wage earner. Neither husband nor wife can, in these circumstances, bring professionalism to either occupation. It is not realistic to expect many large corporations to alter their working hours for the benefit of working mothers when there are employable men.

It is realistic, however, to expect universities to become more flexible so that women who have completed their child-rearing duties can retrain for either their old careers or new ones. It is realistic to demand that government and businesses alike give maternity leaves. It is realistic to demand that women's salaries be equal to men's, not only because they are doing the same work, but also because women may have to bear the cost of surrogate child care. It is realistic to demand that the tax structure be revised so that single people are not penalized.

Lack of Women in the Public Sphere

It is realistic to expect a change of attitude toward women on the part of all thinking people. For thousands of years, women have been excluded from the public sphere. As a result, there have been no checks on the male pattern of culture building. Unquestionably, cultural development has been impressive.

Man has succeeded in becoming the dominant species on earth. His numbers have increased enormously. He has bent nature to his will, and placed all the earth's resources at his command. He has exercised domination over the earth and over other men. But, in our time, we are beginning to understand the effects of such ruthless domination, and to feel the problems created by it. The earth's resources, having been mined rapaciously for generations, are rapidly being depleted. The industrial system which has provided both comfort and safety for millions, is proving to be dehumanizing in its effects on workers and consumer alike. Man's exploitation of other men has become dangerous to the existence of the species. Wars, given present technology, can no longer be won. People cannot be bombed into submission without destroying the earth, the bomber, as well as the bombed. Terrorism, violence, crime in the streets, all attest to the inability of present systems to administer fairly to all people. The elevation of crime in the street to the level of governmental applied violence has already occurred in various places and times, and is possible everywhere.

Men do not seem capable of new solutions. This may be due to the nature of the problems, but it may also be due to the nature of men. Perhaps the very capacities for domination and exploitation which brought industrial civilization this far are the wrong capabilities necessary to carry it further. Perhaps the greatest need in our time is for the conciliatory and nurturing propensities which women, over the ages, have developed. Perhaps women, with their highly developed skills of mediation, empathy, and concern for the individual can provide a new perception of world order, and with it help to solve modern problems.

A Joint Effort Toward a Better World

The problems which now afflict our civilization are worldwide in scope, and appear most difficult to solve. It will take the abilities cultivated by both men and women to reach any solution. It is past time for women to make their unique contribution to the human species, while it still exists.

Bibliography

Abramova, Z. A., 1962, *Paleolithic Art in the U.S.S.R.* Soviet Union.

Adams, James P., 1964, Adolescent personal problems as a function of age and sex. *Journal of Genetic Psychology*, 104:207–214.

Ames, L. B., and Frances L. Ilg, 1964, Sex differences in test performance of matched girl-boy pairs in the 5–9 year old range. *Journal of Genetic Psychology*, 104: 25–34.

Aschenbrenner, Joyce, 1974, *Lifelines: Black Families in Chicago.* New York: Holt, Rinehart and Winston.

Barron, Patricia, Richard Heeschen, and Robert Widman, 1968, Body Build and Performance, Sex Differences. Unpublished dissertation.

Barry, H., Margaret K. Bacon, and E. L. Child, 1957, A cross-cultural survey of some sex differences in socialization. *Journal of Abnormal Social Psychology*, 55:327–332.

Basehart, Harry W., 1961, "Ashanti" in *Matrilineal Kinship*, David Schneider and Kathleen Gough, eds. Berkeley: University of California Press.

Beller, E. K., 1962, Personality correlates of perceptual discrimination in children. Progress report.

Beller, E. K., and P. B. Neubauer, 1963, Sex differences and symptom patterns in early childhood. *Journal of Child Psychiatry*, No. 2:414–433.

Bock, Philip K., 1967, Love magic, menstrual taboos and the facts of geography. *American Anthropologist*, 69 (2):213–216.

Bohannan, Paul, 1965, "The Tiv of Nigeria," in *Peoples of Africa*, J. L. Gibbs, Jr., ed. New York: Holt, Rinehart and Winston.

Borgatta, E. F., and J. Stimson, 1963, Sex differences in interaction characteristics. *Journal of Social Psychology*, 60:89–100.

Boserup, Ester, 1970, *Woman's Role in Economic Development*. London: George Allen and Unwin Ltd.

Bronowski, J., 1974, *The Ascent of Man*. Boston: Little Brown and Company.

———, 1965, *Science and Human Values*. New York. Harper & Row, Publishers.

Brown, Judith, 1963, A cross-cultural study of female initiation rites. *American Anthropologist*, 65 (5):837.

———, 1970, A note on the division of labor by sex. *American Anthropologist*, 72 (5):1073.

Buitrago-Ortiz, C., 1973, *Esperanza: An Ethnographic Study of a Peasant Community in Puerto Rico*. Viking Fund Publications in Anthropology, No. 50. Tucson: University of Arizona Press.

Cancion, Francesca, 1964, Interaction patterns in Zina Canteca families. *American Sociological Review*, 29:540–558.

Campbell, J. K., 1974, *Honour, Family and Patronage*. New York: Oxford University Press.

Chagnon, Napoleon, 1968, *Yąnomamö: The Fierce People*. New York: Holt, Rinehart and Winston.

Chance, Norman, 1966, *The Eskimo of North Alaska*. New York: Holt, Rinehart and Winston.

Chesler, Phyllis, 1972, *Women and Madness*. New York: Doubleday & Company, Inc.

Chiñas, Beverly, 1973, *The Isthmus Zapotecs: Women's Roles in Cultural Context*. New York: Holt, Rinehart and Winston.

Chodorow, Nancy, 1974, "Family Structure and Feminine Personality" in *Women, Culture and Society*, Michelle Rosaldo and Louise Lamphere, eds. Stanford, Calif., Stanford University Press, pp. 45–56.

Coult, Allen D., 1963, Unconscious inferences and culture origins. *American Anthropologist*, 65:32–35.

Crandall, V. J., and Alice Rabson, 1960, Children's repetition choices in an intellectual achievement situation following success and failure. *Journal of Genetic Psychology*, 97:161–168.

D'Andrade, Roy G., 1966, "Sex Differences and Cultural Institutions," in *The Development of Sex Differences*, Eleanor Maccoby, ed. Stanford, Calif.: Stanford University Press.

De Jesus, Carolina, 1962, *Child of the Dark*. New York: E. P. Dutton & Co., Inc.

De Vries, Herbert A., 1966, *The Physiology of Exercise for Physical Education and Athletics*. Iowa: Wm. C. Brown Company, Publishers.

Donovan, B. T., 1963, "The Timing of Puberty." in *The Scientific Basis of Medicine Annual Review*. London: Athlone Press.

Eber, Dorothy, 1971, *Pitseolak: Pictures Out of My Life*. Seattle: University of Washington Press.

Ekvall, Robert B., 1968, *Fields on the Hoof: Nexus of Tibetan Nomadic Pastoralism*. New York: Holt, Rinehart and Winston.

Evans-Pritchard, E. E., 1974, *Man and Woman among the Azande*. New York: The Free Press.

Fortune, Reo, 1932, *Sorcerers of Dobu*. New York: E. P. Dutton & Co., Inc.

Foster, George M., 1965, Peasant society and the image of limited good. *American Anthropologist*, 67 (2):293–315.

Friedl, Ernestine, 1959, *Dowry and Inheritance in Modern Greece.* Transactions of the New York Academy of Science, Series II, Vol. 22, No. 1.
———, 1967, The position of women: appearance and reality. *Anthropological Quarterly,* 40:97–108.
———, 1975, *Women and Men: An Anthropologist's View.* New York: Holt, Rinehart and Winston.
Galbraith, John K., 1973, *Economics and the Public Purpose.* Boston: Houghton Mifflin Company.
Gibbs, James L., Jr., 1965, *Peoples of Africa.* New York: Holt, Rinehart and Winston.
Goodale, Jane C., 1971, *Tiwi Wives.* Seattle: University of Washington Press.
Gough, H. G., 1952, Identifying psychological femininity. *Education Psychological Measurement,* 12:427–439.
Hall, C. A., 1964, A modest confirmation of Freud's theory of a distinction between the super ego of men and women. *Journal of Abnormal Social Psychology,* 69:440–442.
Halsell, Grace, 1973, *Bessie Longhair.* New York: William Morrow and Company, Inc.
Hamburg, David A., and Donald T. Lunde, 1972, "Sex Hormones in the Development of Sex Differences in Human Behavior," in *The Development of Sex Differences,* Eleanor E. Maccoby, ed. Stanford, Calif.: Stanford University Press.
Harris, Marvin, 1975, *Culture, People and Nature.* New York: Thomas Y. Crowell Company.
———, 1972, *Culture, Man and Nature.* New York: Thomas Y. Crowell Company.
Hart, C. W. M., and Arnold R. Pilling, 1960, *The Tiwi of North Australia.* New York: Holt, Rinehart and Winston.
Henry, Jules, 1971, *Pathways to Madness.* New York: Random House, Inc.
Hogbin, Ian, 1970, *The Island of Menstruating Men. Religion in Wogeo, New Guinea.* Scranton, Pa.: Chandler Publishing Company.
Honzik, Marjorie P., and J. P. McKee, 1962, The sex difference in thumb-sucking. *Journal of Pediatrics,* 61:726–732.
Ingham, John M., 1971, Are the Siriono raw or cooked? *American Anthropologist,* 73 (5):1092–1099.
Jacobs, Jerry, 1974, *Fun City.* New York: Holt, Rinehart and Winston.
Kaberry, Phyllis, M., 1939, *Aboriginal Woman.* London: Routledge & Kegan Paul Ltd.
Kloos, Peter, 1969, Female initiation among the Maroni River Caribs. *American Anthropologist,* 71 (5):898.
Kohlberg, Lawrence, 1966, "A Cognitive-Developmental Analysis of Children's Sex Role Concepts and Attitudes," in *The Development of Sex Differences.* Eleanor Maccoby, ed. Stanford, Calif.: Stanford University Press.
Krige, Eileen, and J. D. Krige, 1943, *The Realm of a Rain-Queen: A Study of the Patterns of Lovedu Society.* New York: Oxford University Press.
Lee, Richard B., 1968, "What Hunters Do for a Living, or How to Make Out on Scarce Resources," in *Man and the Hunter,* Richard B. Lee and Irven DeVore, eds. Chicago: Aldine Publishing Company.
Kuper, Hilda, 1965, "The Swazi of Swaziland," in *Peoples of Africa,* James L. Gibbs, Jr., ed. New York: Holt, Rinehart and Winston.
Lévi-Strauss, Claude, 1969, *The Raw and the Cooked Transactions.* New York: J. and D. Weightman.
———, 1969a, *The Elementary Structure of Kinship.* Boston: Beacon Press.

Lewis, Oscar, 1961, *Children of Sanchez.* New York: Random House, Inc.
———, 1964, *Pedro Martinez.* New York: Random House, Inc.
———, 1965, *La Vida.* New York: Random House, Inc.
Maccoby, Eleanor E., 1972, *The Development of Sex Differences.* Stanford, Calif.: Stanford Univeristy Press.
Marshack, Alexander, 1972, *The Roots of Civilization.* New York: McGraw-Hill, Inc.
Mead, Margaret, 1935, *Sex and Temperament in Three Primitive Societies.* New York: Dell Publishing Co., Inc.
———, 1949, *Male and Female: A Study of the Sexes in a Changing World.* New York: Dell Publishing Co., Inc., Laurel edition.
———, 1970, *Culture and Commitment.* New York: Doubleday & Company, Inc.
———, 1972, *Blackberry Winter.* New York: William Morrrow and Company, Inc.
Meggitt, Mervyn, 1964, Male-female relationships in the highlands of Australian New Guinea. *American Anthropologist,* 66 (4).
Money, J., 1961, "Sex Hormones and Other Variables in Human Eroticism," in *Sex and Internal Secretions,* W.C. Young, ed., Vol. 2. Baltimore: The Williams & Wilkins Co.
———, 1965, "Psychosexual Differentiation," in *Sex Research: New Developments,* J. Money, ed. New York: Holt, Rinehart and Winston.
Montagu, Ashley, 1954, *The Natural Superiority of Women.* New York: Crowell Collier and MacMillan, Inc.
Murphy, Robert, 1956, Matrilocality and patrilineality in Mundurucu society. *American Anthropologist,* 50:414–434.
Murphy, Yolanda, and Robert F. Murphy, 1974, *Women of the Forest.* New York: Columbia University Press.
Myrdal, Jan, 1965, *Report from a Chinese Village.* New York: New American Library, Inc., Signet Book.
Nadel, S. F., 1952, Witchcraft in four societies: an essay in comparison. *American Anthropologist,* 54: 18–29.
Netting, Robert, 1969, Women's weapons: the politics of domesticity among the Kofyar. *American Anthropologist,* 71 (6):1037.
Oliver, Douglas, 1949, *Studies in the Anthropology of Bougainville, Soloman Island.* Papers of the Peabody Museum of American Archaeology and Ethnology, Vol. XXIX, Nos. 1–4, Cambridge, Mass.: Harvard University.
Ortner, Sherry, 1974, "Is Female to Male as Nature Is to Culture" in *Woman, Culture and Society,* Michelle Rosaldo and Louise Lamphere, eds. Stanford, Calif.: Stanford University Press.
Raphael, Dana, 1973, *The Tender Gift: Breastfeeding.* Englewood Cliffs, N.J.: Prentice-Hall, Inc.
Redfield, Robert, 1930, *Tepoztlan: A Mexican Village.* Chicago: University of Chicago Press.
———, 1955, *The Little Community.* Chicago: University of Chicago Press.
Richards, Audry I., 1956, *Chisungu.* London: Faber & Faber, Ltd.
Rosaldo, Michelle, 1974, "Woman, Culture and Society: A Theoretical Overview," in *Woman, Culture and Society,* Michelle Rosaldo and Louise Lamphere, eds. Stanford, Calif.: Stanford University Press.
Sacks, Karen, 1974, "Engels Revisited," in *Woman, Culture and Society,* Michelle Rosaldo and Louise Lamphere, eds. Stanford, Calif.: Stanford University Press.

Sanday, Peggy R., 1974, "Female Status in the Public Domain," in *Woman, Culture and Society*, Michelle Rosaldo and Louise Lamphere, eds. Stanford, Calif.: Stanford University Press.

————, 1973, Theory of the status of women. *American Anthropologist*, 75:1682–1700.

Schebesta, Paul, 1938–1950, *Die Bambute-Pygmaen vom Ituri*. Memoires de l'Institut Royal Colonial Belge, Section des Sciences Morales et Poligoes 1, 2, 4.

Schneider, David and Kathleen Gough, 1961, *Matrilineal Kinship*. Berkeley: University of California Press.

Smith, S., 1939, Age and sex differences in children's opinion concerning sex differences. *Journal of Genetic Psychology*, 54:17–25.

Stack, Carol B., 1974, "Sex Roles and Survival Strategies," in *Woman, Culture and Society*, Michelle Rosaldo and Louise Lamphere, eds. Stanford, Calif.: Stanford University Press.

Tuddenham, R. D., 1951, Studies in reputation, 111, Correlates of popularity among elementary school children. *Journal of Educational Psychology*, 42:257–276.

Turnbull, Colin, 1961, *The Forest People*. New York: Simon & Schuster, Inc.

————, 1968, *The Lonely African*. New York: Simon & Schuster, Inc.

————, 1973, *The Mountain People*. New York: Simon & Schuster, Inc.

Uchendu, Victor C., 1965, *The Igbo of Southeast Nigeria*. New York: Holt, Rinehart and Winston.

Van Gennep, Arnold, 1960, *The Rites of Passage*. Chicago: University of Chicago Press.

Weatherley, D., 1964, Self-perceived rate of physical maturation and personality in late adolescence. *Child Development*, 35:1197–1210.

Wilkins, L., *et al.*, 1958, Masculinization of the female fetus associated with administration of oral and intra-muscular progestins during gestation: non-adrenal female pseudo-hermaphrodism. *Journal of Clinical Endocrinology*, 18:559–585.

————, 1965, *The Diagnosis and Treatment of Endocrine Disorders in Childhood and Adolescence*, 3d ed. Springfield, Ill.: Charles C Thomas, Publishers.

Williams, Juanita, in press, *Psychology of Women*. New York: W. W. Norton & Company.

Wilson, Clyde H., 1964, On the origin of menstrual taboos. *American Anthropologist*, 66, no. 3, part 1.

Wolf, Eric R., 1966, *Peasants*. Englewood Cliffs, N.J.: Prentice-Hall, Inc.

Wolf, Margery, 1974, "Chinese Women," in *Woman, Culture and Society*, Michelle Rosaldo and Louise Lamphere, eds. Stanford, Calif.: Stanford University Press.

Woodburn, James, 1968, "An Introduction to Hadza Ecology," in *Man the Hunter*, Richard Blee and Irven Devore, eds. Chicago: Aldine Publications.

Young, Frank W., 1965, *Initiation Ceremonies*. New York: The Bobbs-Merrill Company, Inc.

Index

Name Index

Subject Index